To Be Honest

To Be Honest

Michael Leviton

Abrams Press, New York

To Mom and Dad and "Eve" and all
the others who managed to love me even
when I was most unpleasantly myself

Library of Congress Control Number: 2019939894

ISBN: 978-1-4197-4305-4

eISBN: 978-1-68335-822-0

Printed and bound in the United States

10 9 8 7 6 5 4 3 2 1

Abrams books are available at special discounts when purchased in quantity
for premiums and promotions as well as fundraising or educational use.
Special editions can also be created to specification. For details, contact
specialsales@abramsbooks.com or the address below.

Abrams Press® is a registered trademark of Harry N. Abrams, Inc.

ABRAMS The Art of Books
195 Broadway, New York, NY 10007
abramsbooks.com

Contents

Part 3: The Dishonest Days

A Postscript on Truth

Acknowledgments

Prologue

THIS WAS THE end of the honest days. I'd held out my whole life, but even I had to admit it was time to surrender and start lying. I wasn't sure what I could stomach; my three previous attempts at falsity—one at age five, one again at eighteen, and a third at twenty-six, one lie each decade—had been nauseating, but I had to at least try. My moment of truth was my moment of untruth.

I slumped on the couch in the low light of the Brooklyn apartment Eve and I had shared until a few months before. I'd intentionally left on only one dim lamp. I'd always prided myself on being able to face anything, no matter how painful, but I couldn't look at the world Eve and I had built together over the last seven years: the vintage vanity I'd given her where she got ready every morning, her easel and paintings and drawings and musical instruments everywhere, the dining table we'd made by attaching a walnut tabletop to the wrought iron base of a 1930s Singer sewing machine. I couldn't bear to look so I sat in the dark.

Authenticity was supposed to attract the rare people who would appreciate me for who I really was. That was how it had felt with Eve. But my terrible sincerity had eventually poisoned us just as it had poisoned everything else.

There were no support groups for people who wanted to be less honest. Therapy was about "speaking your truth," not "shutting up for once." Whatever advice everybody else needed, I needed the opposite.

I brought a pen and paper to the sewing machine table, sat down, and wrote myself some new rules:

> — *Hide your feelings.*
> — *Avoid answering questions. No one really wants to know.*
> — *When someone claims to like honesty, don't believe it. To them, the word has a different meaning.*
> — *Do NOT be yourself.*

These rules struck me as comically stupid, the worst possible advice. I wanted to call Eve and ask her what she thought, but I reminded myself that calling my ex-girlfriend to update her about how I was dealing with our breakup was a perfect example of the sort of thing I needed to stop doing.

Despite having inspired thousands of grimaces, glares, and uneasy retreats, it still surprised me that my honesty bothered people so much. Even as I clutched that pen to begin training my brain to lie, my mind Rolodexed through dozens of famous quotes about how great it felt to speak your truth. So many people never said what they most longed to say. Someone once told me she wished for a day that no one else would remember, a day to tell everyone what she really thought. For me, every day was that free. Telling the truth felt like singing. But it also made most people want to strangle me.

Everyone else was well-acquainted with the countless reasons to hold tongues and plug ears, but I couldn't fathom them. Why wouldn't you want to hear what others thought? Why wouldn't you tell them what you thought? I found the whole situation vexing and unrelatable. People claimed to appreciate honesty but lied or encouraged lying dozens of times a day, if not hundreds. When I met someone new, I often gave them permission to be honest with me, but they never took me up on it. The more I pushed for honesty, the more they lied, and the more annoyed we all became. And no one was willing or able to give me a satisfying explanation why.

With a heartbreak-shaky hand, I wrote down more rules:

— *Don't treat others the way you'd like to be treated. They hate that.*
— *Learn to small talk.*
— *Instead of searching for those who will appreciate who you really are, try to be what the person in front of you wants.*

As far as I could see, dishonesty made others genuinely happy. They had to know something I didn't. Why else would the world be so hell-bent on pressuring me to lie? Pretty much everyone insisted that what I called dishonesty wasn't dishonest at all, that I sounded ridiculous casually referring to perfectly normal behavior as "fraud." It was time to take off my lie-colored glasses.

WHEN I TELL the stories of my honest days and my dishonest days, many get mad at me or sad at me. Honesty-lovers don't like when I suggest that expressing myself could be so destructive. Honesty-haters resent me for realizing so late that it was wrong to make people uncomfortable. Some have tried to tell me that "everyone respects honesty" mere moments before advising that I shouldn't tell my story. Some suggest that my writing this book reveals I'm not sufficiently ashamed, that I haven't learned my lesson, or at least that I'm ignoring it. I can see their point: I've supposedly resolved not to tell all and here I am writing a "tell-all." Maybe this book is just an excuse to relapse, to rekindle my tragic romance with truth-telling. Ill-advised as it may be, I'm going to tell you stories that risk making you mad or sad at me. Usually, when you ask someone to be honest, you can count on them knowing you don't mean it. With this book, that is not the case. By continuing to read, you're asking for honesty. And I'm going to give it to you.

Part 1

Just Being Honest

Chapter 1

Most People

MY PARENTS PREPARED me far in advance for life's inevitable tragedies (death, rejection, failure, etc.). By age four, I'd heard about many scary things, but I was particularly fixated on vaccinations. I'd lie in bed envisioning the giant dripping syringes I'd seen in cartoons. Eventually, in August of 1984, Mom tipped me off that I'd be getting a shot the next day.

At the time, we lived an hour outside Los Angeles in Claremont, a tree-lined college town with a little park every few blocks. My parents had settled in Claremont out of desperation. After their college graduations, no one would hire them—they were too honest to make it past job interviews—so Mom put together Dad's encyclopedic knowledge of music and the fact that Claremont didn't have a record store and suggested they start one. It was an honest living.

The nursery school I was about to attend had set up an immunization tent across the street at the edge of a park. The trip to get my shot felt like a typical family outing, but with added dread. The summer sidewalk warmed through my canvas shoes and the sun darkened my freckles. I was an indoor child. Whenever I went outside, I complained that the sun was too hot.

We stepped onto the park's grass and I spotted the blue-tarped immunization tent of doom. I turned to Mom and Dad, scratched my bowl-cut head, and said, "This is like when Bugs Bunny walks to the firing squad."

Mom laughed with enough force to skew her oversize prescription sunglasses. "You're so funny, Michael," she said. "Even when you're scared, you're hilarious!" Mom's wild laugh made me nervous that my baby brother, Josh, would tumble out of the pouch hanging from her chest. But I was also happy to see Mom laughing, because the whole morning she'd been frowning and fidgeting with her wristwatch.*

The crowd of four-year-olds and parents reclined on provided blankets or lawn chairs, swung on the swings, dug in the sandbox, and teeter-tottered, showing no concern. Dad lit up. "I have a prediction," he said. Dad often made a game of predicting the behavior of strangers. He was always right, always knew exactly what everyone else would say and do; to me, it was magic.

Dad scratched his short, brown beard, prolonging the suspense. "I bet," he said, raising a thick, dark eyebrow, "most of these parents didn't warn their kids about the shots." Dad's predictions were about "most people," never "all people." He told me to dismiss those who generalized about "all people" because nothing was true of everyone.

Dad only predicted the most normal behavior. When he took

---

* I don't think Mom and Dad could've hidden their emotions if they tried, but I also don't think they tried.

me to my first concert, he said, "Watch this: Ringo is gonna ask the audience how they're feeling tonight and most of the audience will cheer." When he brought me with him shopping, he said, "When I tell the salesman how much I'm willing to spend, he'll immediately show me something more expensive."

When I asked Dad how he read minds and told the future, he explained, "Most people imitate whatever everyone else is doing. They follow a script and recite lines we've heard hundreds of times, lines somebody else wrote." When I asked why people didn't make up something new, Dad replied, "They're afraid that if they really express themselves, someone might not like them. And they're incredibly scared of someone not liking them." Dad would shake his head and say, "It's ridiculous."

Delivering his newest prediction, Dad smirked and paused, building suspense before elaborating. "I suspect that most of these kids think they're on a regular trip to the park."

"Their parents *tricked* them!?" I asked in horror.*

"Most people think lying is good parenting." Dad grinned with laugh-wrinkles around his eyes as he always did when he mocked "most people."†

We stepped from the sidewalk onto the grass and sat down, and Dad stretched out his long, hairy legs. I only remember him wearing one outfit for my whole childhood: a worn-out T-shirt emblazoned with a band name, often tie-dye, with beige shorts. I remember Mom dressing with more variation, sometimes in baggy T-shirts and jeans, sometimes in loose black dresses that ballooned behind her.

---

* It didn't occur to me that while I'd spent the whole morning in a panic, these kids had enjoyed a regular day.
† Both sides of my family line had been at war with "most people" for generations. We fought this war with full knowledge we'd lose. "Most people" had us surrounded.

I observed the families in the grass around us to get a sense of how many children knew why we were here. The blue tent opened and a mother emerged, red-faced, dragging her sobbing son by the wrist. Children's heads turned. A crew-cut boy on a blanket next to us shifted and wiggled. This boy gestured toward the crying child and asked his father, "Why is he sad?"

The boy's father rubbed the scruff of his neck and replied, "He's fine."

I took in this lying father: blond, clean-shaven, wearing a button-up collared shirt with the sleeves rolled over his muscled forearms. His son squirmed harder and the neck-massaging slowed. The boy asked again, "But why is he crying?"

At this, the father said nothing. The crew-cut boy gazed at his unresponsive father. I felt sorry for him.

Dad muttered mournfully, "It's ridiculous."*

Nearby children eavesdropped on each other's exchanges and repeated the same questions to their own families. The lying parents either said the shot wouldn't hurt or avoided discussing it. One mother said, "I'll never let anyone hurt you." One by one, each kid erupted into his or her own style of tantrum.

I knew the shot would be painful, but I wasn't sure how painful, so I asked Mom, "What does a shot feel like?"

"It stings," Mom whispered. "About as much as a splinter. But the pain goes away much faster." My splinter-foot experience had been one of my most traumatic. It soothed me to know I'd already survived worse. I felt confident that her assessment of the pain would be accurate. I imagined how maddening it'd be if I couldn't trust my parents, to have questions and no one reliable to ask, no certainty, no floor or ceiling.

---

* Despite his gripes about listening to the same old lines recited ad nauseam, Dad used the word "ridiculous" in almost every conversation.

A nurse* emerged from the tent and called my name. I could tell she was from the tribe of "most people." We followed her into the tent. Inside, it was spare and shady, with a grass floor. I noticed a single poster hanging on the wall: a drawing of a winking bunny giving a thumbs-up.

The shot chair was child size, so my legs didn't swing. The nurse eyed me, readying herself for the jittery boy in front of her to freak out. When she uncovered the needle, I saw it was smaller than the ones in cartoons. I twisted my neck to watch as the nurse brought the shot to where my short sleeve ended.

"Look over there," the nurse said, pointing at the tent wall. "At the bunny."

"I want to look at the shot," I told her.

"Look at the bunny," she repeated.

The nurse hesitated and glanced at my parents, who were watching wide-eyed, enthralled by what they were witnessing. The nurse shrugged and I said, "I told you I want to see. Don't you believe me?"

The nurse's squint hardened into a baffled scowl. I'd been rude, but in a way she found unfamiliar.[†]

The nurse pushed in the needle and I gaped in awe. The sting set me off wincing and squirming, but it was exactly what Mom had described. I smiled, admiring Mom's precision. My expression confused the nurse. She bent down to my level, warmly shook my little hand, and told me, "You're the bravest boy I've ever seen." I inflated with pride. I trusted her expertise because she'd given so many shots. And it sounded true that few children would smile at their first shot, if any. I basked in her comment,

---

* None of us remember the nurse's appearance—those details were filtered out of the family retellings.

† I'd soon grow accustomed to this reaction. I had a talent for unintentionally inventing new genres of rudeness.

official evidence that I was the world's bravest kid.* I felt as if I'd been given an award. I was about to launch into a speech about how I owed it all to my parents when Dad interrupted to give one himself.

"All these kids would be brave if they were given the chance," Dad said. "Their parents can't even admit that a shot *exists.*"

Mom beamed, her glasses crooked again. "These kids aren't really crying about shots," she added. "They're crying because they've been betrayed by their parents."†

The nurse heard my parents going on, frowned, and turned back to me. "*I* think you're the bravest boy I've ever met." I suspected she felt sorry for me because my parents were behaving very differently from other parents, and that led her to assume they'd raise me to be a lunatic.‡

I strode out of the tent, my arm bearing a cotton swab and a Band-Aid. I envisioned the glorious future awaiting the bravest kid in the world, the thrilling things I'd see while others were too frightened to look. I imagined other kids wasting their lives with eyes trained on winking bunnies, missing everything of interest.

I turned around to thank Mom and Dad for telling me the truth. But they didn't look proud anymore. Mom's head rested on Dad's shoulder, and his arm curled around her.

"It's so unfair," Mom said.

Dad sighed. "She saw the proof: Michael didn't cry. She lies to children and we called her out. She's embarrassed and taking it out on us."

Mom moped along, cry-speaking, "She didn't like us."

---

* It didn't occur to me that she might recite this line to everyone, even to cowards.
† In that moment, I was impressed by my parents' wisdom, but now, I doubt these conclusions. After all, some kids panic over shots no matter how much you warn them. Many find true comfort in untrue kindness. Many kids would have loved the nurse's compliment even if they knew she said it to everyone.
‡ She wasn't exactly *wrong.*

Dad slid his arm off her and his walk stiffened. "Her opinion shouldn't matter. *At all*. She's a random stranger."*

"We were just being honest,"† Mom said, hanging her head. I considered hugging her and telling her I loved her, but then I sensed Dad's irritation and I took his side instead. I wanted Mom to accept that people wouldn't like us and that it was worth it. We couldn't be both normal *and* special. The bravest child in the world couldn't simply *fit in*. I'd been well-prepared for the glamorous isolation of the honest.

My parents would have argued that children are born truth-tellers, that we revel in self-expression until parents, teachers, and friends punish or shame our honesty away. Most consider it more natural and common for children to have trouble expressing themselves, to instead imitate, do whatever it takes to get attention and love. There are studies that say kids start lying around age two unless you specifically condition them not to. Either way, my parents didn't set out to make our family into a little honesty cult. They were only being themselves. As in most families, any brainwashing was unintentional.

Nice Isn't Respectful

IN MY EARLY childhood, before I started school, Mom spent every day with me making games out of sharing our thoughts. I'd dictate stories for Mom to write down, and then we'd take turns illustrating. When I'd watch TV or movies, I'd dash back

---

* This conversation between my parents would play out over and over throughout my childhood with barely different situations and details. My childhood is easy to remember because of its redundancy.
† This line is a favorite for jerks who just want to be insulting. Most who use it have no actual interest in honesty. My family spoke aloud as many thoughts and feelings as we could, literally *just being honest*.

and forth between Mom and the TV, describing whatever I'd seen. I liked talking about TV more than watching it. Mom recognized how much I liked talking and even made a game out of interviewing me. Sometimes it resembled "Would You Rather?" or "Truth or Dare" without the dares. Coming up with opinions, deciding what I thought and articulating it: these were my favorite games. By the time I was four, Mom loved my talking so much that she decided to record it.

Mom rested a tape recorder in front of me at my little plastic table and invited me to speak freely. She listened, hunched meekly, with the shy giddiness of a fan who had won a contest to interview her favorite celebrity. "When I press the button, tell me all your thoughts," she said. I gazed through the tape recorder's window at the revolving spindles and went off on a stream-of-consciousness philosophical improvisation without "umms" or pauses, pronouncing my r's like w's: "If you got love to add," I said on one of the tapes, "you got love for everybody in the whole world!" I went on for a while explaining that I'd no longer eat gum because I'd seen a commercial that warned about "gum disease." I talked on and on until the recorder clicked off. Mom returned to the table, the corners of her smile extended high enough to reach the frames of her giant glasses, and embraced me. A hug from Mom was like being hit by an affectionate truck. "I love you, I love you, I love you, I love you," she'd say. "I love all your thoughts!" I named these recordings "Michael Talking Tapes" and Mom left them in the tape player next to my bed so I could listen to them as I fell asleep, lulled in the dark by my own uncensored voice.

Dad cared so much about talking that he couldn't engage below a certain standard of conversational clarity. So, Dad didn't know how to hang out with toddlers. At four, the best I could do was listen to music with him in his "record room."

He'd spread out on his hard little gray couch surrounded by ceiling-high shelves of records like fortress walls and I'd sit on the gray-carpeted floor or on the little stepladder Dad used to reach his highest records. Sometimes I'd wobble or dance around. Dad would play me music he thought I'd like. My favorite song was "Boris the Spider" by the Who. I understood that when I got older I'd be able to talk more like Dad and conversation would become a suitable game.

Mom and I sat Dad down to play him the first Michael Talking Tape; Dad took the spot next to Mom on the couch that only barely fit in the room. He propped his right foot on his hairy left knee and faced the TV and speakers, running his hand over his bulbous, bearded chin, his pose identical to when he listened to records. My voice emanated from the speakers. I loved hearing myself so loud. My eyes darted back and forth between Mom and Dad's expressions. Mom laughed and glowed and smiled, but Dad only listened, his forehead lined, his wide, dark-brown eyes unwavering. When the Michael Talking Tape ended with a mid-sentence click, Dad shifted on the couch, planted both his bare feet on the carpet, and clasped his hands with his elbows on his knees. "First of all," Dad said, "Gum disease isn't about chewing gum. It's a disease that affects this pink part below your teeth." He illustrated by lifting his lip to show me his gums. "Beyond that, I didn't understand most of it."

"Well, *I* like the Michael Talking Tape," Mom must have said.

Dad likely noticed Mom's disapproval and got indignant, which provoked "the chocolate defense."

"This is like getting upset because I don't like chocolate!"* Dad would say. "Whether *I* like chocolate has no effect

---

* The way Dad talked, you'd think the whole world was furious at him for his taste in candy. I don't know what personal experience gave him this idea.

on whether *you* like it. So, who cares what I think?" In these moments, Dad's movements would become frustrated; he'd shake his head and drop his hand onto his leg with an unintentionally loud swat. "I'm happy if *you* like the Michael Talking Tape! I can't help it if *I* don't. We don't choose what we like. It's not my fault I don't like chocolate either!"

As Dad went on about the ridiculousness of anyone else caring whether he liked chocolate, I listened carefully, clenching my jaw and forehead as if to wring more thoughts from my brain. I could feel an idea soaking in and it wasn't painful at all, but freeing: I could like the tape even if Dad didn't. We didn't have to agree. I could have opinions without anyone's permission, not even my parents'.

After that, when I listened to the Michael Talking Tape in bed, I'd hold Dad's opinion and mine in my mind simultaneously. I could feel the temptation to agree with him, but I didn't fall for it because Dad had told me specifically that I shouldn't care. I loved deciding for myself. To me, that freedom was better than a million compliments.

The only trouble was that I wanted to be happy when someone liked me without having to be sad if they didn't. I couldn't articulate any of this at four, of course, but my feelings naturally settled into a kind of balance, that I could still be pleasantly surprised if someone liked me, but I didn't *need* to be liked.

I WANTED TO play with Dad but he had no interest in drawing, and I wasn't old enough to converse in a way that he could enjoy. One weekend, I wandered into his record room, where I found him in his usual spot on the couch, staring at a record cover. "Dad," I said. "Can we play a game?"

Dad leaned the record cover against the back of the couch to brainstorm potential games. "Well, you can't read yet, so we can't play Scrabble.* Maybe you're old enough for chess?" he said. I'd never heard of chess, but I hoped I was old enough.

Dad fetched a little wooden chessboard from the garage and placed it on the gray carpet. I watched him set up the pieces in an impossibly complicated arrangement. "This is the king," Dad said, lifting the second-tallest piece and tapping the little cross on its head. "The king can move one square in any direction." He moved the king around the board to show me. I concentrated, desperate to remember the rules. My whole childhood, I listened like this, training myself to observe closely and remember everything that was said.†

I don't know how long Dad spent teaching me the rules and testing me on the movements of each piece, but soon we were able to play through a game. Dad showed me how he'd trapped my king so anywhere it moved it still landed in check. Then he flicked my king so it toppled onto its side and rolled slightly back and forth.

"Checkmate," he said.

"What does that mean?" I asked.

"It means I win."

I watched my king wobble slower and slower and started crying. Dad just asked, "Want to play again?"

Once I'd learned to play chess, it was all I wanted to do when Dad was home. Sometimes Mom would sit in the room silently reading or knitting or doing work while we played. After inevitably losing each game, Dad would ask, "Want to play again?" I always said yes.

Chess was my first competitive game; the drawing and

---

* It cracks me up that Dad had to rack his brain for a game to play with a four-year-old; he didn't even think of catch or hide-and-seek.
† To this day, I'm still impressed with my memory for dialogue and bothered by how little I remember about everything else.

storytelling games Mom played didn't involve winning or losing, so I wasn't used to the concept. One day, we visited my
cousins' house for a family event. My cousin Seth liked to run
around and make everything a contest. When he'd suggest that
we race across the backyard, I'd ask, "Does it have to be a race?
Why don't you just run if you want to?"

Alone with me at a table in his backyard, Seth made a fist,
placed his elbow on the tabletop, and proposed we arm wrestle.

"I'll get hurt," I told him.

"You're a chicken," he said.

I thought about that, whether I was a chicken. I decided that
being afraid of arm wrestling counted as being chicken. Luckily,
I didn't care if I *was* a chicken or what my cousin thought as
long as it meant I didn't have to arm wrestle. "Yes," I told him,
with an informational, almost scientific tone. "I'm a chicken."

Seth hopped up from the table, considering running away
to find someone else to play with, but swiveled in silence on
one foot instead. Then he turned back to me. "I'll play easy,"
he offered.

"What's playing easy?" I asked.

"I won't wrestle my hardest. I'll let you win."

I leapt to my feet. "*Really?*"

"Yeah," he said, amused that I'd never heard of this. "When
I arm wrestle with my dad, he plays easy."

At the realization that Dad could've been playing chess easy
on me all this time, I crumbled. I started crying, which confused
Seth even more.

The next Saturday, on Dad's record room floor with the
chessboard between us, I asked him, "Why don't you play easy?"

Dad waved his hand in the air as if shooing a fly I couldn't
see. "If I played easy, how would you know if you improved?
How would you know if you ever won for real? How would

you ever trust me?" Dad laughed to himself and mumbled, "It's so weird, playing easy. I don't see what there is to gain from it."

"It's nice?" I suggested.

Dad frowned. "Sometimes nice isn't respectful,"* he said. "Being respectful means trusting someone to be able to handle the truth, or at least giving them the chance to *try!*"

I couldn't follow Dad's next rant.† "If everyone plays easy, you never learn to lose. And then when you finally encounter something honest, you're blindsided. You're too fragile. You haven't been prepared to be brave or to manage your feelings. You've never needed to because you've been encouraged to run off and hide with your sycophants and nice people who play easy. So we end up with millions of cowards who freak out at the slightest hint of reality, who think it's the world's moral responsibility to perpetually swaddle them in pillows." Dad tilted his head down, disappointed in the world. "With you, I don't play easy," he said. "I respect you too much."

I took in this last line. Dad respected me. I could see why respect was better than niceness and why I couldn't have both. As we continued playing, Dad kept silently shaking his head. I imagined he was thinking about my less fortunate cousin and his father, who were too fragile to be respectful like us.

Drinking Sour Milk

MY FAMILY HAD always been like windup toys, moving mechanically regardless of obstruction, marching infinitely

---

* Dad often imbued common words with his own personal definitions.
† Luckily, he'd tell it to me over and over my whole childhood.

into walls. We couldn't stop our internal gears. At best, we
could only strain against them.

My parents loved to tell me stories from their own upbringings so, even as a child, I had a sense of why my parents had
ended up so honest. Mom and Dad met in high school when
they were fourteen, in 1966. Mom knew Dad from around
school as a class clown who cracked witty remarks and satirized
the teachers. On their first date, Dad took Mom to see the movie
adaptation of Truman Capote's *In Cold Blood*, perhaps the least
appropriate first-date movie of all time. They both cried at the
end when the sad murderer was executed. It impressed Mom
how different Dad was from other boys, that he wasn't ashamed
to cry, even in front of a girl he barely knew.

By the time I was born, fourteen years later, they'd evolved a
general like-mindedness. But their distinctive upbringings left
them with a few philosophical incompatibilities.

Mom's family split time between Los Angeles and Las Vegas
because her parents, Grammy and Pa, sold cake decorations
and ornaments, moving back and forth between the two cities
that hosted the most weddings. Pa's persona reminded me of
traveling salesmen in old movies, men who met on trains and
asked, "Hey pal, what racket are ya' in?" Pa spoke mostly of his
successes with sports, war, and women and the foolishness of
his wife or kids, most of it exaggerated or fabricated. He was
gregarious, good-looking, and occasionally even charming, but
offered nothing of himself. I doubt he ever shared his true feelings with anyone.

Grammy's pill-addict mother and abusive father had left her
with a chaotic mind and a bottomless, indiscriminate demand
for approval from anyone she encountered, especially strangers.
Grammy experienced every interaction as insulting, occupying
a state of perpetual offense, her feelings hurt by microscopic

slights far beyond anything dreamed of in etiquette. For Grammy, a person was either "sweet" or "nasty" depending on their ability to anticipate and deliver what she wanted. Grammy groused most about the nastiness of waiters who didn't compliment her enough, show her the appropriate gratitude for her presence.

She also harbored a unique resentment for doctors who committed the crimes of asking her age, inquiring about what she ate, or suggesting she might not be in perfect health. She considered a negative diagnosis rude.

Grammy understood that no one would like her if she accused them of nastiness twenty times an hour: being liked required constant self-censorship. "No one knows what I really think of them," Grammy bragged to Mom, as if it were an enviable ideal.

All of Grammy's motherly wisdom revolved around how best to embody what others wanted. According to Grammy, men wanted Mom to play dumb, feign happiness, and be as pretty and feminine as she could manage. For women, Mom was supposed to hide her flaws and portray herself as perfect while still remaining complimentary enough to make even those she despised feel special.

Though many people, especially women, are raised to sacrifice themselves to please others, the oppressiveness of Mom's family pushed her to extremes.

My vision of Mom's mentality at age fourteen when she met Dad comes from a story she told me when I was four or five. One of Mom's high school friends invited her over for lunch. They asked what Mom wanted to drink and she asked for milk. At the table with her friend's family, Mom drank their milk and immediately recognized it was sour. No one else at the table was drinking milk. Mom had internalized Grammy's sense of manners, believed that commenting on the sour milk would be impolite. She also knew it was rude to ask for milk and not drink it. Mom understood that etiquette was all about secretly taking on discomfort to spare others embarrassment. So fourteen-year-old Mom kept drinking the sour milk until she threw up.

When Mom told me this story, she said to me, "You wouldn't drink sour milk. Right, Michael?" I told her I wouldn't and she squeezed me. "I don't want you to ever feel like you have to drink sour milk."

EXPLAINING DAD'S PARENTS requires starting with his grandmother, the outcast of Worcester, Massachusetts. In the one photo of my great-grandmother (shot in the 1930s, the period when she wreaked the most havoc) she wears loose pants and a wide-lapel jacket like the flamboyant costume of a Shakespearean prince, with fox fur draped over her shoulder as if carrying home her own kill. Her hair is short, her face hard. Her sister stands next to her, nondescript, smiling, perfectly normal except for my great-grandmother's arms eeling around her, long, ringed fingers laced against her back. My great-grandmother stares down the camera, showing preemptive contempt for anyone who might eventually behold this photograph.

She'd emigrated from eastern Europe with her family before World War I and settled in Worcester, Massachusetts, where she married another immigrant and had eight children. Dad's mother, who we knew as Bubbe, was born in 1927, the fifth child. Because my grandmother was Bubbe, we called her mother Big Bubbe. When Bubbe was nine, Big Bubbe got fed up with her husband, exiled him from the house, and instructed her children to cross the street whenever they ran into their father. Even in the Lithuanian section of Worcester, where everyone knew one another and crossed paths daily, Big Bubbe saw estrangement as a legitimate method of problem-solving. Those present at this time (and for her numerous future marriages and divorces) say she'd leave a man the first time he told her no. So, Bubbe grew up crossing the street whenever her father passed.

Big Bubbe had already been greatly disliked, but a woman banishing and publicly humiliating her husband was scandalous beyond comprehension. Raised without a father by a brutal woman hated in their community, Bubbe was desperate to get out of Worcester. Big Bubbe had always dreamed of moving to California—no one knows why—so Bubbe inherited the idea. When she was twenty-two, she married my grandfather, who was twenty-seven, and told him, "I'm moving to Los Angeles. Are you coming with me?"

Neither Bubbe or my grandfather, Zayde, had ever left Worcester. Zayde was a short, simple man who enjoyed telling jokes and napping, not the sort of person to seek adventure or leave the only family he knew. But Bubbe asked him to move to Los Angeles anyway. She'd found a husband who wouldn't say no.

When Bubbe moved to Los Angeles in 1950, her mother and siblings followed her. Zayde's family remained in Worcester. Zayde visited Worcester often, but Bubbe refused to ever go back.

Dad described Bubbe's parenting style as normal for Jews raised during the Great Depression, but my family tends to have skewed perceptions of normal.

Dad told me, "She thought you needed to be tough or you'd die. When I was a kid, if I said I was cold, she'd say, 'No, you're not. This isn't cold.'"

Bubbe would take Dad to a toy store and tell him he could

have whatever he wanted. He'd pick a toy and she'd veto his choice.

Dad felt a lot of anxiety around holiday gift-giving because, as a child, he'd seen his mother open gifts from his father and announce that she didn't want them. Dad had tried to calm himself by asking his mother to tell him in advance what present she'd like. She replied, "No one does that."

In Mom's stories, she depicted Bubbe as tyrannical and cruel. Dad told the same stories without complaint or negativity. If any of us suggested anything bad about Bubbe, Dad would defend her, insisting that she'd been a loving mother.

Still, a direct line can be drawn from these childhood experiences to Dad's oft-repeated sentiments. "No one should expect you to read their minds," he often told me. "It's their responsibility to let you know what they want. And you should always be allowed to ask. Guessing feelings is presumptuous. Our emotions don't all work the same. I don't want anyone assuming how I feel. They should ask and I'll tell them." Bubbe's line "no one does that" tied to Dad's insistence on human variety. "Anthropologists and psychologists know that the weirdest thing you can imagine has been considered perfectly normal in at least one culture sometime in world history."

When Dad was eight, he had the idea to keep a journal. He saved his allowance to buy a blank notebook. He wrote his name on the inside cover and the date on the first page and began his first sentence. A few words in, he stopped the pen. It occurred to him that Bubbe would search his room and read this journal and that she wouldn't like the first line he'd intended to write. So he crossed out those first few words to start over with an opening his mother would approve of. Then he realized the pointlessness of writing this to please his mother. Dad's journal began and ended with that one crossed-out half sentence.

When Dad told me this story, I asked what he'd wanted to say. He didn't remember, and said that the journal had been thrown away, that Bubbe threw away a lot of his stuff without asking. I wondered if she'd opened it before she threw it out. Maybe Bubbe saw the crossed-out half sentence without putting together what it meant. Now I know that many parents may not want to know everything that goes on in the minds of their kids. But at the time, I only knew what it was like to have parents who wanted to know what I thought and who wanted to tell me what they thought. Dad's story read as the most tragic I'd ever heard, a story of a child whose mother didn't want to know him.

As a teenager in the late '60s, Dad wrote for his school paper and discovered that he could get free records and concert tickets by writing music reviews. He wrote every music magazine he could find to inquire about writing for them and many said yes, sending him free stuff to review. Dad traded the records he didn't want for ones he did. Having inherited from his mother and grandmother an enthusiasm for criticism, his teenage reviews were works of merciless ridicule. When Dad told me about his youth as a music critic, he laughed at his young self's unbridled negativity, "I wrote a letter to the *Los Angeles Times* criticizing their complimentary review of the *Exile on Main St.* tour in 1972. I described the Rolling Stones as wheezing old men who could barely make it across the stage!" In Dad's best music-critic stories, he'd ask insulting questions and accidentally offend his favorite artists. Apparently, when he interviewed Black Flag, Henry Rollins threatened to beat the shit out of him.

In the late '70s, Dad got to interview Randy Newman, one of his heroes. "I'd listened to his new album," Dad told me, "and the rhymes were out of a rhyming dictionary, like 'sad' and 'mad,' you know? I asked him why his rhymes on this album weren't as unique, if it was a choice to not focus as much on the lyrics." When Dad recounted this, he shook his head, laughing at himself. "He thought I was the craziest interviewer he'd ever met. He said he liked the rhymes, something like, 'Sorry if they disappointed you.' But I didn't let it go. I listed examples of bad rhymes from the album and he kept insisting that he liked them!" He imagined Newman would think he must really care to pay such close critical attention. Criticism was Dad's way of showing admiration and respect.

Dad's friends also spoke like critics, constantly debating art and politics. Mom's friends talked about people they knew. Dad didn't get along with Mom's friends any more than she got along with his.

In 1979, a year before I was born, Dad applied for a job at a corporate record label in Los Angeles managing their back catalog of recordings and was invited to interview with a man who had, for years, been a big deal in the music business. He met this executive and his secretary for lunch at a restaurant in Hollywood. Once they were seated, this man turned to Dad and launched into a diatribe about how much he hated the paintings of Pablo Picasso. Then he glared and demanded Dad's opinion. Dad explained why he liked Picasso and why Cubism was influential regardless of personal taste. The interviewer told Dad he sounded like an idiot and moved on to a speech about something else he hated. The interviewer put Dad through the same cycle over and over, spitting out an opinion, harassing Dad to give his own, then insulting whatever he'd said. The secretary just watched silently. Despite his confusion, Dad continued responding to each question. He went home and told Mom about his weird interview, how he'd certainly not be hired. The next day, Dad received the news that he'd gotten the job. When he arrived at work, his boss's demeanor was still prickly, but not nearly as angry as he'd been in the interview. Dad made a remark to the secretary about his not expecting to be hired after the strange interview, and she explained that he'd been given a "stress test" that measured his willingness to engage with authority, and his calmness and rationality in the face of conflict. *That* was a test Dad could pass.

A Jewish Christmas Miracle

THOUGH MY PARENTS assured me that most people enjoyed lying and being lied to, I didn't witness it myself until my grandmother brought me to meet Santa. My parents hadn't told me much about Christmas because we were Jewish.* For months, Grammy had been offering to take me to Vegas with them for a weekend and had been repeatedly offended by Mom turning her down. Being a seasoned grudge-holder and guilt-monger, Grammy persisted, asking, "What kind of mother keeps a four-year-old child from his grandparents!?!"†

In truth, at four years old, I spent plenty of time with Grammy. I'd stare at her, inspecting the color difference between her powdered face and her neck. Her purple sunglasses matched her long, painted fingernails and coordinated with her bright

---

* Grammy so hated being Jewish that she demanded Pa change his last name. Pa's brothers' wives joined Grammy in insisting that Pitkowski was too Jewish. But they couldn't agree on an alternative so the three brothers ended up with different last names: Pitt, Powell, and Powers. Mom grew up as a Powers, passing as Christian, and celebrating Christmas. Now, Grammy resented Mom raising me Jewish, denying her Christmas with her grandson.
† The real question was: What kind of grandmother can't be trusted to be left alone with her grandson?

pink lipstick. She had the uneasy, practiced smile of a beauty pageant contestant sure to lose. I'd never liked her, but she disliked me just as much if not more. I knew a lot about it because every time she visited, Mom would sit me down afterward to relay Grammy's grievances: I didn't smile at her enough or tell her how thin she looked, I asked too many questions, I criticized her driving, I embarrassed her by saying she was crushing me in the chair we were sharing, and so on. When Mom finished listing Grammy's complaints, she told me, "But you were right about everything. Grammy shouldn't go through her purse while she's driving, and you should only smile and compliment her when you feel like it. You should ask questions about anything you'd like to know. And you *should* call for help if someone sits on you!"

With each of Mom's refusals, Grammy's nagging and accusations escalated until Mom could no longer stand to say no. On the night-drive to Vegas, I slept the whole way. In the morning, Grammy shepherded me back into her car and peeled off. I'd never been in a car without being told our destination. I asked Grammy where we were going and, with her hands on the steering wheel and her face turned fully toward me, she said, "Guess!" I gripped my seat belt, terrified that Grammy would crash the car while her eyes were on me instead of the road. My parents had warned me about the commonness of car accidents. "We're going to meet Santa!" Grammy said, eyes still on my face, excited to watch me light up.

Focused on Grammy's terrifying driving, I absently muttered, "Santa?"

Grammy sighed. "Your mommy never told you about Santa?" She turned back to the windshield in disappointment. Then it dawned on her that she'd get to be the first person to tell me about Christmas, and her hands hopped from the steering wheel to my shoulders. "Santa brings everyone their Christmas presents!"

"Grammy!" I shrieked. "Put your hands on the wheel!" She kept her palms on my shoulders for a couple seconds before begrudgingly taking the wheel again.

"Without Santa, there wouldn't be any Christmas," Grammy said.

"But," I replied, "we're Jewish."

"Christmas is for everyone," Grammy said. "On Christmas Eve, Santa flies in his magical sleigh to every house in the whole world and climbs down the chimneys to put presents beneath your Christmas tree."

I concentrated my hardest to understand what was going on. I imagined the inside of my head, pictured a throbbing brain pulsing in a jar. Now I was motion sick with an accompanying headache.

"We don't have a chimney or a Christmas tree," I told her.

Mom always praised me for being perceptive, but Grammy did not. We drove in bitter silence until we reached the mall's little Christmas scene and joined the line of parents and grandparents with their hopping children.

Grammy pointed to a display of plastic trees with white foam. "See the snow!"

I'd heard Las Vegas was a desert and that it didn't snow in deserts. I dashed under the velvet rope to feel the snow. It felt like fabric and wasn't even cold.

Grammy called after me, her voice muffled through her clenched teeth, avoiding a scene. "Michael! Don't touch the snow!" She pulled my hand away from the fake snow and led me back to the line.

I couldn't imagine why Grammy would lie about foam being snow and, even stranger, why she'd expect me to believe her over what I could observe myself.

Grammy interrupted my furious thinking. "Look!" she said, her mouth open with a playful exaggerated awe that I found condescending. "That's Santa!"

At the end of the line, Santa sat in a throne, posing for photos. As the line moved, Grammy explained, "When you meet him, you tell him what present you want for Christmas." All I wanted for Christmas was proof that Grammy was lying.

As we got closer, I heard Santa's voice. "Why does he say 'Ho Ho Ho' all the time?"

"That's how Santa laughs," Grammy muttered, dismissively flashing her purple fingernails.

Eventually, frazzled Grammy lifted me onto Santa's lap and watched from the side of the stage. I inspected him for evidence of magic. Santa said, "Ho ho ho, hello *Michael*!" I gasped, unable to solve how this man could know my name. I concluded that magic was the best explanation and opened my mind at least a little to the possibility that this strange person possessed supernatural powers. But I had to attempt more tests.

"Ho ho ho, Michael," Santa said, milking my shock at his use of my name. "What do you want for Christmas?"

I trained my eyes on him to scrutinize his reaction and said, "I'm Jewish."

Santa's head fell back with a human-sounding laugh. Then, he leaned in close and whispered, "Me too, kid. Me too!"

Santa and I cracked up together. There was nothing more fun than the airing of a forbidden truth. This mall-Santa's frankness was my personal Christmas miracle.

When I got off his lap and returned to Grammy, she was ecstatic. "You were laughing so much with Santa!" she said.

My fervor to debunk Grammy congealed into nervousness. I knew telling her the story would hurt her feelings, but it seemed a shame to keep quiet about the wild thing I'd just experienced.

I told her what Santa had said. Grammy doubled over in hysterics. "Oh, Michael!" she said. "That's the funniest thing I've ever heard!"

"It is?" I asked. "I thought you'd be embarrassed because you lied."

Grammy stopped laughing. "I didn't lie," she said. Then she went back to laughing. "I can't wait to tell your mommy about what you said to Santa."

Once home, Grammy perched on the brown couch in our little living room and told Mom the story. I looked back and forth, contrasting them: Grammy's peacock colors against Mom's muted earth tones. It was hard to believe these two were related.

When Grammy mentioned that she'd taken me to see Santa, Mom's usually warm demeanor chilled. She interrupted, "You took Michael to meet Santa even though you knew I wouldn't want you to?"

Grammy ignored this question and continued the story. The way she told it, I'd been excited to meet Santa. She edited out my skeptical questions. Then she described the dialogue with Santa as if she had been right next to us to witness it herself. I watched Mom's face to see if she spotted Grammy's lies. When Grammy reached the part when I told Santa I was Jewish, Mom burst out laughing. Grammy ended the story there, omitting the part when I called her a liar. It shocked me that she thought she could get away with these distortions when I was right there to correct her.

When Grammy finished, Mom was still in a laughing fit. I interrupted, "Mom, she told it wrong."

Grammy ignored me but I knew she'd whine to Mom privately later about me embarrassing her. Mom's closed-mouth smile meant she knew who to believe, that she trusted me more than her own mother. I knew she was right to trust me. I marveled at how easy it was to be trustworthy, even for a four-year-old, and how bizarre it was that Grammy and other adults couldn't manage it.*

When Grammy finally left, Mom sighed and braced herself to explain to me why the parents at the mall lied to their children and why the children were so overjoyed to be lied to. Mom told me that when she was my age, she had similar suspicions about Santa. She asked Grammy about it and Grammy replied, "Santa brings you your presents! You're so ungrateful! You think your own mother would lie to you? And all your friends' parents would lie? What kind of a child thinks such nasty things?" Years later, when Mom learned conclusively that Santa wasn't real, she asked Grammy why she hadn't just admitted the truth when asked the first time. "Because believing in Santa is so fun," she replied. "I wanted you to have fun."

Mom did her best to explain why kids believed in Santa despite the story being so obviously false. She said that most people prioritized fun and fitting in over truthfulness.

I replied, "But we make up stories and see movies and we know it's not real and it's still fun!"

Mom laughed. "That's true, Michael! I don't know why they don't just say it's a fun story. They don't want to do it that way, I guess." Then, in an uncharacteristic move, Mom suspended her principles and advised me to hold myself back

---

* I know now that "trust" doesn't only refer to believing that someone would tell the truth. It also means certainty of support, that someone would have your back. Grammy couldn't trust me; I'd criticize her, expose her lies. I had no loyalty to her, only to the truth.

from correcting other kids about Santa. "Next year, in kindergarten, if they ask you about Santa, tell them you're Jewish so
you only talk about Hanukkah. Maybe tell them the story of
the menorah instead."

I was shocked. "Isn't that lying!?!"

Mom hesitated a moment, conflicted, but stuck with her
position. "Yes," Mom said. "But just this once, it'll be better if
you don't tell them the truth."

Dad would never have given that advice.

The Hypocrites of Kindergarten

In KINDERGARTEN, THE roving mobs of cavorting children
either barely spoke or spoke inarticulately, as if they'd never
spent an hour alone talking into a tape recorder. I invited them
to make up songs and jokes and stories but received mostly
nervous squints. The boys couldn't sit still or pay attention for
the games I knew, like asking each other questions or making
up captions for each other's drawings. They'd leap up in the
middle of my explanation to run around and scream. The girls
were better with language and more attentive but wouldn't
play with or talk to me. I wanted friends, but only under condi-
tions that disqualified the whole school.

My teacher, Mrs. Smith, wore metal-rimmed glasses and her
white hair in a messy bun with clumps and strands poking out
all over. She appeared to me older than my grandparents, with
a quiet strictness and devotion to propriety.

Once, I was sitting alone at a desk drawing while the other
kindergarten boys nearby shouted impressions of machine-gun
fire. Mrs. Smith came up behind me and rested her hand on my
shoulder. I shrugged away from her hand, which I could tell she

found rude, but I considered perfectly justified. After all, Mom had told me people should ask permission before touching me and that I could always say no if I wanted.

"Michael, why don't you go play?" Mrs. Smith said.

"I *am* playing," I told her. "I'm playing '*drawing.*'" This line was intended to satirize her suggestion that the games I liked weren't considered games, but Mrs. Smith assumed I'd misunderstood her.

She clarified, "Why don't you go play with the other boys?"*

"We don't like the same games," I said.

She knelt down to my level. "What if we go together and ask if you can play too?"

The way I saw it, I'd told her clearly that I didn't like their games and she'd responded by suggesting that I ask permission to play them? I felt certain something was wrong with her. I rolled my eyes at the exhausting prospect of having to explain something so simple to an adult. But then, before I spoke, another possibility occurred to me: she thought I *did* want to play but that I was saying I didn't because I was shy. Mrs. Smith had accused me of lying.

I corrected her in the slow, condescending tone that she and other adults used when correcting kids. "I'm not shy. I don't like their games because the screaming hurts my ears and the running makes me tired."

Mrs. Smith grabbed my arm and lifted me from the seat. "I'm sure you'd rather play with the other kids than sit here all alone."

I tried to pull away from her. "Being alone is fun," I said. She ignored me and tugged me toward the boys. I said, "This is ridiculous."

---

* Unaccustomed to indirect communication and implied demands, I took this question literally. I thought she genuinely wanted to know why I preferred to play by myself.

Mrs. Smith stopped pulling and frowned. "*Excuse me?*"

"I told you I don't want to play. You don't believe me."

Mrs. Smith's lips curled.* She gasped as if I'd cursed and sentenced me to a time-out. This was my first time ever getting into trouble. Even my parents had never punished me. I started sobbing. "Why?" I asked.

"You're being mean," she said, pulling me across the room again.

I gave her a variation of Dad's chocolate defense. "It's not mean to like a different game. You probably like different games than me, don't you? You don't play *my* games. Does that make *you* mean?" Mrs. Smith ignored this argument. Grammy was the only one I'd seen go silent like that instead of defending herself. To me, it meant Mrs. Smith knew I was right and was too embarrassed to admit it. She left me in the corner in the time-out chair. I faced the wall, crying. Then I thought about the absurdity of receiving a time-out as punishment for wanting to be alone. I laughed. I considered this the cleverest thought I'd ever had.

The next time I played chess with Dad, I bragged about this observation. Dad laughed and said, "That's called irony." I loved that there was already a word for it, because that meant others noticed what I noticed and laughed at; more like me were out there somewhere, even when everyone at school acted like I was crazy.

"Can you believe these people?" Dad said, laughing with me at Mrs. Smith. "There's no rule in school that you have to play

---

* This particular look was one I'd soon encounter regularly. First, it expressed surprise—she'd misread me as a sensitive child left out by meaner kids. Second, it showed anger—not about my obnoxious dismissal of the other boys, but about my judging and mocking *her*. I'd imagine that adults would shrug off accusations from children, but I found the opposite. There's a special fury grown-ups feel when shamed by kids.

games you don't like with people you don't like. She made it up! What were you supposed to do? Play games that you don't find fun?"*

"The other kids should play better games," I added excitedly.

Dad scoffed, and I felt his criticism switch its aim to me. "They should play whatever games they want. Why should they have to play your games if you don't have to play theirs?" I started crying, but Dad continued. "You can't go around criticizing other people for doing the same thing you do. You're being a hypocrite." I immediately knew this new word would be helpful.

MOM TOLD THE story of the Jewish Santa to anyone who would listen. Once, she told it to Bubbe and Zayde while we all sat around the glass coffee table in their frozen-in-the-1950s suburban house. Zayde was drifting in and out of sleep, like usual. Even when awake, he appeared distracted by nothing in particular. On the other hand, Bubbe reminded me of an alligator I'd seen on TV, eyes judging everything through an uncertain number of transparent, layered eyelids. When Mom had finished the story, I remembered my new favorite word and asked, "Mom! Is Grammy a hypocrite?"

Mom replied immediately, "Well, Grammy certainly does a lot of hypocritical things."

Bubbe leaned forward and, in her abrasive depression-era Massachusetts Jewish accent, said, "Don't tell him that! Michael should think his grandmother is the greatest person in the world."

Mom laughed grimly. "Believe me, Michael would notice on his own that my mother isn't the greatest person in the world."

---

* Yes, that's exactly what I was supposed to do.

Bubbe's face twisted into her most burning, condemnatory glare. She turned in my direction as if considering whether to somehow blame this conversation on me.

Mom continued, "If Michael asks if Grammy is a hypocrite and I claim she isn't, he'll either stop trusting me or stop trusting himself. And I don't like either of those outcomes."

Mom turned to Dad, hoping he'd defend her, but Dad only stared through the glass coffee table.

DURING MY FIRST few years of school, I cried in class most days. When I was inevitably called a "crybaby," I'd repeat what Dad had told me about how holding back crying was like holding back laughing and explain why crying should be considered normal, why it was much more embarrassing to hide your feelings or make fun of people who weren't afraid to express their emotions. None of my classmates found these arguments convincing.

One day, the boy who most often called other kids crybabies scraped his knee on the playground and fell to the blacktop crying himself. In my mind, this kid had already been the class's biggest embarrassment for being so afraid of emotion that he had to make fun of anyone who showed it. But now, crying on the ground, he'd been exposed as a hypocrite too. I looked on the bright side, though: he'd learned the hard way to stop calling everybody crybabies.

The boy's knee still had a bandage taped over it when I next witnessed him call someone a crybaby. A classmate had tripped and started crying, and this boy stood over the fallen kid, chanting "Crybaby! Crybaby!"

I approached and interrupted his chant. I tried Dad's method, explaining by asking questions. "You cried when you scraped your knee," I said. "Why didn't you call yourself a crybaby?"

His body flexed. I recognized this posture from angry fighting men on TV, and it struck me as very funny to see a little boy try it. "I'm not a crybaby!" he barked.

"Everyone saw you cry," I shrugged.

"No, they didn't!" he screamed. "I'm not a crybaby!" Then he took off running. "I'm telling," he called back.

I chased after him, explaining: "You call people tattletales too! You can't call people tattletales if you tattle!"

When he reached Mrs. Smith, he hugged her leg. "Michael called me a crybaby!"

With this alleged non-crybaby clinging to her leg, his eyes wide and teary, Mrs. Smith bent down to reprimand me. "That's not nice," she said.

"I'd never call someone a crybaby!" I told her. "I like crying. I cry every day. Crying is good. I was calling him a *hypocrite*." Mrs. Smith hesitated, and I became concerned she might not know what the word meant. "He cries himself and then calls everybody crybabies. He's a hypocrite." Mrs. Smith squinted at me, still uncertain what to say. "I'm helping him. It's hard to see if you're a hypocrite without someone else pointing it out. It's like telling him he has food in his teeth."

Mrs. Smith finally came up with a response. "Michael, how would you feel if someone called *you* a hypocrite?"

"I would be glad they told me," I said.

Mrs. Smith shook her head, exhausted already. " 'Hypocrite' is a mean word."

I laughed, "No, it isn't! My dad calls me a hypocrite all the time!"

Mrs. Smith recoiled and rose again to her full height. Then, without saying anything, she retreated with this boy following along, still clutching her pant leg. I took her walking away to mean that she'd again recognized I was right.

When I boasted to Dad over the chessboard, he laughed, "What were you *supposed* to do? Not notice the contradiction? Ignore it? Cut him a break? Stay quiet?"*

IN THE CAR on the way home from school each day, I'd tell Mom stories of all the lies and hypocrisies I'd witnessed.

"Mrs. Smith made everyone shake hands after kickball to pretend to be good sports! And we played telephone and the other kids kept messing it up *on purpose*! And when I hurt myself on the playground, Mrs. Smith told me I was brave even though I didn't do anything brave!"

Mom would laugh and tell me how right I was. "Nothing gets by you, Michael!"

"Nothing gets by me," I'd say.

The fact that I could tell my parents all my experiences and observations made school's daily injustices tolerable, even occasionally fun. In a tense moment of confrontation with a teacher or another child, I'd sometimes burst out laughing about what a funny story this would make.

Mom and Dad mostly sided with me against the other kids and teachers, but that was only because they mostly thought I was right. When they thought I was being unfair, closed-minded, or hypocritical, they'd tell me that too. It was the criticism that convinced me they were really listening, that made me feel like I mattered. In my family, silence was suffering, confession was connection, and criticism was love.†

LATER THAT YEAR, I experienced a kindergarten Christmas, everyone raving about Santa while I kept quiet about what I

---

* Yes, any of those responses would have been fine.
† This is the brain I'm working with here.

knew, an excruciating introduction to lies of omission. I've heard many describe the pulse pounding and cheek burning of sharing feelings, but it was the bottling up that made me ill. I dreaded the day that these kids would find out they'd been duped. I knew I couldn't resist confessing that I'd been complicit, that I'd known all along.

These kids didn't figure out the truth about Santa for a few more years, a lifetime of holding my tongue. In the wake of the reveal, I witnessed no dramatic scenes, no displays of shame or anger at this betrayal. When I confessed that I'd always known the truth, the other kids lied and claimed they'd always known too. It was as if they cared less about the truth than about the communal experience they'd had with their friends and families. "It's ridiculous," I mumbled to myself, pacing the playground. "It's ridiculous."

A Butt Show-Off

WHEN I WAS eight, Dad, Mom, and new baby Miriam sat in our backyard and listened while Josh, now four years old, told jokes. As he spoke, Josh danced around, his gangly limbs flailing in simultaneous multidirectional motion. Sometimes he'd pick up an inflatable rubber ball twice as big as his torso to bounce and punch and bump against his head. His "jokes" were meandering stories connected with "and then." He'd slow down each time he said "and then" to give himself time to think of the next thing to say. It would be something like: "A penguin walked up to a duck and said he was thirsty. *And then* the duck gave him a cup of water. But it was ice! *And then* the penguin sucked the ice! *And then* . . ." He'd go on, reveling in the attention, until we stopped him.

As we watched Josh's experimental comedy routine, Mom laughed with him, happy to see him smiling with his deep dimples and his long-eyelashed eyes so joyful. I was also laughing, but mostly because I loved his misunderstandings about how jokes worked. Our laughter emboldened Josh to get louder and faster. Eventually, he was forgetting to take breaths, panting while he carried on.

Dad laughed too, but behind it I could sense an impatient discomfort. Eventually, he broke down and interrupted. "Josh," he said. "One thing you should know about jokes: they usually *end*!" Dad's delivery didn't read as mean; we all laughed and Josh laughed with us, though I'm not sure he knew he was being criticized. Dad made this a teaching moment: "The ending of a joke is called a punch line . . ."

Josh interrupted by shouting "Punch line!" and punching the inflatable ball. Josh loved punching things. His favorite toy was a punchable balloon man.

Dad laughed at Josh's interpretation of the word, but continued to explain it. "A punch line is supposed to be so funny and surprising that it feels like a punch."

Josh ran off mid-sentence to chase after the inflatable ball he'd just punched across the yard. Then he breathlessly asked Mom if he could go inside to punch the balloon man. This conversation had inspired him.

"Let's try making up a punch line," Dad suggested, thinking he was inviting Josh to play a fun game. But Josh tensed as if he might erupt in rage or flop to the ground crying.

I interrupted to explain in a different way. "Josh," I said. "Here's what you do. Whenever you want to end a joke, say, 'I just flew in last night. And boy are my arms tired!'" Everyone laughed, including Josh, though I sensed he didn't get the joke. "If you say you just flew here, they think you mean on a plane.

But then when you say your arms are tired, they see that you meant you flew like a bird." I mimed flying with my arms. "The joke is that no one flies with their arms!"

Josh hopped up and down smiling and said the line cutely and we all applauded.*

Not long after that, Dad mentioned to me over the chessboard that he'd tried to teach Josh to play chess. "He moved the pieces wherever he wanted!" Dad said, exasperated. "He just wanted to knock over the pieces." Dad shook his head with bona fide anguish. "I told him I wouldn't play chess with him if he was gonna throw the pieces, but he only laughed and got wilder."

I understood why this disturbed him. Josh wasn't like the rest of us. I'd noticed it too. I didn't know what happened when a younger brother didn't match his family, but I imagined it wasn't good.†

When Josh went to kindergarten, he got along with the other kids, which was even more concerning. His friends would come over and run around in the yard with him, yapping and yelling incoherently like most children.

In 1989, Dad got sick of driving more than an hour to and from work and we moved away from Claremont to the San Fernando Valley. I remember Mom hugging five-year-old Josh on the couch, comforting him as he cried about leaving behind his friends, listing the names of all the boys he'd miss. It struck me as ridiculous to have become attached to so many friends in half a year of kindergarten. I chalked it up to his having low standards.

---

* For the next year or two, Josh would tell a joke, watching for my signal. Then he'd blush and say he just flew in and his arms were tired.

† For our whole childhoods, when Dad described us to other people, he'd say, "Michael's a writer and Josh has great hand–eye coordination."

Josh and I joined a new school halfway through the year. Soon after we started there, Josh came home from first grade sobbing. He collapsed on the carpeted living room floor and told me the other kids had spread a rumor that he had a green butt.

"I don't have a green butt!" he cried from the carpet. "My butt isn't green!"

"You don't have to convince *me*!" I said seriously. "Why would they think your butt was green? Maybe they saw a green tag on your pants or something and thought it was your butt? That's pretty dumb, even for five-year-olds."* Josh gazed up at me tearfully, in need of older-brother wisdom. "First of all," I said. "You shouldn't feel embarrassed. If you *did* have a green butt, they'd be wrong to make fun of it. It's okay to be different."

Josh then burst into tears again, protesting that he didn't have a green butt.

I tried to calm him down with advice.† "Just bring them to the bathroom and show them your butt." Josh wiped away a tear with a new sense of hope.

When he came home from school the next day, he was crying again. "I told them to come to the bathroom!" Josh said. "But they wouldn't go! They said I wanted to show them my green butt. They said I was a 'butt show-off'!"

I shook my head, disappointed in humanity. "You mean you tried to give them evidence and they refused to even look at it? It's like they don't want to be right! Like they don't care what's true!" Josh squinted, thinking his hardest; I imagined him considering whether he, himself, cared what was true. I wondered if he'd yet figured out that caring what was true meant not having friends.

---

* At age nine, I still naively took a lot at face value.
† I must note here that I was genuinely trying to help; the worst possible advice was the best I had to offer.

Josh asked Mom and Dad for clothes, shoes, and haircuts that matched the other kids' at school. His speech took on an unfamiliar laid-back accent that bore no resemblance to our wordy, long-winded fast-talking. Both Mom and Dad referred to Josh's friends as bad influences and worried about his wanting to do whatever his friends did.

I remember Dad asking Josh, "If all your friends jumped off a cliff, would you?"

Without hesitation, Josh said, "Yeah!"

It soon became clear he'd imagined jumping off a cliff into a lake but, misunderstanding aside, Josh's allegiance was clear.

Chapter 2

My Miseducation

In the San Fernando Valley, Dad and I found a new weekend activity: walking miles to and from synagogue. On Saturday mornings, I'd put on a little black suit and a yarmulke for the epic sweaty pilgrimage in the Los Angeles heat, following Dad through the suburban neighborhoods of Granada Hills, an area usually driven past, traversed only by dog owners. I was unaccustomed to long walks, so my legs ached and burned, each step harder than the last, but the physical discomfort was worth it for Dad's games.

Dad would point at billboards we passed, inviting me to analyze how each ad aimed to trick us into spending money. It was during this game that he explained to me that stores priced everything to end at ninety-nine cents to trick people into feeling they were spending less. I asked Dad who would be stupid enough to fall for that. He answered, "Most people."

Another game we'd play involved my guessing how various things worked and seeing how close I could get. Once, Dad asked me to guess the job of the person who made the most money from my favorite cereal, Frosted Flakes. I guessed the cook who invented the flake. Dad explained that it was the investor, a job I'd never heard of; the investor always made more money than the workers, even though it was the workers who invented the flake and drew the tiger and wrote the slogan and played the tiger's voice. After that, when I heard the tiger say, "They're grrrrreat!" it no longer felt great.

When we'd see other people on our walks, we'd discuss their style choices and guess at their lives. Dad might ask me why I thought someone would want a tattoo of a skull. I'd guess that he wanted to look scary. Then Dad would ask if the skull proved he *was* scary or only meant that he wanted to *appear* scary. Each inquiry led to the same conclusion: many tried to appear to be things they weren't, and many were duped by these performances; being perceived as something had nothing to do with really being that thing.* Any time an expensive car drove by, he'd give the same rant: "You know, almost everyone with an expensive car is leasing it? They borrowed the money to look richer than they really are. And even if that guy *can* afford that car, he expects us not to notice that he could've given that money to charity. He'd rather spend his money on appearing rich than on something meaningful. He's an embarrassment. He thinks the car makes him look cool, but it should be a badge of shame."

For each newspaper Dad read, he also subscribed to three media watchdog pamphlets debunking it. So, Dad made a game

---

* Despite all this discussion about the differences between a person's reality, what they presented the world, and how they were perceived, it somehow never occurred to me to consider how I'd be seen.

of challenging me to identify inaccuracies and biases in news stories. Once Dad asked me, "Why do you think newspapers print corrections?"

"Because they made a mistake and they want the news to be right?" I answered.

"That's what they want you to think," Dad said. "They print corrections to make the rest of the paper appear accurate."

Dad and I would role-play debates on political and philosophical subjects and he'd show me how the script usually went and invite me to dismantle why certain arguments were tricky or misleading. He'd use examples from the news and politics and history, both recent and ancient, explaining that people used the same faulty arguments over and over because they weren't creative enough to make up new ones. He taught me the ancient Greek logical fallacies to help give names to the different kinds of bad arguments and lies. As we spoke, Dad's eyes remained ahead, never on me; he had the concentrated gaze of a tightrope walker. Half the time, his voice boomed, low and certain. The other half, he'd sound like a comedian at a roast.

It made me proud that Dad considered me mature enough to take on these adult subjects. None of the children at school could identify the biases in the news or list the ancient Greek logical fallacies. My teachers at school seemed unaware of the flaws in our country's versions of capitalism, democracy, and the legal system. School wasn't honest enough to be taken seriously. Dad was my education.

Through these games, I learned in specific terms why school was bullshit, the justice system was bullshit, success was bullshit, coolness was bullshit, gender norms were bullshit, authority was bullshit, white supremacy was bullshit, conventional romance and friendship were bullshit. Anything slippery or disingenuous stood out as if highlighted red.

I remember spacing out in school, trying to understand why someone would lie. It took me a while to come up with a single example of how lying could be useful. I eventually came up with a potential lie: I could hear a funny joke on TV, repeat it, and claim I'd made it up myself. But it was immediately clear to me why this lie was pointless. I didn't want to be the type of person who took credit for someone else's jokes. I wanted to be the type of person who wrote my own jokes, even if they weren't as good, or who told other people's jokes and admitted I didn't write them. Knowing I'd stolen a joke didn't sound fun at all, even if I managed to trick everyone, because *I'd* know.

Most dishonesty read as comedy. Liars reminded me of the Wizard of Oz frantically saying, "Pay no attention to that man behind the curtain!" Though everyone could see the humor in *The Wizard of Oz*, they regarded the unraveling of their own lies with dire seriousness.

THE BETTER I became at talking, the more Dad criticized what I said. As I got older, he made a game of interrogating me with classic questions of moral philosophy. "If a hospital has five people who will die without organ transplants and one healthy person walks in with organs that could save them all, do you kill one person to save five? Or let the five die?" If I answered that we should kill him, he'd say, "Seriously? You'd tear the organs out of a random innocent person?" If I changed my answer, he'd say, "You'd really let five people die to save one?" He'd often add new information to make the hypotheticals more difficult. "What if the man with the good organs is a bad person and the five dying are heroes? What if the five who need the organs are teenagers and the one with good organs is seventy-five with a terminal illness?" This variation on "Would You Rather?" with moral questions was thrilling but stressful because Dad would hold me to what I said and demand that I justify my answers. To this day, when I'm asked a hypothetical question, I flood with adrenalin.

At night, I'd lie awake in bed, haunted by recent arguments, reasoning them out in my head. I believed that if I thought enough, my mind could be clear and correct, and I'd be able to express my reasoning unassailably and be convincing. When Dad and I talked, I concentrated on remembering every word we said for later consideration. If Dad claimed he hadn't said something or that I'd misunderstood him, I needed to be able to depend on my memory.

Sometimes I'd feel certain Dad was wrong and that I was explaining why perfectly, but he'd still insist I wasn't making sense. When I'd call out Dad contradicting himself or avoiding a question I'd posed, he'd get accusatory: "That's nonsense," he might say. Or, "You don't even mean what you're saying." I particularly hated, "You're wasting my time." These lines bothered me, I think, not because they were critical, but because they were the same evasions Dad had taught me to see through. Sometimes I wondered if Dad was testing me to make sure I'd call out vagueness and avoidance and bad arguments, even with him. I *hoped* he was testing me.

Once, I noticed Dad stomping through the house. I saw him accidentally slam his shoulder into the side of a doorway and asked him, "Dad, why are you mad?"

"I'm not mad," he growled.

"But you seem mad."

Dad glared down at me. "You think you know how I feel better than I do?"

"No," I said.

"Don't think about how I *seem*," he snapped. "Listen to what I *say*. If you don't believe me, that's calling me a liar." He loomed with his arms at his sides and feet together like a soldier. "No one else knows as much about my feelings as I do. That's why it's so presumptuous to try and read someone's mind. If you want to know what someone is feeling, *ask*. And when they tell you, believe them."*

Everybody's a Critic

BECAUSE I WASN'T playing with other children, I spent most of my playtime at home reading and writing. I wrote stories constantly, hundreds of them, and I'd show my favorites to my parents. Mom found my stories amusing. She'd be diplomatic without lying, telling me the parts she liked and sometimes telling me if there were previous stories that she liked better and why. But I always got the sense that she meant everything she said, and she was always responding specifically and seriously no matter the nutty eight-year-old subject matter. Dad didn't share Mom's diplomacy. I remember most clearly his thoughts on a mystery short story I'd written about a boy who could win every chess game, no matter who he played. In the story, everyone was certain he was cheating, but no one knew how. At the end, a detective-like child revealed that this mysterious sham chess master had been playing with weighted pieces. I knew this ending made no sense; I was good at setups, not payoffs. I figured payoffs were too hard for an eight-year-old but Dad didn't see my age as an excuse.

We sat in the record room, Dad waving a marked-up copy of my story. "Why would weighted pieces benefit a chess player?"

---

* I think it's safe to say this was the worst advice I ever received. Wrong or right, these were the lessons I learned and the style in which I was taught. Please keep them in mind in case you want to forgive me for obnoxious things I do later.

"You caught me!" I answered, laughing. "I couldn't come up with an answer to the mystery!"

But Dad wasn't laughing. His seriousness in these criticism sessions made them even funnier. Dad studied his notes on the manuscript. "Did you think the reader wouldn't notice that the ending doesn't make sense?"* Dad asked. "Were you counting on your reader being an idiot?"†

"It was a test!" I said, laughing. "You passed!"

Dad continued without responding to my joke. "Also, chess competitions don't let players use their own pieces! Didn't you do any research?" It had never occurred to me to do research. I decided that the next time I wrote a story, I'd ask the school librarian to fact-check.

"How did he sneak his weighted pieces onto the board anyway?" Dad asked. "Is this kid a *sleight-of-hand artist*?"

I took that as an actual suggestion. "Ooh, maybe at the end he should be a magician!"

"That's not what I meant—" Dad clarified.

"Wait, better idea!" I said. "What if it turned out he had magical powers? Maybe he won because he could read their minds!"

"That could be better," Dad said. "Depends on your execution."

Often these criticism sessions ended with Dad being reminded of a similar story or movie or an episode of the *Twilight Zone* or *Outer Limits* that he'd describe to me for inspiration. Sometimes, he'd read me aloud a Ray Bradbury story.

"Oh wow, that's *way* better!" I'd chirp and rush off to try a new ending or write something else entirely.

I showed Dad every story I wrote that I liked, maybe one out of ten. He'd read anything I showed him and give me written

---

* Dad had an unpleasant habit of asking literal questions without realizing they sounded rhetorical. It was a habit I'd, unfortunately, inherit.
† Mom and Dad were my only readers.

notes. Over the course of my childhood, Dad must've read and commented on a hundred of my stories, maybe even more. He didn't have anything positive to say about any of them. I didn't mind because *I* liked the stories and that was all that mattered. There was no reason my stories had to be good. I understood that it was rare to be a great artist. Dad told me openly that he himself had never written a good story. "I always liked fiction and poetry but I had no talent," Dad said. So, I was off the hook. I could write stories for enjoyment. Criticism was part of the fun.

Eventually, an adult told me I had "thick skin" and explained to me what the phrase meant. It didn't sound like me. Other people armored themselves; I wanted to be like the ancient Greek Stoics Dad had told me about who were as sensitive as anyone but strong enough to bear the full weight of their feelings. That sometimes meant crying but more often meant laughing at myself.

MRS. RACINE, MY fourth-grade teacher, had a stiff '80s perm and smelled like hair spray. She gave me a B- on a story I wrote for class, a noir caper about rats who robbed a cheese store.

I raised my hand and asked Mrs. Racine, in front of the class, why she'd given me a B-. I agreed that the story deserved a B-; I hadn't liked it enough to show it to Dad. But I was testing my hypothesis that Mrs. Racine had no reasoning behind the grade, that she wasn't a good enough teacher to know how to criticize. To me, this situation was win-win. If Mrs. Racine proved herself a better teacher than I expected, good for her! If she failed to justify the grade, she'd have confirmed my hunch that she gave out grades based on personal feelings about the students or on whims that we had no reason to entertain. If Mrs. Racine were publicly discredited, other kids in class who might have felt bad about their grades could be freed from her baseless judgments.

Mrs. Racine replied, "Michael, you need to learn to take criticism." I laughed out loud at how little she knew about me.

"I *like* criticism," I told her. "The problem is you didn't give me criticism. You wrote the grade without an explanation."

Mrs. Racine called me out into the hall as if I was in big trouble. I started crying, as always. Once outside in the echoey school hallway, she repeated that I needed to learn to take criticism. I told her, through tears, "But when you're not specific, no one can decide if your opinion is worth listening to."

I didn't anticipate that she'd be insulted by this remark. I assumed teachers knew they had to earn their authority. But Mrs. Racine reddened; her hands flew to her hips. "I'm the teacher!"

Luckily, my eyes could cry and roll at the same time. "Think of it this way," I said. "If I was grading you on how good you are at giving criticism, what grade do you think I'd give you?" Mrs. Racine's mouth fell open. And I wasn't even finished. "Actually, the question that really matters is: what grade would you give *yourself*?" At this, she flinched and took a step back.

I braced myself for her to punish me or send me to the principal, but instead Mrs. Racine muttered an excuse about having to get back to class and dashed away, leaving me in the hallway. I chased her through the classroom door and called out, "Mrs. Racine, *you're* the one who needs to learn to take criticism!" This retort would have landed better if I weren't still crying.*

---

* I'm now aware that Mrs. Racine probably didn't give her students specific comments because she was overworked. She'd probably read fifty student stories and didn't want to admit that she had no memory of mine. But if someone had been there to direct my attention to this possibility, I would have replied without compassion, "Why didn't she just say that?"

When I told Dad about this confrontation, he tilted his head against the cushion of the record room couch and stared at the ceiling. "If she can't handle criticism from a child, how does she expect to make it through life?"

It seemed true that if Mrs. Racine got this sore over questions from me, under the smallest fraction of what I received from Dad, she'd shatter.

Ask the Rabbi

THERE WERE SHOCKINGLY few conversational lulls on our walks to and from synagogue, but whenever a silence struck, I'd tell Dad about any theories or questions that had been recently on my mind. I'd never found a question that Dad wouldn't answer; I doubted that such a question existed. That's why one Saturday morning, hurrying after Dad in my little suit and yarmulke, I considered it perfectly appropriate to ask, "Dad, what does the Torah say about fetishes?"

Dad laughed, charmed. "That's a great question!" he said, his voice rising in pitch.

I'd learned the word "fetish" earlier that week from Mom, even though I'd been saying fetishistic things since I started talking. In one section of the first Michael Talking Tape, Mom asked me what TV shows I liked and I answered, "*Inspector Gadget* because Penny gets tied up." When she asked what other shows I liked, I said, "He-Man, because sometimes Teela gets tied up. And Betty Boop because sometimes she gets tied up."

On the tape, you can hear Mom laugh knowingly. She says, "Well, Michael, it's good to know you're a feminist."

I'd often brought up these things in school, thinking it was a matter of taste; some kids liked cartoons about soldiers or unicorns, and I liked cartoons about girls tied up. In earlier childhood, teachers had shrugged off my remarks, but by age nine, I'd noticed that the subject made adults mysteriously uncomfortable. So, one afternoon with Mom, I asked her why it bothered them.

Mom didn't need to pause to decide how to discuss this. With the unvarnished truth, answers required no hesitation. "You like girls tied up because you have a 'fetish.' That's what it's called when you really like a special thing that other people don't even think about." She said it matter-of-factly, the way my teachers spoke about photosynthesis or the gold rush. "Lots of people have fetishes," Mom said. "Liking girls tied up is one of the most common ones. And lots of girls like being tied up too."

I stopped drawing. "They do? Why?"

"Why do you like what you like?" Mom asked me.

"I don't know," I said.

"That's because no one knows why they like what they like. But some people get upset when they're reminded that not everyone likes the same things."

I could tell this answer wasn't the whole story, but it was satisfying because she made it sound like anyone thrown off by my fetish was unreasonable.

When I brought up fetishes on this sweltering walk to synagogue, Dad told me, "The Talmud is supposed to discuss everything. That should include fetishes." Then he laughed. "But I have a feeling you've found something they missed." I blushed with pride. "Do you have a specific question?"

"My question is . . . does the Torah say it's okay to imagine girls from your school tied up?"

Dad answered casually, "In Judaism, you're allowed to think anything you want. It's Catholics that believe thoughts can be sinful."

I considered this some more. "Also," I said, "I've imagined girls tied up since I was born . . ."

"Since you can remember," Dad corrected. "Memory develops at three or four."

"Oh yeah," I said. "So if there's a God, he gave me a fetish."

"That's an interesting argument," Dad said.

"Why does God give kids fetishes? Does God like fetishes?"

"Hmmm," Dad said. His brow folded, and I wondered if his head hurt as much as mine when he thought. "I don't know," he said. "You should ask the rabbi."*

The next morning, at the big wooden table in the synagogue where I had my one-on-one Hebrew School lessons, I opened with the question: "What does the Talmud say about fetishes?"

Rabbi Minsky was in his sixties, with a wizard-like red beard and nicotine-stained yellow teeth. He always reeked of cigarette smoke.

The rabbi's light green eyes trained on me and I watched his wild red eyebrows rise. "Fetishes?"

"Yeah," I said. "Like if someone imagines girls tied up, but doesn't tie up girls in real life."

"Tied up?" he repeated, wagging his head and waving his hands in a cartoonish caricature of confusion that might very well have been bad acting. Mom had presented fetishism as commonly understood. This scholarly rabbi was either unaware of fetishism or pretending to be.

I told him, "I imagine tying up girls all the time. God must want me to think about that, right?"

Rabbi Minsky said, "Why are you thinking of this? This tying up?"

---

* This may sound like a joke, but he was not joking.

"No one knows why they like what they like," I said, surprised that a nine-year-old would know more about life than an allegedly wise old rabbi. "If the Talmud doesn't mention fetishes, why not? Isn't it an important subject? Are there some things God doesn't want us to talk about?" Rabbi Minsky hesitated, so I spelled it out for him. "If God wants us to talk about everything, we *have* to talk about this," I said. "Either God isn't honest or *you're* not honest."

"Now, hey now," Rabbi Minsky said. "That's not nice." This always puzzled me, when dishonest people found it insulting to be described as what they were. If they thought dishonesty was so bad, why did they insist on practicing it? The rabbi sighed and said, "Let's get started. We have a lot to talk about today."

He began lecturing about something much less interesting than fetishism, and at first I felt pretty salty about the whole exchange. But then my feelings shifted and I found it hilarious. As Rabbi Minsky went on, clearly still tense, I kept smiling and occasionally bursting out laughing. He got irritated enough to pause and tell me I seemed distracted. I said, "I'm laughing because I might be more honest than God!"

Make Fun of Something True

My NEW SCHOOL was close enough to our house that Mom and I walked there, but most of the students arrived in buses. I liked the kids on the buses because they struck me as critical thinkers, unlike the white blond kids back in Claremont who swallowed the ridiculous lies school fed them, who really believed that grades and memorization and pleasing teachers proved your intelligence. These new kids resented the absurdities and injustices of school as much as I did. They told personal stories and cursed and talked dirty, their conversations full of words and sentiments the white kids plainly couldn't handle.

Robert and Manuel led the group of friends I most liked, and I followed them around as much as they let me. They regarded me with confusion, but must've found me an amusing curiosity. They wore expensive sneakers and baseball hats with sports team names, their hair buzz cut, slicked back, or combed into stiff waves. I didn't do any of those things. The barbers at Supercuts would ask Dad how he wanted my hair and he'd say, "I'm not a hair expert. Just do what you think is best." I was the only one in the group who wore glasses. My thick wire-rimmed glasses, at the time, were considered the epitome of nerdiness, and Mom hadn't changed my clothing style much since kindergarten.

One day, I was crouched on the playground blacktop with my back against the handball wall, watching them pass a basketball back and forth, racking my brain for a game or conversation topic that would entertain them enough that they'd give up on this boring dribbling.

Robert chased the ball with each bounce; he was much bigger than the rest of us, moving with the controlled clumsiness of a clownish physical comedian. His huge head bobbed up and down, his round face jolly. He was usually the one who broke any silence, guiding the conversation.

"Michael's nasty," Robert said. "He picks his nose. I saw it." His friends laughed riotously. I had no complaint about this remark because it was true; I did pick my nose, and it was entirely possible Robert had caught me. "Michael picked his nose and then ate the booger!" Robert continued, darting after the ball.

"And then he shit out the boogers!" Manuel said. He only spoke when he really had something to say. He was small but athletic and handsome, with thick, sculpted black hair and dimpled cheeks.

"Wait a minute," I said. "That's ridiculous." The boys turned to me with reluctant interest. They'd expected me to respond with a similar jab, to join in the banter. "I believe that you saw me pick my nose," I told them, rising from the blacktop. "But I obviously didn't eat my boogers. Why would anyone eat boogers?" The boys looked at each other nervously. "It's true that if I did eat boogers, they'd come out in my poop. That's science," I continued. I considered it evenhanded of me to compliment the part they'd gotten right. The boys laughed at my mentioning shit again and I got the feeling they weren't catching my meaning. "If you're gonna make fun of someone," I concluded, "only make fun of what really happened."*

Manuel did a nimble little dance in place and said, "Michael picks his nose! He admitted it!" The boys half-laughed, but the scene felt mirthless and awkward.

"Of course I pick my nose!" I said. "Everybody does. You do too—"

"Shut up! No, I don't!" Manuel interrupted, his fists suddenly clenched, his face taut. "Take it back!"

"Come on, Manuel, you're really trying to tell me that you've never picked your nose?" I turned to the others and said, "Does anybody believe that Manuel has *never* picked his nose?"

"Shut up!" Manuel shouted, stepping close to intimidate me.

I continued addressing the other boys. "See how Manuel is threatening to punch me?" Then I parroted what Dad had told

---

* I can only imagine how bizarre it must have been to deal with me at age nine—this joyfully argumentative nerd smiling through his gratuitous sermons.

me about displays of masculinity. "He's pretending to be tough to hide his embarrassment. He's so ashamed of picking his nose that he can't handle someone acknowledging it."

"Shut up!" Manuel said again, too upset to think up a comeback.

"If he was really tough, he wouldn't care. He'd admit he picks his nose. He's too scared to express his feelings. That's why all he says is 'shut up.'"

"Shut up!" Manuel sputtered.

I laughed and pointed. "See, *that's* funny." No one else was laughing so I tried to explain, but they still didn't see the humor. I sighed, "Make fun of *true* things, okay? And only make fun of what isn't also true about you. For example, you can make fun of me about wearing glasses because I wear glasses and you don't." I thought more. "Or because I'm clumsy and I hurt myself every time I play sports. Because you guys aren't as clumsy." I thought of more things that were unique to me that they might ridicule. "And I cry about everything. And I like girls. And I try to talk to them and they run away." The boys watched me in a horrified trance. I felt so energized that I started stepping back and forth in random directions, an awkward, chaotic hopscotch. "And my shoes are from Payless. And I have freckles and I'm ugly. And I get good grades and I'm a nerd. And I don't like the games everyone likes." Confessing my flaws felt unexpectedly powerful. If I could accept all the unfortunate truths about myself, no one could embarrass me by mocking them. My words sped up and rose in volume as if I were delivering an inspiring, climactic speech. "And I don't use gel! And no one laughs at my jokes! And I have no friends! And I don't like wearing a hat!" In the desolate silence that followed, an idea struck me. "Hey!" I said, hopping on my toes. "I invented a new game that maybe all of us would like!" Manuel shifted weight from his right leg to his left and back. A couple boys instinctively backed away. Others listened in dread. "Let's take turns telling true things about ourselves that could be made fun of!"

That weekend, I told Dad this story and how they'd run off to get away from me. He said, "Wow, these kids are so immature!"*

Checkmate

DAD AND I still played chess in his record room in our new house in the San Fernando Valley. By age ten, I'd been losing dozens of games each weekend for six years. These thousands of losses had dulled my chess-related emotions; nothing felt more commonplace and expected than losing.

One game, I spotted an opening to fork Dad's bishop and queen with my knight. Because I'd never before had such an opportunity, I assumed I had to be overlooking something, that Dad was luring me into brilliant trap. I scoured the board for any threat to that square and didn't see any. It appeared Dad had made a mistake. My hand shook as I slid my knight into place. I continued scrutinizing the board as I moved, not yet taking my hand off. Dad's expression betrayed no recognition of his blunder, or sign that he was impressed by my exploiting it. I took my hand off the knight.

"Well, look at that," Dad said. "I'm in trouble." Dad surveyed the board, tapping his fingers on the carpet. This went on for a while. "I don't think there's anything I can do," he said. He searched the board some more and determined he couldn't protect one piece without endangering the other. He gave up,

---

* It wasn't until I was much older that I recognized the ridiculousness of referring to nine-year-olds as "immature."

moved his queen away, and I took his bishop without any sacrifice of my own. This was my first time in a chess game experiencing a moment of advantage.

As the game continued, Dad's playing became erratic and unconsidered. He lost more pieces unnecessarily and said, "I don't think I can recover, but let's play out the rest of the game anyway."

When I checkmated him, he flicked over his own king. I'd knocked over my king thousands of times, but it threw me off to see Dad do it. I'd always hated that gesture. We both already knew who had lost; I didn't see why we had to add this symbolic moment of submission. Watching Dad topple his king felt even worse than toppling my own.

As the king's rocking slowed, I watched Dad, in suspense about what he would say. "Want to play again?" he asked, exactly as he always did.

"Yeah," I told him.

"Okay," he said, already lining up his pawns.

I picked up pieces too and began arranging them. "I thought you'd say something about me finally beating you."

Dad didn't stop setting up the pieces. "What did you think I'd say?"

"I thought you'd say that it was worth it that you never played easy on me," I said. "Because now I can be sure that I really won."

"You know that already," Dad said. "Why would I point out what you already know?"

I scratched my head. "I guess I thought you'd say you were proud of me or something."

Dad laughed uncomfortably. "Beating me isn't much of an accomplishment," he said. "I'm not even good at chess."

The Falsely Accused

THE FIRST WEEK of sixth grade, Mr. Gelman and Mrs. Johnson announced that a crime had been committed and that class wouldn't continue until someone confessed. The class remained silent as Mr. Gelman, pink, bald, and enormously tall, and Mrs. Johnson, elderly, hunched, and dead-eyed, called on Manuel, Robert, and their friends, interrogating them in front of the class, asking things like, "So, Manuel, do you have anything you'd like to tell us?" And "Well, Robert, I have to say, you look pretty nervous."

I interrupted. "What was the crime?"

Mrs. Johnson replied, "They know what they did."

I'd spent a few years at this school already aware that the white teachers mistreated the black and Mexican kids. To me, it was impossible to miss. The teachers spoke to them in harsher, colder, more suspicious voices. When they raised their hands to answer a question, the teachers called on them with condescension and skepticism. In fact, whenever a teacher spoke one of their names, it was with a tone of accusation or punishment, to humiliate them for not knowing something or not paying attention. I noticed that the kids with the darkest skin were treated worst. I'd brought up these observations with Robert and Manuel and their friends many times, but they clearly didn't want to discuss the subject.

With all that Dad had taught me about the justice system, America's racist history, and the methods police and lawyers used to trick the innocent into confessing or make the innocent seem guilty, I knew what a racist sham trial sounded like, and one was happening in my sixth grade class.

"You have to explain the charges," I said, interrupting Mrs.

Johnson. "And the only reason you're trying to get a confession is because you don't know who did it or you have no evidence." I expected the class to laugh, but they were unresponsive, probably stressed out.

Mr. Gelman ignored me and ordered Robert to follow him into the hall. In only a few minutes, he returned saying it was all over now and we could continue class. "Wait," I said. "How do you know it was Robert?" Mr. Gelman said something else about how it was all over now, but it wasn't over for me. "If you knew from the start that it was Robert, you wouldn't have gone around class interrogating people. Did you blame him without evidence?" The teachers ignored me, left me fuming in my seat.

When Robert returned the next day, I asked him what happened. They'd sent him to the principal for graffiti in the bathroom and called his parents. On the playground, Robert told us, "I still don't even know what the graffiti was like, if it was words or a picture or anything!" He told us he didn't do it, but said the principal and his parents didn't believe him.

"Your parents trust the teachers more than *you*!?!" I asked, appalled by the thought.

It wasn't long before Mr. Gelman and Mrs. Johnson stopped class for another interrogation. This time they said something about a stolen candy bar and once again directed their questions exclusively to Manuel and Robert and their friends.

"Why do you always accuse the same people?" I asked, knowing why.

Mrs. Johnson asked to talk to me in the hall. I immediately started crying, which she naively mistook as a sign I'd fold, a common misinterpretation. My tears were a manifestation of anger and should have been taken as a warning that I was about to become aggressive and merciless.

"Michael Leviton," Mrs. Johnson said in the hall, "you can't talk like that."

"It's school. We're allowed to ask questions," I said. "Teachers are supposed to answer."

Mrs. Johnson remained callous and unmoved. "Those boys are a bad influence on you," she said. "You should stay away from them."

"You blame whoever isn't white," I said through my tears. "Just like the newspapers."

Like Mrs. Racine a couple years before, Mrs. Johnson clearly wanted to punish me, but something mysterious prevented her. My previous best guess had been that these teachers feared me telling the principal my side of the story because I spoke well enough that I might be believed. In this moment, I put together that Robert could speak clearly too, but that the teachers didn't worry about anyone believing him. The answer flooded through me: they didn't punish me because of the color of my skin.

In an unprecedented rage, I told Mrs. Johnson this realization. She kept repeating that Robert and Manuel were bad kids.

"How do you know?" I asked again. "What's your evidence?"

"I know what kind of kids they are," Mrs. Johnson said, eyeing the classroom door, preparing to make a run for it.

"All you know is they're not white."

Like Mrs. Racine before her, Mrs. Johnson fled, hurried back into class, leaving me crying in the hall. I followed Mrs. Johnson back inside and found that the interrogation had run its course undeterred while she kept me occupied. I sat back down at my desk, consumed by plotting what I'd do differently next time.

I now understood that my teachers feared embarrassment more than they feared being immoral. They were emotionally unprepared to be questioned or exposed; that left them vulnerable, fragile. Mrs. Johnson and Mr. Gelman had already shown me that they wouldn't send me to the principal. Besides, I'd already told my parents about the racism I'd witnessed and I knew they'd support any attempt to stop it. My lack of respect for authority and total comfort about confrontation meant Mr. Gelman and Mrs. Johnson had no way to make me shut up.

I told Robert and Manuel about all of this, but they wouldn't look at me.* Robert said that I never got in trouble because I was the teacher's pet. I started crying, insisting Robert had seen how I hated the teachers, how I called them out. They remained unresponsive to all my best arguments, so through tears I assured them that next time the teachers interrogated the class, they'd see.

It wasn't long before my teachers held the class hostage over some new crime. I immediately asked Mrs. Johnson outright why she didn't accuse the white kids.† Mrs. Johnson and Mr. Gelman acted as if I hadn't said anything. "Why aren't you asking *me* if I did the graffiti?" They didn't respond to that either. The fact that I was crying in no way hindered my assault.‡ "Why are these questions so hard for you? Why are you afraid to answer?"

Eventually, Mrs. Johnson acknowledged me, saying, "Michael, you're being distracting."

I said, "I'll be quiet if you'll be honest."

---

* I didn't have the perspective to understand what these kids were going through and why they wouldn't want to talk about it.
† It didn't occur to me that I might be embarrassing or disturbing or endangering the kids I thought I was helping. I spoke the truth recklessly; I found honesty's destruction unpredictable.
‡ In the moment, I envisioned myself as powerful, but I'm sure my questions read as whimpers.

Chapter 3

Teenage Truths

AT THIRTEEN, I was old enough that Dad would take me to concerts a few times a week with free tickets from work, mostly to see acts I'd not yet heard of: Ray Davies, Neil Young, X, Rufus Thomas, Joni Mitchell, the Allman Brothers, Bradford Marsalis, Ministry, Mose Allison, the Grateful Dead. The bus to and from junior high played KROQ, providing me with my first opportunity to discover music on my own. Because Dad listened to everything new that came out, he'd already heard every new band I could find.

One of the first bands we saw that I'd actually heard of was Nirvana. Dad was a bigger fan than I was; I'd only heard the hits. This was also the first concert we'd attended where Dad was the only adult in sight. As we waited for the bands to start, I looked around in disgust at this stadium of flannelled drones, a grunge-themed ant farm.*

---

* My style was unique because Mom still bought my clothes and she had no idea how thirteen-year-olds in 1993 dressed. My baggy pants and button-up shirts still bore flamboyant colorful 1980s patterns. My pattern-mixing must have looked pretty unhinged.

A comedian, Bobcat Goldthwait, opened the show. Dad and I respected this eccentric decision, Nirvana flouting convention. I loved Bobcat's unique hoarse screech, a voice purely his own. He began his routine by mockingly asking the audience how many of them shopped at the Gap's new grunge section. The stadium erupted with laughter. I was surprised; I didn't expect people to have a sense of humor about their embarrassing trend-chasing.

A few songs into Nirvana's set, I could sense that something was bothering Dad. He said, "This band is so incredible, so authentic and personal." I could feel a "but" coming. "But I hate their stage outfits. I can't stop imagining them cutting their jeans with scissors and using hairspray to mess up their hair. It's the least punk thing I can imagine. They put in all this effort to look like they don't care." Dad shook his head. "Plenty of great musicians wear costumes, but they *admit* to wearing a costume. Grace Jones and David Bowie don't pretend they just rolled out of bed. Nirvana are lying."

"Totally," I said, impressed by Dad's insight. "It's so fake."

"Well, they're still young, I guess," Dad said. "Maybe they'll get more comfortable with their real selves when they're older."

EAVESDROPPING ON MY school bus felt like watching bad movies, sitting through clichéd dialogue and overacting. Kids around me bragged about crimes and sexual exploits that had obviously never happened. In their preposterous stories of dangerous older siblings and sex-crazed romantic interests at other schools, they couldn't even keep track of the names they'd invented. Yet, I never heard any of them doubted.

That summer, I attended an educational program on a college campus often referred to as "nerd camp." The first day, when we'd all just met, the circle of boys I sat with on the grass

wanted to take turns saying how far we'd gotten with girls. I'd heard conversations like this on the bus, but always from boys much older and cooler. Most of the kids in this circle were smaller and less physically developed than me. The child nerds defined second base as touching breasts, third base as getting a blow job, and a home run as having sex. At thirteen, I couldn't imagine how I would've ended up friends with a girl, let alone kissing one. The boys went around the circle, each announcing that they'd gotten to second or third base. I knew they had to be lying so I asked follow-up questions, pressing them to tell the full detailed stories of these alleged blow jobs. The little blond boy who had initiated the game quickly blew up at me, told me to shut up and stop interrupting. He took his turn, cocked his head and smirked in an inadequate impression of a man. "I got into a pickle between third and home," he said. The circle was impressed.

When my turn came, I said, "I haven't gotten to any bases." The blond boy didn't allow a pause for this to sink in before gesturing to the next kid in the circle, who announced that he'd also gotten to third base. I listened, stewing. When we'd gone all the way around the circle, I said, "I didn't realize this was supposed to be a game of pretend."

The boys' eyes darted around the circle, each one hoping someone else would know how to respond. The blond boy ended the silence by standing up and suggesting that they go get sodas.

I didn't know if these boys really believed one another's lies or if their bonding didn't depend on the truth. But I left with a pretty good method for spotting false stories.

It seemed that many lied for the purpose of giving off a particular social impression. These boys boasted about non-existent sexual experiences because they wanted to look cool and adult. Because they weren't particularly creative, quick-minded, or imaginative, they couldn't invent realistic details or unique scenarios. They'd remain vague and adapt stories they'd heard elsewhere to be about themselves, assuming no one would ask follow-up questions. So, to spot this kind of lie, I only had to ask two questions: first, does this lie help them make some kind of desirable impression? Second, if they wanted this impression, is this the story they'd use? Once I had these two questions at my disposal, almost every story a boy told me read as a lie.

I felt certain girls weren't like this. I'd listened in on their conversations and watched them from afar. Girls talked about their experiences and feelings. They wrote in locked diaries; I'd daydreamed about what thoughts or stories could merit such secrecy. Girls wanted to express themselves. I set myself to the task of figuring out how to be friends with them as soon as possible.

High Self-Esteem

AT FOURTEEN, I went back to summer nerd camp and met a girl named Maya who liked personal questions. In our first conversation, Maya told me the story of her birth: her mother wanted a child but not a husband so convinced an ex-boyfriend to father a child he wouldn't raise. Maya also told me about her eighteen-year-old boyfriend back home in Washington and shared with me her observations about sex. She theorized that there was no way to be universally good at it, that sexual chemistry was about the lucky coincidence of two people having compatible interests. She wore a tie-dye shirt and shorts, so I told her she dressed like my dad. She said her mom dressed the same way. It was the first interesting conversation I'd ever had with someone outside my family.

The next day, Maya said I'd made her realize she should break up with her boyfriend. She'd written a break-up letter and mailed it that morning. She told me now she wanted to kiss me. She spread a picnic blanket under a tree in an isolated area and we stretched out, facing up. She leaned over and kissed me from above. When I kissed back, she pulled away. "Let me show you how to do it," she said. "Stay still." I'd seen people press closed lips together or stick tongues in each other's mouths, but she did neither; she sucked on each lip, one at a time. I tried the same thing on her and it felt like how I'd hoped kissing would feel. This was a big relief; I'd feared that kissing was something else everyone pretended to like just to fit in.

I said, "Wow, I guess some stuff is popular because it's genuinely beautiful."

Maya laughed and said, "Kissing can be real or fake like talking can be real or fake." She smiled dreamily from above me. I thanked her for teaching me how to kiss, and she said she was touched to be the one to teach me.

I told Maya that she was the only person who'd ever really liked me and she didn't believe it. After talking about me with other camp nerds, she reported back and said, "It's true! Most people really don't like you! They explained why, but the stories they told made you sound really funny and interesting."

"We both like honesty, so it's hard for us to imagine why other people wouldn't," I told her. "But trust me, they hate it. Or at least they hate it when *I'm* honest."

She nodded. "People mostly like me, but now that I think about it, it does feel like the ones who don't probably turned against me because I said something honest."

Maya was my "girlfriend" for the rest of nerd camp. After that, we wrote letters and talked on the phone long-distance as often as our parents were willing to pay for, once every few months.

Having met one girl who liked me, I felt even more justified in my plan to hold out for the few who were capable of honesty and forget about everybody else.

A YEAR OR so later, I started regularly passing notes with a girl in my sophomore Spanish class. Tamar wasn't like Maya; when it came to my personal questions, she was evasive. Though she never answered, she appeared to enjoy my asking. She'd write me just as personal questions back, provoking me to say more and more. It wasn't long before I was raving in these notes about my fetishistic fantasies, getting a thrill out of watching her big eyes widen as she read them during class. She'd finish a note and give me a sly look with a closed-lipped grin. I started to write about how I felt about her, telling her the sexiest and most romantic things I could come up with. I asked her directly how she felt about me and she told me she thought I was cute and emotional, that I was a sexual person like her. She told me about seeing the British band Pulp play, how she couldn't stop imagining Jarvis Cocker's long hands moving over her. We never had these dirty conversations face-to-face—we never even spent time alone—it was all in notes in Spanish class, as if real things had to be kept secret. I'd seen in teen movies how notes could be intercepted and read by the teacher in front of the class, humiliating everyone involved. I wrote Tamar that I would love it if that happened, that I was proud of our notes. I told her I thought we wrote stuff so dirty that this teacher would be too embarrassed to read it aloud. I asked Tamar if she'd be upset about one of our notes being read to the class and she avoided the question.

I passed her a note asking if she'd like to hang out sometime outside of school. She wrote back "yes" with an exclamation point. I took the exclamation point seriously. That night, I dreamt of exclamation points.

I'd failed my driver's test (not because of truth-telling, just because I was a bad driver), so Tamar picked me up at my house far out in the San Fernando Valley, and drove me around Los Angeles, blasting Billie Holiday's *Music for Torching*. I'd never heard a voice so honest.

At the end of the night, Tamar parked the car outside my house and I asked if I could kiss her. Her shoulders hunched to her ears. "Why did you ask?" she said, squirming. "Why didn't you just do it?" She looked back up at me. "Asking ruins it. I would have kissed you but you *asked*."

Maybe I was supposed to understand this as a polite excuse. Maybe I was supposed to kiss her now without asking. But instead I held her to this philosophical position. "You only want to kiss someone who doesn't ask? Is everyone supposed to read your mind? I don't want to try to kiss someone who doesn't want to kiss me back."

"Don't ask *permission*," she said. "Do what you want."

I thought back to Maya telling me in advance that she wanted to kiss me. "Isn't this just your personal preference?"

"*No one* likes being asked," she insisted. I mentally noted that I should pose this question to Maya in my next letter. "Asking isn't sexy. You should be more confident. If you're confident, you don't have to ask. Because you know everyone wants to kiss you," she said. "Confidence is hot."

"Let me get this straight," I said. "You're saying that if I somehow convince myself that everyone wants to kiss me, that unsubstantiated delusion will be perceived as hot?" Tamar backed against her door, likely considering what to say to politely get me out of her car. I still hoped to turn her around by arguing. "Barely anyone wants to kiss me. That's just factual information. How am I supposed to believe something that's provably false?"

"You have low self-esteem," Tamar said.

I laughed. "No, low self-esteem is when you hold *yourself* in low esteem. I love the way I am. I have a low opinion of *other people*. I have low *other-people-esteem*."

THOUGH TAMAR DIDN'T kiss me and we didn't go out again, we still kept up our note-passing. Maya and I also kept up our letters and phone calls.

Six months later, Josh was having his Bar Mitzvah, and my parents told me I could invite friends. It turned out that we'd be borrowing an RV for the weekend (so Dad, who didn't drive on the Sabbath, could stay next to the synagogue Friday night and avoid walking back and forth). On Saturday night, while it was parked in our driveway waiting to be returned, one of my friends could stay there too.

I invited Maya and two other friends we both knew from nerd camp who lived near me. When Maya arrived, she told me she now had a boyfriend back home and that it would be wrong to kiss me, even though she still loved me. I appreciated her clarity and straightforwardness and respected this boundary. I focused on another fantasy: to introduce her to Tamar and have a conversation with both of them at the same time.

After the Bar Mitzvah that Saturday, we all met up: me, Maya, Tamar, and the two others from camp. Everyone but me wanted to somehow get ahold of alcohol. I'd never gotten drunk before, so I had no thoughts about whether this would be fun. I ran with it because it was what Maya and Tamar wanted.

The nerd boys and I sat in the car in a supermarket parking lot watching from afar as Tamar and Maya asked an older guy to buy them vodka.

We drank the vodka with orange juice in the RV in my parents' driveway. My memory gets hazy here because I was so drunk, but I woke the next morning remembering enough isolated moments to put together what likely happened. I remember suggesting that we all take off our clothes.* I don't remember any discussion that might have followed, but they must have liked the idea, because the five of us ended up naked in the RV bed together, two boys lying with one girl and me alone with the other. The two other guys were older and more experienced.† I'd done nothing but kiss Maya and reach up her shirt. Naked in bed with Tamar, I didn't know what I was supposed to be doing. I might have been the least experienced person to ever start an orgy.

As thrilled as I was to make out with Tamar, it wasn't long before I wanted to stop and talk. "Hey, Tamar," I said. "Is this the only time we're gonna do this? Or is this gonna happen again with just us, alone?"

Tamar kept her eyes closed. "Shut up and kiss me," she said, which I loved; it was like something from a movie. We kissed awhile more, and then I paused again to ask her, "Are you gonna be my girlfriend now?"‡

"Shut up and kiss me," Tamar said again. And again that line served its purpose.

---

* This was particularly odd to suggest because I didn't like my body. Still, I saw it as cowardly and self-destructive to hide my flaws. Seeing others naked required being naked myself. My body was just another unpleasant truth worth exposing.
† Some teen nerds managed to have girlfriends, apparently.
‡ I was oblivious to the fact that we were only a foot away from Maya and these two nerds, who could definitely hear everything I was saying.

A while later, we'd switched. I was with Maya while the other guys were with Tamar. This time I commented to Maya, "You said before that we couldn't kiss because you have a boyfriend."

Maya took Tamar's line. "Michael, shut up and kiss me."

"Are you gonna tell him about this?" I asked.

"Shut up and kiss me," she said again.

Then we were interrupted by Tamar making ecstatic noises. One guy was kissing her while the other was doing something between her legs. I didn't know what exactly he was doing, and I thought to look. But then, when I turned, I realized I didn't want to see it. It was the first time I'd not been able to bear to look at something. I wondered if this was how others felt when they couldn't face the truth. My shame at my cowardice was quickly eclipsed by frustration that I didn't know how to get Tamar to make these noises.

The next morning I woke up in bed with Maya and the two guys. Tamar sat on the opposite side of the RV, fully dressed in the previous night's clothes. She shot me a blushy smile that I adored. I walked over to her, naked, and found my clothes. When I bent over to pick them up from the floor, she ran her hand through my hair. "I should go home," she said.

Once everyone was up and Maya was taking a shower in the house, the other guys deconstructed with me the previous night's events. The taller one said, "Tamar was a screamer! She was sucking my face off!" Though he was technically telling the truth, hearing this disgusted me. I instantly decided I'd never speak to him again. The nerds left and I dropped Maya off at the airport to fly home.

At school the next day, I told the wild story of the orgy, by far the best story I'd ever lived, over and over to my friends. I included all the miserable parts and my continuing uncertainty about whether I'd ever kiss these girls again. In Spanish class, Tamar smiled at me in that same blushy way, so I asked her if she'd like to hang out that night. She said yes.

Once at Tamar's house, I told her how much I wanted to do that again with her alone and asked if she'd teach me what to do. She recoiled, told me she'd thought of it as a one-time drunken thing, and asked me not to tell anybody about it. "Oh," I said. "I didn't realize it was a secret. I've been telling the story all day." She got quiet and didn't want to look at me. I should have just left, but instead I told her what was upsetting me, about the other nerd calling her a screamer and saying she'd sucked his face off. She then told me she felt sick and needed to go to bed.

"You don't have to lie," I told her. "You can tell me you're upset." I naively expected a breath of release. But the more I assured her she could be honest, the more stressed she acted, and the more desperately she repeated that she was fine except for this sudden mysterious illness.

The next day at school, she wouldn't respond to my notes. Maya wasn't returning my calls either.

After dinner that night, my parents and I were in the kitchen talking about various things that had happened at the Bar Mitzvah. "How was it seeing your friends?" Mom asked.

"It was good at first and then really bad," I said. "Everybody hates me now because on Saturday night we got drunk in the RV and I convinced them to get naked and make out and no one liked how I dealt with it."

Mom and Dad sat down at the kitchen table and I told them the entire story (it didn't feel remotely unusual to tell my parents about my teenage orgy). When I described Tamar getting upset the next day, Dad mirrored my indignation. "What were you *supposed* to do?" he asked. "Keep it secret? Hide what had been said about her?"* Dad gave me an approving nod. "I think you handled it well."

---

* Yes, that was what I was supposed to do.

Chapter 4

Family Camp

In 1997, when I was sixteen, my parents sat me down at the dining room table and asked if I wanted to go to family camp.

The rest of my family had gone to this camp without me for the last few years while I was at nerd camp. Mom explained that it was an experimental community created by a famous family therapist. The founder had died ten years before, but it was now run by her protégés. Mom had been studying to become a therapist for the last few years under the mentorship of one of these protégés; that's how she'd originally been invited. Mom said the camp's culture and activities had been designed to exemplify how, in practice, this famous dead therapist's methods could make a better society.

I asked, "Are the therapists there good?"*

"I like the therapists," Mom said. "A few of them at least."

---

* Of all the questions to ask, that was the one that came to mind.

"It's not all about the therapists," Dad said. "Family camp has a whole different culture." Dad paused and got teary. "It's hard to describe," he said in a voice muddled by crying. "It's the only place I know where you won't be punished for being honest."

That was it. I was sold.

So, ALL THE Levitons got into Mom's minivan and drove together the six hours up to the Bay Area. I was seventeen, Josh was fourteen, and Miriam was ten.

I hadn't spent much time with Miriam. By the age she could speak articulately, I was eleven or twelve, already Dad's little disciple. Miriam was only around when Mom or Dad were in the room and they tended to be the focus of my attention. At family dinners, Dad and I would talk about whatever was on our minds, usually leaving out Miriam and Josh, sometimes even leaving out Mom.* Miriam had big curly hair, big cheeks, and a performing streak; she liked to sing and dance and improvise one-girl shows, playing all the characters. While I'd only had to deal with Dad, Miriam received criticism from both Dad and me, like we were Statler and Waldorf from the Muppets, high up in the theater box, joking together obnoxiously. Though Josh and Miriam could have resented being so often ignored, I got the sense they were relieved to avoid Dad's scrutiny. Still, Miriam had endured a trying childhood and, by ten, was already embittered and uninterested in hiding it.

THE ONE-AND-A-HALF-LANE ROAD to family camp runs along the top of a series of cliffs, twisting like crazy, treacherously steep at all times whether going uphill or downhill. It

---

* It didn't occur to us that we should talk about something that would appeal to everyone present.

felt metaphorical, like we were supposed to vomit physically to prepare for vomiting emotionally.

From the road approaching camp, one could see a creek with a cute little bridge and children frolicking among the rocks, hunting crawdads with whittled spears, catching newts in jars and, beyond that, the thick woods. Our van pulled into the camp "parking lot," a big grassy clearing in the forest. Most of the cars there had bumper stickers: "I am the proud parent of my inner child"; "All who wander are not lost"; "Stop child abuse. It shouldn't hurt to be a child." Countless "Practice random acts of kindness and senseless beauty" stickers. One license plate frame read "I'd Rather Be Surfing," and another read "I'd Rather Be Myself."

The bathroom building resembled a cement block dropped haphazardly in the forest. The outside walls of the kitchen building were plastered with posters, each one featuring a quote from the camp's founder over a background of clouds, rainbows, or flowers. I moved poster to poster, rubbing my chin like a snob in a gallery.

"Normal is dysfunctional."

"Ask for what you want, even if you are certain the answer will be 'no.'"

"Criticize without blaming."

"The failures of a family can be measured by the number and severity of its secrets."

We had dinner at our own picnic table in the dining area, and a fidgety man in wire-rimmed glasses with a smattering of unruly gray hair joined us uninvited. I assumed he was friends with Mom or Dad or both, but my parents' awkward greeting suggested otherwise. He introduced himself to me and immediately said that I didn't have to remember his name. "You don't have to remember names here," he said. "We don't

care about politeness." I didn't believe him; a week without
politeness sounded too good to be true. As if to illustrate, Dad
told this man that we'd rather not have him at our table. The
old man showed no sign of offense, said okay, and sat somewhere else. This exchange between adults saying explicitly
what they wanted and accepting each other's boundaries was
my vision of utopia. I'd never realized how much all the indirectness and hostility I usually encountered weighed on me,
how freeing it felt to know I wouldn't be scowled at over every
insignificant interaction.

The next day, I attended the morning ceremony called "temperature reading." I followed everybody to the amphitheater
where most of camp's 150-person population sat freezing on
the old wooden bleachers bundled up with mugs of coffee. The
attendees generally wore camping clothes or sweatpants, a lot
of green family camp hoodies and T-shirts.

Temperature reading began with "warm fuzzies," a time
dedicated to campers taking the stage and giving apprecia-
tions about anything that had happened the previous day. Lots
of campers stepped down from the bleachers to give little
speeches, and I was impressed at how much everyone seemed
to love camp and one another. I'd never witnessed communal
positivity that didn't read to me as empty etiquette. Warm fuzzies was followed by "bugs." Frowning campers now got in line,
three times as many as had come to the stage for warm fuzzies.
Someone complained that the teens made too much noise at
the campfire. Someone else was mad that his favorite jobs had
been signed up for before he'd arrived. A little girl of about five
protested camp's chopping down trees for firewood. Someone
brought up an imposition on the part of another camper and
we had to listen to an indignant rebuttal. Others leapt up taking
sides. Campers started crying, upset by all the fighting. Then

other campers expressed resentment of the ones who didn't like the fighting, refusing to be shamed for being brave enough to work through conflict. After a while, most had lost track of which original bug had started it.

I theorized that this was what happened when those who had been censored their whole lives were suddenly invited to speak: they weren't used to making decisions about what they wanted to say or why.

The "session area" sat at camp's edge, a clearing with a floor of orange and yellow leaves, and a ceiling of trees with little gaps of visible sky. Camp rolled a chalkboard into the clearing to serve as backdrop for the work and added a rug to represent a stage. The audience sat in folding chairs with scattered boxes of tissues. I loved the surreal beauty of the chalkboard in the woods.

The therapists at camp were referred to as "facilitators" and the therapy was called "work." I loved that camp had made up its own unique jargon. Inventing names and phrases felt personalized and expressive; thoughtless inheriting of language was square.*

One of the facilitators, Max, with a beak nose, a bushy beard, and knowing eyes, got up front. He wore a fleece vest and beanie hat and seemed to be perpetually shrugging. He sprayed himself with mosquito repellent and announced that we'd start with a full-group "check-in."

"This is a chance to share with the group what's bubbling for you right now or to catch us up on your life since last camp."

One by one, campers gave soliloquies summarizing their

---

* In retrospect, I wonder if family camp's unique language might have also served some legal purpose. Camp's facilitators were all certified therapists, but it still strikes me as suspicious.

recent pasts, mostly telling devastating stories. Everyone was crying, including me. It was heartbreaking to have real people standing right in front of me with the saddest faces in the world, telling the most important stories of their lives. I loved the flawed beauty of their improvised speech.

One woman started her check-in with a grimace. "Has it ever occurred to you that maybe some of us don't enjoy standing here to hold up our year for judgment?"

Max the facilitator rose. "We all hear your feelings about how check-in doesn't fit for you. How many others here feel uncomfortable at check-in?"

Dozens of hands flew up. I couldn't imagine what there was to feel uncomfortable about. Now, campers took turns sharing feelings about check-in itself, describing their self-inflicted guilt and shame, their "inner critics," their experiences not worth listening to, their lives never good enough. Some spoke about fear of judgment and mockery, even at camp. I knew in theory that these feelings were common, but I'd never heard it confirmed, confessed explicitly before me.

THE NEXT AFTERNOON, we congregated before the blackboard in the woods again for work. Max the facilitator asked the audience of about forty in lawn chairs if anyone wanted to volunteer, and a broad-shouldered giant who towered over all of us raised his hand and lumbered to the leaf-strewn rug. Max asked him what was "percolating," and he told the story of his wife getting pregnant. Only a few sentences in, he broke into a sobbing so intense that it was more like screaming. Through that unbridled crying, he told us that his wife had miscarried and it was unclear now if she could have children and that he blamed himself.

When the man made a particular noise, like mooing, Max

said, "Follow that sound!" The man mooed louder and his huge body curled into itself with the release. Max asked him, "If your pain had a voice, what would it say?"

The giant answered, "You hurt everyone who loves you!"

Max asked the giant to call up someone from the audience to play the role of his pain and recite this line over and over. Hearing this voice externalized destroyed him; his legs buckled. Audience members leapt from their seats to buttress his cumbersome frame.

I knew nothing of self-loathing or loss or grief. I imagined that even the teenagers already acquainted with hospitals, prisons, courtrooms, and funerals hadn't seen a grieving man cry this wildly.

Max called up more volunteers to restrain the giant so he could rage. Almost everyone present got up to hold onto him, including Dad and me. I clutched the giant's shoulder as he flailed under our group grip, bucking and twisting. Dad and I made eye contact; he raised his eyebrows and smiled at this bizarre moment of father/son bonding.

After that, I went to every session I could. I saw work about a doctor bullied by his boss, childhood sexual abuse, a woman who wanted her husband to be more open to rough sex, the toll of years of unemployment, and the troubles with dating over the age of eighty. I felt I was getting views of so many different lives, so much perspective that I'd never find anywhere else. Knowing a person's past helped so much to understand his present. Outside camp, histories were invisible; most people stubbornly refused to discuss why they'd ended up the way they were, leaving me forever in the dark.

Aside from the proper sessions, Dad and I went to "men's group." The "specialty groups"—men's, women's, young adult, teen, elder, children's—acted as confidential sessions where campers could discuss their partners or families privately. Someone could confess an affair in women's group without her family knowing. A grandfather could talk about his dead wife's secret addiction without tarnishing her memory for his kids or grandkids. I didn't like confidentiality; I considered privacy dishonest.

In men's group that first year, I watched Dad do work about his anger at his father. Once Dad had chosen someone from group to play Zayde, Max asked Dad how he should be posed. Dad said, "He's always asleep." So the camper cast as Zayde feigned sleep on a folding chair. Dad kept describing him as "weak" and "cowardly," so Max asked him to call someone up to play Zayde's weakness. Dad picked a young, muscular guy and everyone laughed. Dad was surprised by the laughter. "The irony didn't occur to me," he said. "I thought of my father's weakness as carrying him through life. Like he'd droop on the floor without it. So, to play weakness, you'd have to be strong."

Dad didn't go as wild as others I'd seen, but he did cry a lot and talk about not wanting to be like his father. Once he'd calmed, the facilitator asked me to tell him whether I thought he was like his father.

I said, "Are you kidding? You're the least asleep person I know." The group was moved. I shrugged and added, "For better or for worse. Pros and cons." That got a laugh out of the men's group.

In less than a week, I'd already watched a few dozen people do therapy in front of me. Beyond that, camp had a magical power to transform every conversation into therapy. At camp, somehow we only told personal stories or discussed types of interaction or communication and how we felt about them; so many talks ended up commenting on the very conversation we were in the middle of. But this all felt right to me. And when I didn't like a discussion, I could walk off without anyone being offended.

My only objection was that in about a third of the sessions, either the person doing work or an audience volunteer would play someone's infant self, curling up on the rug in the fetal position. The person doing work would apologize to his infant self or make promises. Someone might play their own infant self with other campers in roles as family around the "cradle." I didn't know how anyone else felt about having an adult onstage pretending to be a baby, but I found it unpleasantly distracting.

Going to family therapy camp as a teenager had many unexpected side effects. Afterward, I couldn't help viewing all strangers as vessels of hidden pain and fear. I imagined what the world would look like if pain glowed, if we could know on sight how much someone was suffering. Some would be candle flames and others would look like furnaces. Some would be blinding to behold.

I came home from camp with whole new lists of manipulations, defense mechanisms, and coping styles, new categories of distorted thinking and delusion. Camp's endless stories of abusers, narcissists, and gaslighters contributed to my brain's compendium of lies. It was getting harder and harder for me to fall for anything.

Truth or Dare

WHEN I RETURNED to high school for junior year, everyone read as even more shallow and fake than before. I remember standing outside the venue where my school's teen bands played, accosting a smoking acquaintance with my gratuitous running commentary about what was *really* going on, gesturing at a cool, attractive boy near us and bloviating, "Look at that guy! Think of how much he's hiding! What's his family like? What does he really feel about his friends or the girls he goes out with? We'll never know! No one knows! It's crazy! He'll never tell!"

Though I was having trouble appreciating anyone in my high school, the teenagers in my drama class interested me most. They were charismatic and talented, hilarious improvisers, impressive dancers. I felt an affinity for artistic people because they tended to be more open to discussing feelings, as if being expressive in one way encouraged a person to be more open in others. Regardless, the fact that I admired the drama kids didn't mean they wanted to be around me. In most social situations, I could find one or two friends who enjoyed my presence and couldn't see what everyone else disliked so much. But even those who liked me would eventually remark on how angry others became when my name was mentioned and the general unease that descended wherever I went. One actor I admired would glower at me so brutally that I'd leave any room he occupied. A friend who brought me up to him reported his response: "One thing I've gotta give Michael Leviton. He knows I don't like him and he never makes a big thing about it. I've never met anybody who was so cool with me not liking him."

"That's so nice that he noticed!" I replied, flattered by what I considered a compliment.

On the first night of the drama class camping trip, I ended up crowded in a flashlight-lit tent with all my favorites from class to play Truth or Dare. I'd never played before but I'd heard about this game that felt ideal for me, a situation when everyone told the truth and any question was permitted. Because the drama kids appreciated spectacle, the dares tended to be pretty humiliating, so most picked truth. This was convenient because I had no interest in the dares. In fact, I interrupted the game to suggest that we skip the dare half and play "truth."

"Maybe you'll realize that telling the truth is fun and you'll start answering questions truthfully all the time," I said. The group was unresponsive to this suggestion.

My turn came to pose a question for the biggest heartthrob in our drama class. I considered what I wanted to know most about him. I wondered a lot about the experience of being the boy all the girls liked. It occurred to me to ask whether he felt like he could be himself with the girls he dated, but I decided against that one because I already knew the answer was no. One thing I didn't know was how much sex the most desired boy in school actually had. I didn't want to ask for a number—I wanted to make it personal somehow, have him tell us something about his emotional life—so I asked how many girls he'd had sex with, who was his favorite, and why.

The tent erupted with protests, claiming I couldn't ask that question. I scoffed, "It's Truth or Dare! The whole concept is about answering any question!" The group continued to demand that I ask something else. "What's wrong with what I asked?" I said. "And since when does Truth or Dare have forbidden questions?"* The heartthrob waved down the objections, told them it was okay. He made a show of mentally counting the girls he'd slept with and said twenty. It was hard to say if he was telling the truth or exaggerating in either direction. He said his current girlfriend was his favorite, which I figured he felt he had to say. "Because," he said, thinking. "She's smart? And fun?" I cracked up, expecting everybody to laugh with me at this

---

* I suspect the trouble was that he'd slept with a couple girls in the game and that everyone there knew his current girlfriend, who wasn't present.

avoidant, pandering answer that expressed nothing. "Come on!" I said. "That's not an answer! You really don't have anything to say about why you like sex with your girlfriend? You're hiding your feelings, even in Truth or Dare!"

The group again yelled at me, arguing that he'd been charitable enough to answer a bad question, that it was time to move on. Even while others performed truths and dares, the tension in the tent remained, everyone aware that I could ask an inappropriate question or call out someone for lying at any time. At one point, someone asked me a truth question; I can't remember the specific question but I remember it being boring. "You could ask me *anything*!" I said. "Is that really what you most want to know!?!" Eventually, it was my turn to pick another question for a random girl I'd just met on this trip and barely spoken to. Without any personal context, I asked her one I'd want to ask anybody: "What are your sexual fantasies about?"

Again, the tent freaked out, but this time was worse than the last. "What's wrong with you?" one of her friends shouted.

"You're such a pervert!"

"Ask something else!" another one of her friends said.

"Okay," I said bitterly, "but how am I supposed to know which questions are off-limits?"

"Common sense!" she said. "Like, you wouldn't dare someone to stab himself in the eye."

"Apparently, in our society, sexuality is so taboo that confessing your fantasies is the equivalent of stabbing yourself in the eye!" The room was silent. "Are your fantasies even that bad? Are you fantasizing about something particularly dirty or immoral or something?" After more bickering, I backed down, "Okay, okay, I won't ask any more sexual questions. How about this: 'What are the three things you're most insecure about?'"

The tent hated that question too. "You're so mean!" someone shouted at me.

The girl who had been asked the question barked, "I'm not insecure!"

I laughed at that. "Oh, come on. Everybody's insecure! Do you expect anyone to believe you're not insecure about *anything*?"

"You're so pretentious," someone shouted.

"Stop asking questions," someone else said.

Though I found this all very funny, it also aggravated me enough that I didn't want to play anymore, so I got up to leave. I had to climb over a bunch of people so it made a scene and gave them time to accuse me of taking the game too seriously and childishly storming out. When I finally reached the flap and unzipped it, I delivered my parting line. "You guys should rename the game 'Hide Your Feelings and Dare.'"

Michael Leviton Is Lying

MY SECOND YEAR at family camp, I saw Amanda do work. I'd only had one interaction with her in the lunch line, but I'd noticed how much she irritated everyone with her conniptions in temperature reading over minor slights that only she cared about. If she couldn't keep it together at camp, I couldn't imagine what she was like in the rest of the world.

When Amanda volunteered to work, she plodded to the front as if wearing rusty armor, stood in front of the chalkboard, and gazed into the audience, her face hard. "This is terrifying," she said. The campers in lawn chairs kept their heads down to avoid eye contact.

"This audience is here to support you, not to judge," Max

said. The audience clearly disliked her and would definitely judge. "So," Max said to Amanda. "What's bubbling today?"

"I'm lonely. I'm just very lonely. I date a lot, and it never works out. Men are so fucked up. I don't want to shut my mouth and act like I don't have feelings."

"I'm hearing," Max said, "that you think men don't like when you show your feelings."

"For instance, I have herpes," Amanda said. Audience members recoiled and quickly recomposed themselves to act as if they hadn't. "I was on my third date with this guy I really liked and it was getting sexual so I told him and he pulled back, totally disgusted. He left me for doing the right thing."

Max replied, "Why don't you call up someone to represent your support?"

Amanda peered into the audience with wet eyes and stopped at Dawn. Dawn had been a cheerleader in high school forty years before and was often typecast as support. She joined Amanda in front of the blackboard.

Max asked, "Where do you want her?"

Amanda said, "Behind me. With her arms around my waist."

Dawn embraced Amanda from behind.

"Now," Max said. "Call someone up to play the role of a man you'd like to be with."

"Wow, really?" Amanda laughed. "This'll be fun! I can have anyone I want?" Amanda searched the audience, giggling, looking the men up and down, licking her lips in mock-lechery. "Aww, man, Jack isn't here!" she said, referencing the camp teenage Adonis who didn't attend sessions, opting instead to work out shirtless within view of the picnic tables. Then she looked at me. "Michael Leviton?"

Whenever they cast a role that wasn't a proxy baby, I irrationally hoped to be picked. I knew this was stupid, but I felt it anyway. I was moved that Amanda would choose me, especially in the role of an attractive man, a part I'd never played, in life or in therapy.*

Max asked me, "Michael, are you comfortable in that role?"

"Sure," I said.

Once onstage, only a few feet from Amanda, I watched her zigzagging teardrops navigating her wrinkles, landing on her thin lips. From where I stood, one of her eyes reflected more light than the other, one dark brown and the other amber.

"What's happening inside right now?" Max asked her.

Amanda could barely speak. "I looked into his eyes and thought, 'I want some of that! I want some of that for myself! And why can't I have it? I know my worth. I deserve some of that!'"

Dawn began to chant, "You deserve some of that! You know your worth!"

"Yeah!" Amanda said. "I do! I know I do."

"You deserve a man like that," Dawn said. The audience joined in on this chant.

I noticed Mom in her lawn chair up front, drawing Amanda. Mom often sketched the sessions. This time, she drew a caricature of Amanda waving her arms, spouting a word bubble that said: "I know my worth!"

The audience chanted in unison about Amanda deserving love and then Dawn went off on her own improv: "You're fine how you are! You're strong! You're right!"

Amanda's legs folded and Dawn caught her, now supporting her physically too. "Let's get more support," Max said. Audience members rose to lift her.

---

* I was so flattered that it didn't occur to me that it was odd for this woman in her fifties to pick an eighteen-year-old for this part.

Amanda howled, "I want to be loved! I want to be loved!" Her keening echoed through the woods. "I'm so loooooonely!"

After a while of Amanda whimpering in a net of arms, she quieted and stood on her feet again and the attention fell on me, the metaphorical representation of the type of man she'd want to be with. Max instructed her to ask me anything she wanted.

Amanda had wearied in the last half hour. She asked me, timidly, "Do you think the right person will understand my personal truth?"

I wanted to tell her that her personal truth was off-putting, like mine, and that she should learn to be happy alone. I racked my brain for different phrasings. I decided to say that I found the terms "right person" and "personal truth" hard to define, which was technically true. But before I went in that direction, it occurred to me that I was playing a role in someone else's session, that I was being asked to recite a specific line, like an actor. As much as it felt wrong to say something untrue, I'd agreed to a job that required it. I felt nauseated and wondered if I could get out of this by vomiting. I'd never heard of someone vomiting mid-session. Amanda's eyebrows twitched; she'd noticed my hesitation. I hadn't lied since letting the kindergartners believe in Santa. I slowly slurred my second lie: "The right person will want to hear your truth—"

Amanda turned to Max and interrupted, "I don't believe him." A nervous grin took over my face. "Look at him!" she said. "He's laughing! He's obviously lying."

Max replied, "I'm hearing that you find it hard to believe that a man you'd want to be with would—"

"No," Amanda interrupted. "I'm talking specifically about *him*." She pointed at me. "This particular man, Michael Leviton, is lying."

The audience groaned. Max tried to diffuse the awkwardness.

"Hold on, let's not make assumptions," he said. "Why don't we ask Michael directly." He turned to me. "Michael, you can discard your role and speak as yourself. And remember, you don't have to answer; everyone has the right to ask as well as the right to not answer." He was giving me an out. I couldn't believe even a therapist would encourage me to lie.

Amanda shot me a death stare. "All right. Michael Leviton. Do you believe that I'll be appreciated if I stay the way I am and continue to speak my truth?"

I said, "It's funny to be in this role because I relate to you. Except I try to live without needing other people. If you're being yourself, it's statistically unlikely that you'll find someone who appreciates you. It'd be like finding a hundred-dollar bill on the ground."

Amanda appeared confused and said, "You deserve someone that appreciates you."

At this, I really lost it. "You keep saying that. What does it mean to *deserve* appreciation?" This came out sounding much angrier than I intended. I tried to soften my tone. "Most people who are liked are just good at putting up a front. If you care about that, do your best impression of what other people want. If you choose to be yourself, don't go around expecting people to like you."

I had been focused on Amanda, who had backed away a bit in befuddlement. I turned to the audience and saw that they were sniffling and crying, not for Amanda, but for me.

Max said, "Michael, it sounds as if you don't think you deserve love." I was about to explode when Max switched gears, realizing that the attention had been shifted from Amanda, who was waiting, arms crossed. Max said, "Thank you, Michael, for sharing."

Afterward, I talked to my parents about what had happened.

Dad hugged me, dying of laughter. "Oh my god, that was so funny. Your response was so perfect!"

"Poor Amanda," Mom said. "She doesn't understand how annoying she is."

"I should have told her," I said. "I can't believe I lied." But I knew that even those who hated Amanda would have said telling the truth in that session was wrong. When it came down to it, even family therapy camp wasn't honest.

For my college application essay, I wrote about family camp. I ranted about learning how much people kept hidden, about my longing to see behind everyone's facades.* Despite the essay, I got into college. I've heard that they don't always read the essays.

Singing My Complaints

I SPENT MY first year of college annoying everybody in all the same old ways, treating every conversation like a game of Truth or Dare that only I knew about, that only I'd agreed to. My non sequitur personal questions read as forced, but even if I'd segued into them naturally, I offered no reason to answer.

Inspired by memories of the Michael Talking Tape, I started carrying a tape recorder and asking for "interviews." I anticipated questions about how the interviews might be used.† I decided I'd just tell the truth: that I suspected the tape recorder might convince people to answer questions they wouldn't normally, making conversation more interesting and entertaining

---

* I don't think my parents or I were aware of how insane this essay made me look. But even if it had occurred to us, we'd have likely applied our classic line: "I'd only want to attend a school that appreciated an essay about family therapy camp."
† This was 1998. Social media wouldn't exist for another few years.

for everyone involved. Luckily, my desired interview subjects didn't ask why; to my amazement, they were just excited to speak to the tape recorder. I'd ask them to tell the story of their favorite kiss they'd ever had, and they'd get emotional and reply with that improvised, flawed speech I'd loved at family camp. I took this as evidence of my theory that everyone could be interesting if they'd let themselves.

BECAUSE I COULD only stomach most people available for short increments, I had a ton of free time to fill with writing and music. I'd continued writing short stories all through high school, showing Dad my favorites, getting his notes and hearing that he still didn't enjoy anything about them.

In my first year of college, Dad responded to one of my stories saying he'd liked it, but he didn't give me any notes telling me why. It appeared that his vocabulary to discuss what he liked was much more limited. I saw no clear reason Dad would appreciate this story more than my previous; it wasn't better in any substantial way. I wondered if his opinions could be as arbitrary as anyone's, if maybe he'd just read it in a good mood.

We had a phone conversation about it. I reminded him that he'd urged me as a child not to define myself according to his opinion, "I liked lots of my stories that you didn't. It would be hypocritical to call this one my best story purely because you liked it."

"That makes sense," Dad said. "There's no reason why my opinion should matter. I mean, who cares what *I* think?"

I'D STARTED TEACHING myself guitar, ukulele, and piano and was attempting to write songs, setting my grievances to music. I played concerts around school, strumming a ukulele, singing my complaints to small audiences composed of the very people I was complaining about. I sang things like, "Some enjoy mystery, I'd rather know. Some prefer the curtain to the show." They found my songs funny, which led me to believe they didn't realize I was talking about them. Maybe the ukulele accompaniment made the songs feel less hateful. Even when I'd introduce a song with, "This one's about all of you," they'd still laugh as if I didn't mean it.

Now I could play music, sing, and write songs to cheer myself up. I spent so much time cheering myself up that I became a competent musician.

Another Side of the Story

WHEN I WAS home one summer, Mom received a call inviting me to an informal elementary school reunion. I'd never heard of such a thing. A former classmate I didn't remember was throwing a reunion in her backyard, using phone numbers from the sixth grade school roster or written in her yearbook. It was surreal to see the familiar child faces now adult, as if drawn on flaccid balloons and then inflated.

I immediately recognized Robert, whose huge head and jolly round face translated perfectly. He told me he was happy to see me. I was surprised he even remembered me. Robert said when he'd heard about this reunion, I was the one he most hoped would be there. He wanted to tell me his side of the story of what happened when we were kids.

"I always want to hear other people's sides of the story!" I told him. "But they'll never tell me!"

Nineteen-year-old Robert was excited to tell me how bizarre I was as a child. He said I was always whining about their games and conversations; when they took turns joking about mothers and insulting one another, I'd start crying. "And you weren't embarrassed!" Robert said, "You acted like we were supposed to keep talking while you were crying! We didn't know what to do. We'd just run away!"

"Yeah, that sounds like me," I said.

"Then you'd try to bring it up again later and tell us why our joke had hurt your feelings and we'd have to run away again!" Robert was able to laugh about it now. "It was hard to be friends with you," he said. "But we tried!"

I told him the story of when he accused me of picking my nose; he didn't remember that one. When I brought up Mr. Gelman and Mrs. Johnson, it became clear that this was the main subject he'd wanted to talk about.

Robert explained that he and his friends were bused in from faraway neighborhoods, that they woke up at 5 AM while I strolled to school at 7:30 AM. The teachers had labeled him and his friends bad kids from the moment they'd arrived, years before I moved there in third grade. He told me about awful things he and Manuel were going through at home at the time and how it brutally affected their lives when they were blamed for things they didn't do. "You used to try to defend us," Robert told me. "You were this nerdy crying kid, but you'd fight with the teachers in front of everybody. If they messed with us in class, you'd cry and tell them off. It was so crazy. You weren't even really our friend, but you had our backs!"

"Sort of," I sighed, dismayed at having to correct him. "If I'd known you'd committed a crime, I would have snitched without even thinking."

Robert winced. "Really?"

"Yeah. I wasn't loyal to you. I was only loyal to the truth."

Robert shook his head and turned away, disturbed. It was like we were kids again.

It'll Be Okay

MY FIRST NIGHT home from college for summer break in 2000, a week before my fourth year at family camp, I was playing piano downstairs when I heard a door slam from upstairs. I'd heard many things in my family, but never a door slam. Miriam screamed through the door at Mom, the only other person home at the time. Mom appeared at the top of the stairs in tears, hurrying down toward me.

"What's wrong?" I asked.

"Ummmmm. Okay," Mom said. I'd never seen her hesitate like this. I sensed I was supposed to sit down so we moved to the couch. For a moment, she still didn't say anything. Then, she spit it out. "I'm leaving your dad," she said. "We're getting divorced."

"I think that's good," I said without pause. "You guys have always been philosophically incompatible."

Mom looked at me hazily. "What?"

"You like people and Dad doesn't," I told her. "You have hopes that are always being dashed and Dad expects the worst already. Dad loves going to concerts and you don't and he talks about art and politics and morality and you talk about people. And you want everyone to like you and Dad wants to be left alone." Mom lowered her chin and her eyes emptied. I thought I was showing understanding but Mom didn't look comforted. "Is there something you'd like me to say?" I asked. Mom shook her head. "How would *you* describe your reasons for getting divorced?"

Mom sighed and brushed her palm over the couch's arm. "I fell in love with someone else."

Though I was technically against secret-keeping, I was perversely proud of her, impressed that she'd managed a forbidden romance. I'd never known Mom to go out anywhere so I asked the blunt question, "Where did you meet someone to fall in love with?"

Mom faltered again, sighed, and said, "At family camp."

There's a lot I could have thought about in that moment—the forthcoming scandal, the absurdity of leaving one's husband for someone from family therapy camp, the feelings I should have been having and why I wasn't having them—but my brain instead instinctively listed each man at camp to guess which one Mom had fallen for. Mom interrupted my mental guessing with his name: "Joe." She lingered on the "o," relishing the syllable. I could tell she was in love.

I knew Joe, but I'd never even noticed him and Mom conversing. He spoke with a high-pitched voice and slow, jumbled speech. His thick glasses magnified his eyes. It unnerved me to imagine this random acquaintance in a relationship with my mother.

Mom took a deep breath and said, "Dad and I had an open relationship."

"I can understand that," I said, too quickly again.

"You *can*?" Mom said.

I'd never had a girlfriend, but I thought I understood open relationships because the girls I liked were always sleeping with other people.

Also, though Mom thought she was telling me about the open relationship for the first time, I'd sensed it already because my parents were so bad at keeping secrets. She and Dad both brought up monogamy and open relationships often, and with a casualness that implied they'd had one. Mom had mentioned that several of their friends at camp had open relationships. Dad had offhand given me advice as a teenager about how to talk to women that didn't sound like how he'd approached Mom at fourteen. I'd never questioned them because their casualness made asking about it feel square.

"It's so awful to tell you this without Dad here," she said. "We wanted to wait till camp, when we'd all be in the same place and we'd all have support. But now everything's messed up." Mom let out a long sigh. I'd never seen her so lost and devastated. Mom kept wiping her nose with a handkerchief. "Annika at camp suspected Joe and I were together and gossiped to Jane, who called Miriam a few minutes ago to tell her about it."

"Wow, that's not supposed to happen," I said. It hadn't occurred to me that family therapy camp could intervene in actual life.

"So Miriam asked me if the rumor was true," Mom said. "And I couldn't lie."

I wasn't usually physically affectionate, but this seemed a time to hug Mom. "It'll be okay," I blurted emptily, parroting the culture's most popular line of comfort.

We hugged for a moment, her clutching me the hardest she'd clutched me since my childhood. Then Miriam burst from her bedroom in pajamas, stomped down the stairs, and stopped in the middle of the staircase to scream at her. Mom jumped out of our hug and dashed to meet her, but Miriam swatted her away, flew back to her bedroom, and slammed the door again, her muffled yells still audible. Mom chased after her a few steps and stopped halfway up the staircase. She remained awhile on that middle stair, neither of us saying anything. This was what it took to leave us speechless.

AT THE TIME, Dad was visiting a friend in Northern California. When Mom called to tell him that Miriam and I knew about the divorce, he drove the six hours back to L.A. Then Josh, who had been away on a trip with his friends, returned and we had a family meeting in the living room. The chairs and couch surrounded a glass coffee table that Josh used to climb under as a child; he would lie on his back on the carpet, spacing out, staring up through the glass. Now, Josh was a teenager in a muscle shirt with spiky bleach-tipped hair. Mom and Dad told Josh about the divorce and he immediately asked, "So, where do I live then? With you or with Mom?" They explained that Mom would find her own living situation and Josh and Miriam would move back and forth. Josh said, "That's fine as long as I have video games and cable TV at both houses."

Mom said, in a therapist's tone, "Josh, how do you feel about us splitting up?"

Josh shrugged. "It's none of my business. I don't know why Miriam's so mad."

Miriam glowered and said, "It's completely normal to be upset when your parents get divorced!"

Dad sighed and said, "Well, at least this is happening right before camp. It'll be a great chance to process our feelings."

Miriam bolted upright from her slump. "You still want to go to camp?"

"Why wouldn't we?" Dad asked.

"Because everyone knows that Mom's leaving you for some-one else from camp!" Miriam slapped her forehead. I'd never seen that cartoonish gesture in real life.

Dad shrugged coldly. "I see no reason to hide what's hap-pened. It'll be helpful for us all to be able to talk about what we're going through, to tell our sides of the story. Joe's coming too, so his side will also be represented."

Miriam couldn't believe this. "Joe's going too!?!"

Mom started crying again. "I need him. This is a really hard time for me."

"This is crazy," Miriam said. "It's just crazy."

Miriam wasn't crying—she was just sick of the lunacy. She turned to me, hoping I'd serve as an older, more authoritative voice of sanity.

I shrugged. "It makes sense to me."*

Mom and Joe drove separately while Dad drove Josh, Miriam, and me up the treacherous mountain. Miriam cried in the car while I did my best to comfort her. "People break up," I said. "It happens all the time. It should be an easy thing to accept. It's usually good when a couple breaks up; the tragedy is when they stay together while they're unhappy. Technically, almost everyone married should get divorced."

ONE BY ONE, campers I knew greeted me with long hugs, condolences, and assurances that they'd be there for me if I wanted to talk. I kept telling them I was fine—though insisting I was "fine" in an annoyed voice made me sound like I wasn't fine. And beyond that, being fine with your parents' divorce wasn't acceptable either. I resented the suggestion that I was *supposed* to be upset, that even therapy culture believed everyone should be the same.†

I kept noticing Miriam in the distance at a picnic table or on a tree stump crying or yelling at Mom or Dad or both or hugging one of the facilitators. I figured it was best to leave her alone. I'd really bought into a family camp line: "Other people's feelings are none of your business."‡

---

* This was how a lot of the divorce went: Miriam would make a valid argument and we'd take turns shrugging.

† I'm not the expert on my own repression, but I speculate that I wasn't crying for the same reason I didn't cry about my nursery school vaccination: I'd been emotionally prepared. I wasn't raised with a belief that my parents would stay together forever, so I was ready.

‡ This inspirational quote was intended to comfort the neurotic too stuck on what everyone felt about him, not to encourage me to ignore my sister's devastation about my parents' divorce.

Walking back to the dining area from the bathroom, Joe ambushed me. "Hey, Michael!" he said in his overly enthusiastic nasal whine. "How are you doing?" His thick glasses were smudged and crooked. He checked his watch as if he'd written crib notes there about what to say, and asked, "Can I talk to you for a minute?" I knew this conversation would be a nightmare, but I was sometimes willing to watch a train wreck even if it required that I be a passenger. Joe and I walked to the creek bridge; we had a background soundtrack of wind through leaves and river-trickling. "I just wanted to say," Joe said, "that I'm excited to be a part of your family."

"Okay," I said.

"I like your dad a lot," he continued. "I think he's a great guy. But we all know he can be difficult too and, in those times, you can talk to me. I can be like your father."

My first instinct was to laugh. But it only took a second more for this comment to feel more creepy than funny, this random man wanting to take over as my father.

"Joe," I told him. "When someone leaves her husband for another man, generally the kids don't like that man, you know?"

"Yeah," he said vacantly.

"So, that would be good to accept, that no one's gonna welcome you into the family."

"Okay," he said.

"So, I'm gonna go now," I told him.

As much as Mom's love for Joe bothered me, I understood that he likely served as a long-needed relief from Dad's scrutiny and criticism. Still, it disappointed me to see Mom with someone unquestioning, easygoing, and inarticulate, someone defined by qualities that appealed to most people.

At temperature reading, Mom stepped down to the amphitheater floor and said, "My bug is that some people gossiped about me and the rumor got back to my daughter and made things a lot worse for all of us. So, my solution is that everyone should think twice about gossiping."

The woman who had spread the news got up and said, "She's talking about me. I stand by what I did. This community isn't here to help you keep secrets."

This led to a whole back-and-forth about confidentiality which went on for an hour with no resolution.

That afternoon at the check-in, Dad said, "This camp is obviously happening at a weird time. My only request is that if you want to know what's going on with me, *ask*. I'll tell you. And if I tell you, believe me, I'm not gonna lie. No one knows how I feel except me. That's it."

Mom's check-in was more tearful. "I'm afraid that now everyone hates me!" she said. "And I feel like everyone's talking about me and I can't even find out unless someone breaks confidentiality."

I showed up to the first men's group with the knowledge that it would likely involve talking about Dad and Joe. There was no chance that they'd stay quiet to avoid a scene.

I waited in the clearing with a dozen other men, some shifting in their lawn chairs, some perched woodenly, some whittling, some swatting mosquitoes, some glaring into the dirt. The men's and women's groups met simultaneously so the women luxuriated in the picturesque session area while we congregated in the fly-infested clearing by the compost heap. I could hear the groundskeeper's farm animals snorting and squawking as if in the throes of their own group session. I sat in my lawn chair, swarmed by flies.

I heard rustling in the bushes behind me and turned to find not a struggling forest animal, but Joe, his shoulders high, hiding his neck, his hands clasped at his belly. Men around the circle rolled their eyes.

Dad arrived carrying extra folding chairs tucked in his armpits. He dropped the chairs onto the pile and sat across the circle from me without acknowledging Joe or showing any nervousness.

The men went around the circle doing check-ins, but everyone finished quickly. Nothing led into work. No one cried or even paused out of emotion, unlike most years, when everybody spilled their tears as soon as they could. I wondered if they were rushing and remaining detached to make room for Dad and Joe.

When it was Dad's turn, he said, "Men's group has always been my favorite part of camp. I have to censor myself in the main group . . . *a lot*. But I've always felt that this was the place where I could really show my heart."

It bothered me that Dad said he'd been censoring himself. I thought he would tell anyone anything. I zoned out, considering this remark, my attention swinging in and out of Dad's long check-in. "Last year, Joe told my wife that I'd been talking about her. I don't get why it upset her so much, but it did. And now she's leaving me for Joe. Obviously, Joe broke confidentiality to cause problems in my marriage so he could move in."

Joe interrupted. "That's not what happened."

"Did you tell her about our conversation in group last year?" Dad asked.

"She had a right to know," Joe said. The group fell into a chaos of hostile grumbling, so Joe panicked. "I didn't break confidentiality!" he said. "I didn't tell anybody anything."

The circle was enraged, but I laughed; I found nothing funnier than someone too flustered to stick with a story.

Somebody said, "For god's sake, Joe, stop talking."

Joe bent as if stabbed in the belly and said, "I'm not the one who should stop talking! *You* should stop talking."

Dad's eyes bulged, bloodshot and wet, and he leaned forward in his lawn chair, aggressively, even violently. "This is the only place in the whole fucking *world* where we're supposedly able to say what we feel, and you tell me to *shut up*!?! *You're* an untrustworthy lowlife, so *I* have to shut up? Because you're gonna go out and *tattletale* on me?"

Another crying man then broke in. "How am I supposed to speak from the heart in this group when I know somebody might walk out of here and steal my wife?"

This conversation continued uneventfully until men's group was over.

The next day, Mom did work in the main session accusing Dad of using the men's group to turn me and other camp men against her and Joe. Joe had clearly reported to Mom again what had been said in men's group. Her work eventually led her to describe what had gone wrong in their marriage. "He always acted like my feelings weren't justified, like I didn't have to be considered. It's always been this way. Growing up, my feelings didn't matter. And still, my feelings don't matter. I've asked my kids to welcome Joe into the family and they don't. I've asked men's group to stop talking about us and they won't. What other conclusion am I supposed to draw except that I don't matter?"

The next men's group discussed Mom's session. Dad didn't address what she'd said about their marriage; instead, he focused on accusing Joe of breaking confidentiality again.

I FIGURED THAT everyone would move on by next year's camp, but I figured wrong. My parents and Joe weren't going to stop fighting, which meant that everyone else had to hear about it. Men started doing check-ins specifically about how tired they were of talking about Dad and Joe. But, when Dad and Joe weren't being discussed, no one else volunteered to replace them because the group's trust had evaporated.

The following year, camp still wasn't over it. Miriam, who was now fifteen, did work in the main session about the divorce. The camp women jokingly referred to the men's group as "impotent." I started to wonder if the Levitons had broken family therapy camp.

A Deal with the Devil

AFTER CAMP IN 2001, the summer before my senior year of college, a friend of my friend's girlfriend confronted me about how I dressed. Shira had giant brown eyes, wide and kind with others but always narrowed at me. I envied the grace in her movement, how she'd own every object she lifted, how she always stood in photographable poses but still read as authentic. Perhaps most impressive to me, she spoke with her own style of brutal honesty; no one I knew was as comfortable mocking and insulting me. She had no issue complaining openly about my presence. She refused to ride in my car because she didn't trust my driving. When we went bowling, she made a show of covering her eyes for my turns, saying she couldn't handle my awkwardness.

At this particular house party, in a living room full of friends and acquaintances sitting on couches and on the carpet, I made a casual comment about girls not liking me and Shira erupted, "Look at how you dress! How do you expect someone to go out with you?"

I engaged her, legitimately curious. "You think my clothes are the reason girls don't like me?" I asked. "I have a pretty low opinion of people, but even I wouldn't imagine everyone's that superficial."

"It's not *superficial*," Shira said. "You're twenty years old now. You're supposed to have some style. You dress like a child."

I was still wearing khakis, corduroys, and baggy T-shirts. I'd added an overcoat that I thought looked film-noir.* I told her, "If someone cares that much about clothes, she's not my type."

Shira laughed at me. "Dude, you're not in any position to pick and choose. Doesn't it bother you that everyone else has girlfriends? Everyone else has sex?"

"A little," I said. "But I'm good at entertaining myself alone. I can fantasize and play music and write stories." Shira turned to my other friends as if she wanted them to back her up, but they felt too sorry for me. "Okay," I told her. "Let's say I'm convinced: I want to wear clothes that will make girls like me, a disturbing concept. But let's say I'll wear whatever other people will like. How should I dress?"

"Look at other people and wear whatever they wear," she said. "Watch a movie and dress like the actors. Or dress like a band. Anything's better than what you're doing."

"Why don't you take me shopping?" I asked her. "I'll try stuff on and see what you think I should look like."

I thought this would be funny, to see what embarrassing trends she'd tell me to follow. My friends, who had been listening, appeared excited; they'd apparently been unhappy about how I dressed too but were unwilling to say anything. They all pushed Shira to go shopping with me, so she agreed.

I met Shira at her house so she could drive us to the vintage clothing store; she still refused to ride in my car. On the way, she explained why clothes weren't superficial. "Everybody cares

---

* Her description wasn't exactly *wrong*.

about how they dress and how other people dress," she said. "If everybody cares about it, how can it be superficial?"

"Are you kidding?" I said. "Everybody's wrong about almost everything."

"You have the worst attitude," she said. "You talk like you're so superior but you're just insecure. If you listen to me and dress better, people might actually like you."

"But I'd know they only appreciated me because I dressed like them!"

Shira whacked her palms against the steering wheel. "Just be happy if people like you. Stop thinking about why."

At the vintage store, Shira rummaged through shirts, handing me possibilities. "The first thing is to wear clothes that fit. Your shirts are huge. Do you buy large or something?"

"Medium," I said.

"You're thin. Buy small. Maybe extra small." She handed me patterned button-up shirts from the '60s and '70s, jeans, a jean jacket, a denim shirt.

"What's with all the jeans?" I asked. "I'm gonna look like a cowboy."

Shira laughed. "Have you ever looked at anyone? Everyone wears jeans."

In the changing room, I found all these clothes far too tight. I put on a pair of jeans and a plaid button-up and a jean jacket and laughed at my own reflection. I couldn't imagine how everybody else could stand dressing alike. I walked out of the changing room in this preposterous getup, expecting Shira to laugh, but she smiled beautifully. "Wow," she said. "Honestly, you look way better than I expected. You look like a different person."

I tried on a few other outfits, and each time I walked out of the dressing room, Shira gasped. "I can't believe this," she said. "I'm saving your life."

"I can't possibly wear any of this in public," I said. "It'd be like Halloween."

"There's a show tonight," she told me, her eyes practically twinkling. "You should buy this stuff and go with me and wear it and see the difference."

Despite the ridiculousness of this whole experience, I was flattered she would invite me somewhere, and the experiment sounded more interesting than staying home. So I bought this plaid shirt and pair of jeans and jean jacket and went with her to the show.

There were lots of people I knew there, some kids I hadn't seen since high school, some I'd seen around other times when home from college. The moment I walked in, an acquaintance ran up to me, glowing. "Michael! You look so good! I've never seen you dressed like this."

"Yeah," I said. "It's an experiment. Shira told me to wear it. She says dressing differently will make people like me."

"It will!" the acquaintance said. She thought she was being positive.

Each person I ran into told me how good I looked. Friends of friends introduced themselves warmly. Acquaintances who usually avoided me in public acknowledged that they knew me and said hello. Dressed this way, if I stood alone, strangers made eye contact. The difference was staggering. I knew people were easily tricked, but this went beyond my lowest expectations for humanity.

Everyone I spoke to encouraged me to keep dressing like this, so I gave it a try. I bought some smaller T-shirts and pants and some more jeans and vintage button-up shirts. The first time Dad saw me in tight jeans, he said, "You look . . . odd."

"I know," I replied. "This girl convinced me to dress like this and it turns out everyone likes me more. It feels like wearing a costume, and it's insane to me that it makes a difference, but I think I'm gonna try it on occasion. It's the first thing I've ever done to get people to like me."

Dad scratched his beard. "Doesn't sound like the thing to do," he said. "What if you meet someone who actually would understand you and they discount you as a trend-follower because you're dressed like everybody else? Imagine if you met *yourself* when you were dressed like that. What would you think?"

"I'd think I looked embarrassing," I said. "Like a cowboy."

"That's not good," Dad said.

"But what if we're the only ones who think like that?" I asked.

"Why would that matter?" Dad asked. "Who wants to hang out with superficial, trendy idiots?"

I didn't have a good answer. But I kept dressing this way. When I returned to college that fall, everyone told me again how much better I looked.

"I guess if other people like it, that's worth something?" I replied to one friend who brought it up. "I don't know. It's a crazy decision to be forced to make."

"How to dress?" she asked.

"No, whether to pursue the approval of fools or to resign myself to being alone."

Eventually, on one of my vintage shopping trips, I bought some clothes that felt more connected to a style I actually liked. I watched so many film noir movies and admired so much jazz photography, it occurred to me that I could wear suits. After some junk store searching near my college, I found a few fraying suits and an overcoat that fit me and bought some plain white button-up shirts and thin black ties. I didn't fit in anymore, but I was happy to go back to looking like myself.

This was how I dressed when I graduated, went to family therapy camp once more, and then set off for New York, where I'd decided to move.

I'd heard New York had good concerts and jobs in writing and publishing. Some I knew from college were moving there or were originally from there, so I had couches to stay on while I found a job and an apartment. I liked the old buildings and characters and chaos. Los Angeles was famous for being fake and homogenous, but New York was famous for being blunt and eccentric. It seemed my best option.

But I wasn't optimistic about my future. The further from childhood people got, the more frequently they lied, and for pettier and pettier reasons. According to my observations, maturity meant more compromising, less confrontation, more mind-reading, less directness, more conformity, less uniqueness. What I liked about myself would surely be even less appreciated with age.

So, while most kids moved to New York with big dreams, I arrived prepared to be hated.

Part 2

An Honest Living

Chapter 5

Open Mic

ON MY SECOND day in New York, the roommate of the friend whose couch I was occupying recommended that I go to an open mic in the East Village to perform my bitter ukulele songs. I'd never been to an open mic. I'd only seen them in movies, always portrayed negatively, so I went with low expectations.

The Clubhouse was a crowded dive with chipped-painted black tables and a cheesy neon sign behind the stage advertising the place's name. As I hung around waiting for the open mic to start, my attention landed on a couple in the corner, cuddling, making out, and eye-gazing. She wore a black skirt, a white button-up shirt, and a thin black tie. His brown suit seemed much fancier. His reddish blond hair swept wildly about his head, and his dimpled chin was one of the finest I'd seen. Guitar cases leaned beside them. New York didn't wait to show off its fantasies. I wanted to look like him, to feel that girl looking at me like that. I'd accepted long ago those things would never happen to me, that they were the culture's rewards for dishonesty, but I'd trained myself to enjoy marveling at it from afar. After all, I could enjoy a painting without having to own it.

The open mic started with the host, a much older angry nerd that I feared could be my future, playing a set of his own songs for his captive audience of open mic musicians. Then, the next forty-five minutes or so featured various East Village archetypes: a teenager who could barely play, an abrasive elderly punk rocker, a psychedelic poet, an inadequate rapper, a fame-hungry pop duo, but I found even the bad acts enthralling. And whenever I got bored, I spied on the couple in the corner.

About an hour in, a scruffy-haired, Jewish-looking boy my age played guitar and sang in an exquisite low vibrato a song I adored so much it seemed impossible that I'd ended up in the same room as the one who wrote it. He mentioned he was playing a full-length show at the Clubhouse in a few days so I wrote down his name on a napkin to look him up later and see him play again. More bad acts followed, but then a woman with her hair in elaborate curls that must've taken hours to construct played piano and sang a jazz tune she'd written that sounded like a brilliant classic, another one of the best performances I'd ever seen. The open mic went on in this pattern, a few crummy acts followed by something stunning. I felt like I was seeing Woodstock, but from a few feet away in a grungy room with random amateurs playing between the geniuses. My napkin filled with names.

I noticed that the musicians I'd loved were all hanging out with one another, that anyone could walk up and ask to be on their email list or take a show flier or buy a burnt CD of their recordings. I introduced myself to each musician I liked. I told them how much I loved their songs, often complimenting them on specific lyrics or musical moments. People usually fled from my compliments, but these musicians responded with curiosity. I told them this was my second day in New York and they said variations of "You came to the right place!" and "Get ready. You're in for it."

Around midnight, the suited couple in the corner was called to perform. They played raw folk songs, harmonizing in voices that didn't match their put-together exteriors, his nasal and hers hoarse. She sang in the highest part of her range so her voice would crack. The suited couple made vulnerability and imperfection look so cool that I suspected even "most people" could appreciate it.

By the time my name came up to perform, it was 3 AM and almost everyone had gone home. I played my two songs and the host liked them enough that he invited me to play a show there sometime. Before I left, I searched for all my napkin names on the club schedule and wrote their show dates down in my own pocket calendar. My calendar had never been so full.

Standard Questions

MY FIRST DAYS in New York were characterized by humidity and fantasy. My college acquaintance's apartment wasn't air-conditioned. On the way to my first job interview—to be an assistant at an entertainment agency—I descended from his fourth-floor walkup, waited shoulder-to-shoulder on the sweltering subway platform, and slogged a dozen trash-scented blocks. On the way, I anxiously envisioned what would happen if I couldn't get a job. It seemed quite plausible that I was unhireable. I tried to distract myself with the beauty of the Flatiron district, and the elevator ride to a floor that felt awe-inspiringly high. But the fantasy was soiled by the certainty that I'd be rejected here like everywhere else, and the fact that I'd sweat through my suit.

My interviewer, a woman from human resources, likely in her late thirties or early forties, wore her hair in a platinum blonde crew cut. The roundness of her face matched her round-framed glasses and contrasted with the lines of her pinstripe suit. She smiled with her mouth closed and only the left corner of her lips lifting, the smile equivalent of a single raised eyebrow. The phrase "human resources" struck me as refreshingly harsh, an admission that they defined humans as mere cogs in a capitalist scheme. But it was hard to imagine this cool woman in front of me viewing humans as resources. I thought this talent agency should rename their hiring department with something more creative and personalized.

"Okay," my interviewer said, leaning back in her chair. It felt like she might put her feet up on the desk. "Let's see what you've got." I didn't know anything about the protocols of professionalism in corporate life, but I felt certain she was ignoring them and doing as she pleased. I liked that.

"This is my first real job interview," I told her.

Dimples appeared in her forehead and she gave me a side-eyed smile, unsure if I was kidding. "Oh, don't worry," she said, waving her hand in the air, a response that would smooth the moment regardless of whether I was joking. Despite her social grace, I could tell my comment about this being my first interview had thrown her off.

She started asking questions, her voice dry and joyless: why had I chosen to apply there, why did I want to work in entertainment, and so on. After a flurry of questions she'd clearly asked many times a day and abhorred asking, I found a pause and said, "They should let you choose your own interview questions." At that, she perked up. I told her, "I bet we could have a great conversation if you chose the questions." She laughed, which emboldened me. I asked, "Do most people give pretty similar answers?"

She laughed again and said, "Yeah."

"That would drive me crazy," I told her. "It's like water torture, but with interview answers instead of water."

She seemed to enjoy that line, replied with a smile and a shrug, "Sometimes it's pretty boring."

"Do you have a question you'd like to ask everybody, but that you don't? Something you'd personally like to know?"

She grinned one-sidedly again and bounced her fingertip against her forehead. "I'd have to think about that." She sighed to herself, still smiling. Then she looked down at her desk as if to read something written there. "So, where do you see yourself in ten years?"

Given the real conversation we'd just had, I assumed she was joking. But she bristled, all camaraderie instantly gone, believing I'd laughed at her. "Sorry," I said. "I didn't expect to continue immediately with the questions they make you ask."

She sat at attention. "No one makes me—these are standard questions."* She asked me again where I saw myself in ten years and I told her I couldn't speculate because life is chaotic and uncertain. She appeared to find that reply surprising. She moved on to another question and I suffered through watching her unhappily doing her job. But then, out of nowhere, she asked a question I loved: "What's your biggest flaw?" This was something I wanted to know about everyone. The question invited introspection and confession and gave me a chance to show off my honesty.

---

* It's easy to understand now that she didn't see a job interview as a place for great conversation or self-expression. I was the only one who cared if our meeting involved something authentic.

My thoughts jumped to what Dad told me when I was a child about his hiring methods. When a job applicant came in for an interview, Dad would ask them to write a short essay using a provided list of ten vocabulary words. But Dad had invented three of the ten words; they had no meaning. He gave extra points to applicants who admitted they didn't know the fake words and minus points for those who attempted to use them.

I asked my interviewer, "Do you mean my worst flaws according to other people or according to myself? If you asked someone else my worst flaws, they'd list some things I consider my best qualities." The interviewer sat up, engaged again. "Most people say I'm judgmental about perfectly normal behavior, that I think too much, that I'm unnecessarily confrontational, always making a scene . . ." Laugh lines appeared around her eyes, which I interpreted to mean she liked my truthfulness, so I kept riffing. "As far as what *I* consider my worst flaw, I wish I could be more tolerant of other people's cowardice, immorality, and weakness. After all," I said, "we're just the products of our upbringings and genetics, so it's irrational for me to resent people for what they've inherited."

The interviewer bobbled her head, suppressing laughter. "I'm sorry," she said. "I just . . ." She rested her palms flat on the desk and pulled herself together. "I don't feel right letting you go on like this. When someone asks your biggest flaw, you're not supposed to really list your flaws. I thought you were joking."

"People often think I'm joking," I replied. "I'm rarely joking."

The interviewer regarded me with pity. "You should say something good about yourself that sounds like a flaw, but isn't really, like that you're a workaholic."

"But if the only acceptable answer is a lie, why ask?" I was genuinely curious about her hiring methods but, from my mouth, "why" lashed like a whip. Horses would hurry. Lions would straighten.

"It's just how you're supposed to answer," she said.

I pulled a cloth from my suit pocket and cleaned my glasses while I continued. "But what are you trying to find out? Are you testing how convincingly I can recite a predetermined cultural script?"*

She softened, feeling sorry for me again. "None of this stuff you're saying matters," she said. "I'm trying to help you. Lots of interviewers ask these questions. If you react like this, no one will hire you."

It then dawned on me that this exchange might be the real test. Perhaps she was challenging my integrity, seeing if I'd stand by my position.† "I have faith that some employers value honesty," I told her. "But if it turns out you're right, that I'm truly unhireable, I'll have to find another way to make a living that better suits who I am."

The interviewer's concern curdled into bitterness. "Okay," she said, giving up on me. She rose from her seat, forced a broad smile, held out her hand for me to shake, and rattled off things she didn't mean. "In a few days, we'll let you know our decision," she said, already knowing her decision. "It was nice meeting you," she told me, excited to never meet me again.

A Fake Horn on a Real Unicorn

EACH JOB INTERVIEW ended the same way: I'd straightforwardly answer a question and my interviewer would respond

---

* If you can believe it, this atrocity of a question was sincere.
† As crazy as that interpretation may sound, I found it more believable than her claim that getting a job required that I say perfectionism was my biggest flaw.

as if I was joking, rude, crazy, or stupid. Temp agencies considered me insane because I admitted I didn't possess any of the skills on their lists.

During my job search, I spent most evenings at the Clubhouse. I befriended many of the musicians I liked and hung out with them as much as I could, often all night. They didn't have to wake up early because most either lived with parents or crashed on couches or worked at coffee shops, clothing stores, or bookstores. One was an art mover. One constructed window arrangements for a department store. Everyone I'd known in college worked in an office. When I spoke to my new musician friends about my failing job search, they'd say something like, "You're really gonna be somebody's assistant? That doesn't sound good."

A few months after my arrival in New York, I ended up getting another interview to be an assistant to a literary agent. Charlie was around my dad's age, wore a tailored suit and tortoiseshell glasses and spoke in old slang with a cool Rat Pack cadence. I found him very handsome; I liked his rakish smile and freewheeling demeanor. Charlie was always in enthusiastic motion, his arms swinging or his hand dabbing the bald front of his head with a handkerchief. He interviewed me in his hip mid-century modern office, asking me only what he wanted to know. I showed him the literary magazine I'd edited in college and he asked how I worked with writers, how I decided on the cover. He asked how long I'd been in New York and what I thought of it. I told him about the open mic, about how no one this cool had ever liked me before. My story of randomly meeting artists I admired reminded him of how he'd become an agent. A few decades before, Charlie had asked his best friend, an unpublished poet, if he could send his poems around to publishers. This friend ended up the best-selling modern poet in the United States. I confessed to Charlie I'd never heard of his famous poet best friend and he laughed, charmed by the admission. He went on, saying that confidence in one's ability to recognize beauty and talent defined a good agent. I told him I was surprised at how many took opinions from other people, afraid to trust their own observations. I brought up my favorite part of the children's novel and cartoon *The Last Unicorn*. "The unicorn's horn is invisible to most people," I told him. "Only magical people have the vision to tell the difference between a unicorn and a regular horse. At one point, a witch recognizes the unicorn and cages her in a traveling zoo. But the zoo's audience isn't made up of magical people; they only see a regular horse. So the witch attaches a fake horn next to the unicorn's real horn. The crowds are awestruck by this fake horn, which could have been fastened onto any old horse. The fake horn impresses them more than a real unicorn." Charlie said he'd heard all he needed, that I was hired.

On my first day, I hadn't even settled into my freestanding cubicle outside Charlie's office before he told me about a problem. A ghostwriter he represented who wrote best-selling thriller novels under another famous writer's name wanted to sell a book under his own name; but the outline he'd turned in was sloppy. "He refuses to take notes," Charlie said. "He's having an ego freak-out. He's gonna fire me if I don't send out this outline as it is." Charlie asked me to read it and tell him what I thought.

The outline *was* sloppy, but I had suspicions as to why. The ghostwriter's thriller was set in the 1970s in the town where he grew up. The parts describing this town and the teenagers who lived there had been written with more attention than the parts that sounded like a mainstream thriller. I stood in Charlie's office doorway and proposed my theory.

"I think he's scared you're gonna criticize the parts that mean something to him." Charlie listened with a skeptical curiosity. "In his ghostwriting, he's never been allowed to write anything personal or use his own voice. He wants to write about when he was a teenager, but he's afraid no one will let him. He's only sloppy with the parts he feels forced to include. If we only edit those parts and compliment the rest, I bet he'll be moved that we appreciate him for who he really is."

Charlie grinned as if I'd offered a strange wager and said, "What if *you* talk to him?" Charlie mischievously hopped up from his seat. "I'll say I just hired a new assistant, some kid I don't even know. This kid liked the outline and wants to talk. I'll tell him I have no idea what you want to say, that he can skip the conversation if he wants, hang up in the middle, I don't care. See, I think he'll be curious enough to take the call. And if he doesn't like what you have to say, he won't blame me." Charlie sized me up. "Are you comfortable getting on the phone with him yourself?"

"Yeah," I said. "Why wouldn't I be?"*

Charlie held in his laughter with a close-lipped smile and nodded.

My cubicle faced the glass wall of Charlie's office; we could see each other from our desks, but we couldn't hear each other. I watched Charlie call the ghostwriter, swiveling back and forth in his chair. He gave me a thumbs-up, transferred the call to my line, and remained in his office, grinning at me.

I told the ghostwriter that I'd read the outline and that it struck me as more unique than the stuff he'd worked on over

---

* I can understand why I might sound arrogant or cocky here, but I meant this literally: I genuinely couldn't understand why someone would be uncomfortable getting on the phone in this situation.

the last five years, more personal and inspired. I noted the spots where I could feel he wasn't used to being allowed to express himself. I suggested cuts and revisions to every line that felt like he didn't want to write it.

As I went through the piece explaining each suggested edit, he stayed quiet on the line. I had no idea how he was responding. Charlie's eyes stayed on me with anticipation. When I'd finished my comments, the ghostwriter thanked me and asked me to send the call back to Charlie.

Charlie answered the phone and laugh-wrinkles blossomed around his eyes. Then his mouth fell open. He hung up and dashed to my desk.

"I don't know what you said to this guy," Charlie told me, laughter in his voice. "But he wants to take all your notes. He said, 'I don't know where you found this kid, but he's the best editor I've ever worked with.'"

Charlie read my edit of the outline and burst from his office. "I can't believe I'm saying this, but this is good." He gave me the intrigued look I'd already come to love. "But I've gotta ask," he said. "How did you know he'd listen to you?"

"I didn't," I told him. "I just try to give everyone permission to be honest and hope they take me up on it."

I went out to lunch, high off this ridiculous triumph, and when I returned to the office, one of the other agents approached me. "Charlie told me about what you did today. You've got nerve! Your second day at work!" Each agent that passed my cubicle stopped to congratulate me. Unfortunately, my second day was the high point.

In the weeks that followed, it became clear to all of us that I was an awful assistant. I needed every aspect of my job explained to me, and I missed typos in everything I wrote. Eventually,

Charlie called me into his office to tell me I was making too many mistakes, that he couldn't proofread everything for me, that he had to be able to trust me. I said something like, "I've already been trying my best. I think I'm just not good at this job."

At first, Charlie chuckled, amused by the oddness of my essentially firing myself. But then he quickly became stiff and anxious. "This isn't working out here," he said. "You're not an assistant. And, really, you're not cut out to be an agent, either. You're not a salesman. You're a creative person, a writer or editor. I remember what you did on the second day. You're talented. If you can get an interview for a creative job, list me as your reference and I'll tell them that story and talk them into hiring you. But I'm not gonna let you be an assistant. I'm gonna tell them the truth."

"I like the truth," I said.

As hard-boiled as I could be about rejection, Charlie firing me shook me up. First, I was sad that I wouldn't be able to hang out with him anymore. Second, I wasn't sure if I'd be able to get another job. It had been virtually impossible to get this one, and even an eccentric boss I loved and respected didn't want me working for him.

When I told a friend from college that I'd been fired after only three months at the job, she wasn't shocked; she said she'd been doubtful from the start about whether I could hold a job. She advised me to stay quiet about getting fired, to keep it secret. "You have to portray yourself as competent," she said, "Even if you aren't." She suggested that, when I searched for future jobs, I should omit this one from my resume and act as if it never happened. I told her what Charlie had said about being my reference, about how he'd help me become a writer. "You *believed* that?" she said. "He was trying to get you out of the room! Definitely don't list the person who fired you as a reference. That would be *crazy*." At the thought that even Charlie might have lied to me, I was fully depressed.

I'd been fired on a Monday, so I dragged myself to the open mic for some cheering up.

The Clubhouse stood on a filthy, frenzied East Village corner; out front, I always encountered something interesting. Once, an elderly beatnik approached me, announced himself as a "card-carrying homosexual" who usually was in bed by "jazz noon." He said he'd gotten "wise" by "interviewing his brain" and suggested that I follow him into the park "like back in the '60s". Another time, I saw a well-dressed young woman curled inside a much older homeless man's shopping cart. He leaned over the cart's side so she could do his makeup. I watched her gingerly apply his eyeliner, holding still to keep the cart from rolling and ruining his cat-eye. I loved that corner.

On the day of my firing, I showed up to find a bunch of my favorite open-mic musicians smoking out front. I was greeted by my favorite of all, a magnetic girl my age in a camouflage T-shirt.

"Hey Michael," she said. "How's it going?" Each time she acknowledged me, I'd blush, overwhelmed with gratitude.*

"Well," I told the group, "this morning I got fired."

There wasn't a beat before they all broke out in applause. "Congratulations!" she said.

"It happens to the best of us," someone said. ". . . and the worst of us." Everyone laughed.

"Man," said the kid who recorded everybody in his parents' Harlem basement. "Getting fired is so great. I only started playing music because I had free time when I got fired."

---

* There were times when I even thanked her for including me, which made everybody present uncomfortable.

"I got fired from every job I ever had," my favorite, the most brilliant person I knew, told me. "I even got fired from my best job working for a private detective. I was supposed to be following somebody and I spaced out and lost him."

We stood on that corner for a while, telling stories of failure. Then we went inside and I watched them play their songs, their lyrics full of sentiments others wouldn't dare admit.

Having exhausted all my connections, I applied to every writing-adjacent job I could find that didn't have "assistant" in the title. I sent out dozens of resumes that listed my three months as an assistant as my only office work experience and received only one response: from a writing and editing job at a literacy program. I interviewed with a woman in a suit who struck me as an incognito oddball passing as a professional. The whole interview, she stifled charmed laughter. I asked her about the job and she said it involved producing books for schools to help below-level readers. Everything had to be written simply, at the lowest reading levels, but with subject matter appropriate to kids older than ten, sometimes for teenagers. I found this fascinating and asked a lot of questions about the program's teaching techniques; I was impressed by everything she told me. She remarked that I was the most curious and enthusiastic job applicant she'd ever had.

Eventually, the interviewer told me she'd noticed my previous job had only lasted three months and ended a few weeks ago. "It's actually an amazing story," I said. I launched into telling her about my past trouble with interviews and how Charlie had been idiosyncratic enough to hire me, and then about being an awful assistant. "Charlie said he'd recommend me for a creative job like this but he won't let me be an assistant."

My interviewer finally let herself freely laugh. "I'm definitely calling him," she said.

I was hired, and my first day she told me about her phone call with Charlie. "His side of the story was even funnier than yours! He said you're a nut but that I'd be crazy not to hire you."

"I think that's fair," I told her.

Chapter 6

This Is Not Normal

THAT FIRST NIGHT at the Clubhouse, I'd written down the name of the woman in the suit: Eve. When she played again, I was sure to be there. She got onstage wearing a black hoodie with the hood up, gray torn jeans, and black cowboy boots. I gathered that this was her usual look, that she'd only worn a suit that first night to match the suited man. I searched the room for the suited man, but didn't see him; I wondered if they'd broken up. I assumed that a boyfriend would attend all his genius girlfriend's performances.

She played a thin three-stringed wooden instrument I'd never seen before, a thinner dulcimer she hung from a shoulder strap and strummed like a guitar. We both played small instruments. Onstage, Eve was controlled and serious, her eyes aimed above the crowd. She didn't speak between songs.

I saw Eve play often at the weekly open mic and showed up at all her shows. She never noticed me. Though I'd usually approach anyone I wanted to meet, Eve made me too nervous. I hoped eventually we'd be introduced through one of our mutual friends.

In my first six months in New York, I played some shows of my own at the Clubhouse, and some new friends invited me to play shows with them at other venues too. I was soon performing a couple times a month on lineups with musicians I loved. But I still hadn't met Eve.

Eventually, I noticed her in the audience at one of my shows, probably there to see the mutual friend I was opening for. Onstage, when I was supposed to be concentrating on my performance, I could only think of Eve's presence. I kept forgetting lyrics and hitting incorrect chords because I was distracted by my sweating under the lights, imagining how repellant I looked.

When I got off the stage and sat down, Eve took the empty seat beside me, which nearly made me spontaneously burst into tears. "Hey, I like your songs," she said. "I'm Eve."

"I know who you are," I told her. "I like your songs too. I go to all your shows." Her brow knitted and I realized she thought I was mocking her. "I'm not being sarcastic," I said. "A lot of people think I'm joking when I'm not." She eyed me, unsure what to make of this reply. "I really do go to all of your shows," I told her. "I just never introduced myself."

She settled into my earnestness but postponed committing to an opinion on it. She quickly suggested that we play music together sometime, gave me her number, said it was nice to meet me, and returned to her table and the friends she'd arrived with.

The next day, I called her and left a short message with my name and number. Then I spent the whole day worrying that she might not remember me by name, that I should have reminded her who I was. That night, I was playing music alone in my apartment when she called me back and asked me to meet her for a drink at a bar in Brooklyn in thirty minutes. "Weren't we gonna play music?" I asked, immediately regretting the question. Before she could answer, I said, "Never mind. Yes, I'll meet you."

She'd chosen a bar with wrought iron crisscrossing and circling the windows, chairs, and walls; it felt like having a drink inside a birdcage. We looked funny together, Eve in her ripped jeans and black hoodie with the hood up and me in my dark grey fraying junk-shop suit and thick-rimmed black glasses.

Eve started asking me standard questions: where was I from, how long had I lived in New York, how many siblings did I have. Then she asked me what my parents were like, which struck me as an odd thing to ask upon first meeting someone. But it was an easy question to answer. "My parents are really honest," I told her. "My whole family is. My dad, especially, sees through everything. He's really good at spotting fraudulence and hypocrisy."

"Hmmm," Eve said, thrown off by this strange answer but also curious. "Are your parents still together?"

"Actually, it's a crazy story!" I said, excited to tell her about my parents' divorce, which I considered funny and interesting. "My family goes every summer to this place I call family therapy camp . . ." Eve listened to my explanation of family camp, her brow thoroughly furrowed. When I told her that Mom left Dad for someone else from camp, her mouth twisted. "Then we all kept going to camp together anyway: my mom and dad *and* my mom's boyfriend!"

"Wait," Eve said, switching from revulsion to urgent interest. "Your parents got divorced and still spend time together?"

"Yeah," I said.

Eve reached into her hoodie's pocket with her small fidgety hands and produced a ballpoint pen. She bent over her napkin and began to draw, an excuse to look down so her hood would hide her face. "My parents won't be in the same room," she said. "They can't even bear to hear each other's names."

"Because they still love each other or because they hate each other?" I asked.

"They're still in love," Eve said. "Or maybe that's just what I want to think."

In the time it took to say these few lines, Eve's ballpoint drawing had taken form on the napkin: a crosshatched portrait of a young woman's big-cheeked cherubic face. I stopped the conversation to gush about how much I loved it, how crazy it felt to see it come out of her so suddenly and casually when I didn't even know she drew. As I rambled, she added to the drawing a cartoonish buck-toothed tentacled monster growing out of the young woman's head like a parasite. She added a word bubble to the monster's mouth but didn't fill it.

Eve looked thrown off by my praise, so I asked, "Are you one of the people who gets uncomfortable when someone freaks out about your art?" Before she could answer, I told her, "When I say people hate honesty, they assume I'm talking about negative honesty, like criticisms, but I find people are even more bothered by positive honesty, compliments, telling someone you care."

Eve laughed at this, partly unnerved, partly charmed. "You *are* really honest," she said.

"Yeah," I told her. "When I tell people I'm honest, they never believe me."

"Of course not!" Eve said, laughing. "It's the most suspicious line ever!"

I laughed too while simultaneously lingering in the sting of this perfect harsh truth. She continued, "Describing yourself is always suspicious. When someone goes out of their way to call themselves nice, they sound psychotic. It's like saying out of nowhere, 'I'd never murder anyone. I'm definitely not the type who murders people.'" Until now, Eve had come across as very serious, but when she cracked this joke, she had exquisite comic timing.

"Are you honest?" I asked her.

She laughed. "Have you learned nothing from this conversation?" We laughed again but then she looked down, inspecting her drawing. "I try to be honest, but it's hard."

"What about it do you find difficult?"

"I don't know," she said.

"How could you not know?" I asked. Then I figured it out. "Oh, you mean you don't want to tell me." Eve laughed again but still didn't answer the question. She filled in the speech bubble with the leech-like monster saying, "I'm probably a liar."

AT THE END of the night, I didn't dare imagine that she might be romantically interested in me, didn't even consider trying to kiss her, but I did ask for her address so I could write her.

I sent her a handwritten letter without corrections or cross outs and admitted that I achieved this effect by writing numerous drafts. Both of our addresses were on Grand Street, though about a mile apart, so I ended with, "It's like we have a tin can telephone and Grand Street is the string."

In her response, Eve wrote about how her teachers had always punished her for doodling and now she'd submitted a book of her doodles to various comic book publishers. I found it funny that she referred to her drawings as "doodles." I'd seen stuff from Picasso's sketchbook that wasn't as good as what Eve had sketched in front of me, but he'd never called his drawings doodles. I wondered if her doodles would be published. I believed in the beauty of Eve's drawings more than I believed in the wisdom of publishers.

Eve finished her letter with a line suspended at the bottom of the page without context: "This is not normal." If there was ever a line to make Michael Leviton swoon, it was this one.

WHEN EVE INVITED me to her apartment for the first time, she showed me the book of doodles, a lined composition notebook filled with ballpoint tableaus. I looked through it in front of her. Her characters grinned with crooked teeth or bit their own lips, haggard and awkward, with anxious eyes and sweat flying off their foreheads. The characters' thoughts and dialogue appeared in bubbles around them, sometimes so many overlapping bubbles that the characters appeared smothered under their own words and feelings. Eve portrayed herself in many of the scenes too, her eyes sad dots framed in bags and lines, even in happy scenes.

Eve's real eyes were big and green and decidedly not dot-like. She didn't have prominent eye-bags either, but her face read as wise and experienced, like she'd thought and felt a lot, traits I associated with eye-bags. Her portraits of herself did, however, accurately communicate her paper-pale complexion and her hair, black as ballpoint.

There was no way to ignore that Eve's doodles, drawn long before meeting me, showed a preoccupation with dishonesty. Some characters announced plainly in word bubbles that they were liars or truth-tellers; others would translate themselves or each other, clarifying, "When I say 'shut up,' I mean 'you're the greatest.'" In my favorite image, an unflattering portrait of Eve swooned in the arms of a smiling bucktoothed boy who pronounced: "We know what no one else will tell you."

I was so moved by these drawings that I started crying. I explained to Eve that I cried whenever I felt a lot. She said she'd always cried easily too and told me a story about when she visited the Grand Canyon with her family when she was eight. She stood on the cliff with her mom and started sobbing. Her mother asked what was wrong and eight-year-old Eve answered, "I'm crying because the best part of the Grand Canyon is being here with *you.*" Eve got emotional retelling this story and that made me cry again. So, from the start, we were crying.

Later, we drank some wine and she put on a record and asked me to slow-dance. We danced and she moved her mouth toward mine, but I pulled away. "Of course, I want to kiss you," I told her. "But this isn't realistic. You're not gonna be my girlfriend. I'm happy just to be friends and have you in my life." Eve ignored this statement, moved toward me again and, this time, I kissed her back.

I spent the night in her bed. She fell asleep first and I stayed awake next to her, telling myself to enjoy whatever time I had with her because it wouldn't last.

In the morning, I informed her that I was emotionally prepared for this to end at any time, that I didn't want her to feel guilty when she inevitably dumped me; I just wanted to ask that when she did, I'd like her to break up with me straight instead of trying to protect my feelings. Eve laughed this off, made a joke, and kissed me some more. In the same conversation, I told her about my fetish, about mentioning it on the Michael Talking Tape, about Dad suggesting I bring it up to the rabbi. She found the stories hilarious but was surprisingly moved too. "Having a fetish sounds strange and beautiful," she said. "It's so great that you weren't taught to feel shame about it."

Over the next few weeks, I kept asking Eve directly how she felt about me. When she avoided the question, I'd start to tell her how I felt about her. She'd interrupt before I could get out half a sentence. "We just met a month ago," she'd say. "You don't even know me." So I stopped bringing it up.

We'd hang out at the Clubhouse and go see concerts and movies and play music or listen to records or take weekend morning trips deep into Brooklyn to wander junk shops looking for vintage clothes or furniture—nearly everything I owned came from these junk shops, most notably a faux-Victorian three-piece turquoise velvet couch which served as my apartment's centerpiece.

After three months, she called me at work and asked me to have dinner with her. She told me where she wanted to go and when, but when I arrived, Eve wasn't there. I waited twenty minutes and called her. She didn't answer so I figured maybe she'd gotten stuck on the subway. I waited another half hour and she still didn't show. The restaurant filled up and the waiters got anxious, regretting having seated me alone. I gave up the table and waited on the sidewalk outside. I called again and she still didn't answer. When she was more than an hour late and still not responding to my calls, I worried something bad had happened.

I headed to her apartment to see if her roommate might know something. Eve's buzzer didn't work, so I waited for someone to enter the building and open the main door for me. I knocked on her apartment door, and when it opened, Eve was standing there, her nostrils shrinking and flaring as if smelling something rotten. "What are you doing here?" she asked.

"You didn't show up to meet me and you weren't answering your phone."

"You came to my *apartment*?" she said.

"I was worried," I told her. She didn't seem happy to see me and hadn't invited me in, so I asked, "Is everything okay?"

She sighed and gestured that I could come in.

"I didn't plan to see you tonight," she told me.

"You asked me to have dinner," I said.

She jumped back stiffly. "No, I didn't. We left it up in the air."

"You told me where and when to meet you."

Eve moved across the room one step at a time, drifting farther and farther from me. "If that's what you think, then why are you here? If I stood you up like that, you should never speak to me again."

"Never" is a haunting word. It sent my thoughts to an imagined future, a new era known as "never." This conversation would end, and I'd leave the apartment and "never" would begin and that's where I'd live from now on.

I told her, "I don't know what you could do to make me never want to speak to you again." This felt like the most romantic thing I'd ever said, but Eve's expression showed no sign that she'd witnessed anything romantic.

She sat on her bed, her fingers lacing and unlacing. "I didn't want to have dinner with you. You guilted me into it."

"Why are you lying?" I asked her.

"Stop badgering me," she said, suddenly crying. "Leave me alone."

Without thinking, I sat on the bed, embraced her, and told her, "You don't have to lie."

"Yes, I do," she said through sobs.

Here, I started channeling family therapy camp. "What are you afraid will happen if you tell the truth?"

She looked me in the eyes, crying madly, and said, "You'll see that I'm a horrible person."

"What did you do that's so horrible?"

"I can't even say it," she said.

"Tell me."

Eve took a breath to brace herself. "I was lonely and I thought it would make me feel better to see you. And then I changed my mind and decided I didn't want to see you, tonight or anytime."

My arms were still around her, and the thought came to me that this might be the last time I'd touch her. I focused myself on feeling this embrace so I could remember it. Eve continued. "And then you came here like a crazy stalker." She laughed and wiped her eyes. "You didn't even get the hint that I was dumping you."

An interior switch flicked, accepting that Eve wouldn't be my girlfriend, redirecting all hope on staying her friend. "There's nothing wrong with not wanting to see someone anymore," I told her.

"I stood you up!" she said, crying again. "I'm a monster! Why are you still here?"

"Because I'm in love with you," I said.

Eve fell back onto the one pillow on her twin-size bed. I stretched out next to her, my face inches from hers. Her sad eyes moved back and forth, staring into one of my eyes, then the other, and back. I liked watching Eve's eyes darting. She laughed and wiped more tears off her face. Then I kissed her and she kissed me back and the breakup was off.

AFTER THAT, WE saw each other nearly every day. I played in her band and she played in mine. I spent a lot of time with Eve's friends and twin sister. In a few months, Eve agreed to call herself my girlfriend.

One weekend afternoon, Eve and I were in my apartment when she took a phone call from an unknown number. A thrilled shock rolled over her face. "Oh my god," she said. "Wow. Thank you. Wow." She listened on the line awhile, thanked them again, and hung up. "They want to publish my doodles," she said. "They want to publish the book as it is." She explained that she'd been getting rejection letters the whole time we knew each other, that she'd kept them secret. She'd been rejected by everyone she'd sent it to except her favorite publisher, who hadn't written her back. They'd just called, eight months after she'd sent it, to tell her they wanted to publish it. I'd never been so happy. "I love when the world has better taste than I'd expect," I told her.

IN JANUARY OF 2004, Miriam, who was now a senior in high school, visited me in New York. Miriam's hair still puffed with brown curls like it had when she was a child. She wore a lot of flannel with T-shirts and jeans.

Eve changed her style regularly, had now retired her black hoodie for a red-and-blue plaid winter jacket and thin-rimmed glasses.

Miriam and the friend she'd brought with her on the trip showed up at my place straight from the airport. I opened the door for her and watched Miriam take in my one-bedroom apartment cluttered with beautiful old stuff I'd collected and Eve sitting there on my fake-Victorian couch. Eve leapt up and said, "Hi!" in a much higher voice than usual. "I'm Eve! I've been so excited to meet you!"

Miriam looked at Eve and then at me. She'd expected my life here to be much worse. She hugged Eve, shooting me a skeptical look over her shoulder as if she suspected I'd hired an actress to pretend to be my girlfriend. Miriam's friend behaved normally. For her, an older brother with a girlfriend was unremarkable. In my family, it was concerning.

I'd planned to leave Miriam and her friend to find ways to spend the day while I was at work, but Eve volunteered to show them around New York. She spent every afternoon with them, which struck me as nuts. "You really don't have to!" I told her.

"I know! I want to," she insisted.

We threw a party at my apartment for Miriam's seventeenth birthday and invited all of our friends. I made a compilation of doo-wop and soul from the '50s and '60s, leaned my bed against the wall and designated my little bedroom for slow-dancing. Miriam had a disposable camera and shot a photo of me and Eve swaying together, her head against my chest.

On Miriam's last day in town, we got lunch just the two of us. "Eve's so amazing," Miriam said. "She's so pretty and nice and funny and stylish and talented and cool. I'm sort of obsessed with her. I'm gonna buy her same jacket when I get home. I can't believe she's your girlfriend."

"Neither can I," I said.

Miriam was chewing potato chips. "Do you think this is gonna last?"

"Probably not," I said. "But I'm gonna enjoy it while I can."

At that, Miriam relaxed, relieved. "I just wanted to make sure you had realistic expectations."

High Ceilings

THE LITERACY PROGRAM where I worked had hired their freelancers for a defined period of a year and a half. Eve and I had been together for a year when my contract ended. I'd found some freelance writing work to live on for a while and I hoped to get more, but I couldn't afford to keep living alone without a full-time job, and I doubted I could get another one. I'd learned at family camp to ask for what I wanted, even if I knew the answer would be no, so I told Eve I needed to move and asked if she'd like to find an apartment with me and live together. As expected, she said no. She was generally hesitant to commit (it had taken her six months to admit I was her boyfriend) and she was independent, spent a lot of time alone, liked having her own space. I'd also always hated to share living space, but there was nothing I wanted more than to live with Eve. I knew she didn't feel the same way; I'd long since accepted that I loved her more than she loved me. So, I started searching for apartments and talking to other friends and acquaintances about being my roommates if I found a place.

The apartment-hunting situation in Williamsburg, Brooklyn had changed a lot between 2002 and 2004. When I'd found my first apartment, I'd gone through a charming elderly real estate agent with a dirty office that had clearly been there for decades. That place had since closed. Now, every broker I could find had a clean office with a glass storefront like an aquarium full of young, clean-shaven white men with gelled hair and expensive-looking suits who spoke in continuous streams of flimflam.

I told anyone showing me apartments my one deal-breaker: I was too tall to live with a low ceiling. Each time, they'd take me immediately to an apartment with a low ceiling. When I remarked on the low ceiling, they'd reply, "These ceilings are high."

The first time this happened, I laughed. "Come on!" I said. "I'm looking right at it! Do you expect me to believe you over my own eyes? Do people fall for this?" The broker looked at me as if *I'd* been rude.

The second time a broker claimed low ceilings were high, I found it less funny and tried to push past it. "Well, I'd like to only see places with ceilings higher than this."

The broker doubled down, sticking with his script. "With your budget, you're not gonna find a place with a higher ceiling."

At this, I laughed again and did one of the things liars hated most: I leaned into his lie. "Oh, of course," I said. "Well, since this is the highest ceiling you've got, I guess there's no reason to have you show me any other apartments."

At that, the broker backpedaled: "Actually, I just remembered some other apartments with much higher ceilings!"

"Sorry," I told him. "I can't work with people who lie to my face."

It only took a few rounds of this before I determined that they would *all* lie to my face, using the same strategy of showing their worst apartments first, misleading their customers into thinking there weren't better options, a business practice I considered despicable. So, I started telling brokers from the start, "Hey, I know about the trick where you show the worst apartments first. With me, you can skip that." The brokers pretended to laugh and praised me for being clever. Then they'd show me their worst apartments anyway, telling me the low ceilings were high.

After a few weeks of this, one broker infuriated me to the point that I held off on calling him out and asked him to show me another apartment. I walked into the next apartment he showed me, which of course had the higher ceilings that he'd claimed I couldn't afford. "What a *high ceiling!*" I exclaimed. "Isn't this *odd?* You said I couldn't find a higher ceiling, and then look at *this*. How *strange!* It's almost as if you were *lying!*"

The broker, enraged but holding himself back from exploding, avoided my gaze. He muttered bleakly, "It just *looks* higher. It's an optical illusion."*

Around this time, Eve asked me to meet her at a nearby coffee shop I'd never heard of in half an hour. This was suspicious. We always got coffee at the same few spots, and usually it wasn't so spontaneous. Also, she'd stayed over at my apartment the previous night; we'd seen each other that morning. The timing coincided with my few weeks of dismal apartment searching and her telling me repeatedly that she didn't want to move in

---

* I see now that I was unnecessarily torturing real estate agents who were only trying to make a living. Psychological manipulation was part of their job. I'm sure they weren't happy about it either.

with me. I felt certain she'd invited me to coffee to break up. We hadn't had a fight or anything, but I knew that these decisions were made secretly and without elaboration. Even if she wouldn't tell me why, I could think of plenty of perfectly justified reasons.

When I arrived, I found Eve standing outside the coffee shop accompanied by an older woman in business attire. Eve smiled, kissed me, and said she wanted to show me something. The stranger unlocked the door to the building next to the coffee shop, led us up two flights of stairs, and opened the door to an apartment. We entered, and I found myself standing alone with Eve in a sunlight-flooded kitchen. Eve embraced me, smiled, and asked, "Michael, would you like to live with me here?" We both started crying and I told her yes without even looking at the apartment or the height of its ceilings.

When I was no longer in the thrall of the moment, it occurred to me that in order to pull off this surprise, Eve had conducted her own apartment search, concurrent with mine. She'd listened as I told her my miserable experiences and let me keep looking, wasting my time. She'd misled me to believe that she didn't want to live with me, let me think that she didn't love me. Instead of appreciating the surprise, I managed to resent the dishonesty behind the most romantic moment of my life.

Eve and I decorated this shabby one-bedroom railroad with what we found on our junk trips. In the living room, we had my fake-Victorian fainting couch and the decrepit speakeasy piano I'd gotten for free on Craigslist. Our guitar amplifiers served as end tables with flowers in vases, and we used a pile of vintage suitcases as a coffee table. The bedroom in the middle of the apartment was only big enough for our bed so the kitchen doubled as Eve's art studio with a desk and easel and her paintings, drawings, and instruments cramped in one corner. Everything in the apartment was coated in a quick-replenishing dust that neither of us was hung up on removing. Eve collected our pencils in a box and wrote "pencils" in illustrated text. She could make anything beautiful by writing or drawing on it. Even the mundane reminder Post-it notes she left stuck to her computer screen killed me. Sometimes when she wasn't home, I'd stand by the door and gaze at her little office corner in the kitchen as if it was itself a work of art.

We complained often about the constant background noise from the street two stories below (sidewalk conversations, car stereos, revving trucks), but even the racket could be romantic. An out-of-view local child would occasionally call up to a nearby window for someone else named Eve. The child would shout the name with a long "e"—"Eeeeeeeve! Eeeeeeeeeve!"—the same way people in love elongate syllables. We never saw this shouting girl or figured out where her calls originated. Each time I heard her, it felt as if this unseen child were an extension of my own feelings, as if I were the one calling out Eve's name.

THOUGH EVE AND I were both used to spending most of our time alone working on things, we miraculously continued exactly as we always had, except on opposite ends of the same railroad apartment. I'd write or play in the living room while Eve drew or wrote or played in the kitchen. We'd take turns being silent while the other composed or practiced. We'd take breaks to eat together. At night, we'd have band rehearsals or go out to see friends play concerts.

After a few months in the new apartment, we discovered an unusual video store around the corner. The store had no organization system, just a few thousand random DVDs and videotapes on shelves, mostly direct-to-video B movies and low-budget unprofessional stuff, almost nothing good. Eve and I would sometimes spend an hour there showing each other one insane video cover after another, eventually renting whichever one struck us as funniest. Eve called these movies "thrilers" because of their often-misspelled descriptions; one had literally referred to itself as a "thriler." She'd smile romantically and say, "Let's rent a thriler tonight." We'd end up watching some ridiculous monster movie with homemade special effects, commenting on every hilarious detail. Occasionally, a thriler would have an inspired moment; we'd be watching a movie that acted as if a rubber toy alligator was a huge monster, and a character would give a surprisingly moving monologue out of nowhere and Eve would say, "I'm crying at *Killer Croc 3*! Has it really come to this?"

When we felt more in the mood to watch good movies, which Eve sometimes referred to as "tearjerkers," we'd trek to the regular video store. But no matter what we rented, I watched mostly for Eve's commentary. Making it through a movie could take hours because we paused it so often to talk. Sometimes, we'd abandon the movie and stay up talking. We were so great at talking.

Sometimes we'd cover our favorite songs or even whole albums for fun. Other times, we'd take turns showing each other music we'd discovered. It wasn't long before we associated hundreds of songs with our relationship and joked about how a normal couple would have decided by now which one was "our song." Once in a pharmacy, I hugged Eve and said, "The radio's playing our song!" It was that Michael Sembello 1980s hit in which he spends the whole song repeating that a woman he knows is a maniac. This started a running joke suggesting wildly inappropriate possibilities for "our song." Another night when we were listening to records, Eve put on her own suggestion for our song: The Monks' "Shut Up."

We'd often spend time with Eve's twin sister, Lila, who Eve spoke to on the phone every few hours. The closeness of the twins was impressive to witness. Once, when Lila wasn't around, I asked Eve if twins felt this close because they knew everything about each other, a rare human experience. "She's witnessed almost your whole life," I said. "The rest of us see barely any of one another's histories. Even if we all shared as much as we possibly could, we'd never get close to knowing each other like twins."

Eve answered, "I can't imagine not having a twin. It feels to me like without a twin, you'd immediately lose your mind. How do you live without another you? Without a person that's born to understand you?"

"I accepted as a child that I wouldn't be understood," I told her.

"I understand you," Eve said, gazing at me warmly, proud to be the only one who understood me.

"I *think* I understand you," I told her. "In some ways, at least. But I still want to understand you more." Eve smiled, but I could sense her uncertainty about this comment. "I mean, we've been together for a year and there's so much you haven't told me about your past. I don't know any stories about your ex-boyfriends—"

Eve laughed, blushed, and said, "Oh, you don't want to know. It's boring."

"It's not boring!" I said. "I'd like to see you *try* to be boring."

Eve didn't laugh. "It's boring," she repeated until I let it go.

One night, we watched a movie in which Natalie Wood gave an angry speech to Robert Redford about how much she hated him. He interrupted by kissing her, and she fell blissfully into his arms.

"If I told someone that I hated her and she tried to kiss me, I'd be horrified," I grouched, pausing the movie. "If a woman told me she hated me, I'd never even think to try and kiss her! I'd leave! It's so disrespectful to assume she's lying. And I wouldn't want to be with someone who says stuff she doesn't mean just because she's upset."

Eve sighed. "Come on, it's obvious she's in love with him. He just knows what she wants without having to ask or hear her say it."

"I don't find that romantic at all."

"I know," Eve said. "You're romantic too, in your own way." Eve ran her hand through my hair. "You're romantic in a way that isn't in movies."

In Space, No One Can Hear You Lie

AROUND THIS TIME, my friend Sidney called me with a wild offer. Sidney had been one of the few in college who appreciated me. He'd played football, was tall and broad-shouldered and good-looking, could pass as normal when he tried. He'd done such a good job passing that he'd been hired at a studio in Los Angeles to package modern remakes of old movies from their archives. He said this meant he was in a position to hire me to rewrite a horror movie from the 1930s, a dream job I desperately needed.

Very soon after I started working on it, he told me the studio had taken him off my project and replaced him with a more experienced producer based in New York, that I should go into the office to meet him. I looked up this new producer's name and found that he'd worked on a few movies I'd seen. I didn't like them, but they were popular with everyone else I knew. When the receptionist showed me into the producer's office, I was surprised at his appearance: blond and muscular with spiky hair like a surfer, young-looking for his forties. He cockily bragged about his career, about dropping out of high school to work at a movie studio. He described himself as a "wunderkind." I couldn't fathom why he was so intent on impressing me. I theorized that he might feel insecure about taking over for my friend. Maybe my being twenty-four made him feel old so he wanted to tell me he'd been a success younger than me. Maybe he did this with everyone; that possibility disturbed me most. How infinitely tedious and painful to want to impress *everyone*!

As the producer went on about himself, he told me a story from his first week in Hollywood, about the marketing meeting for the movie *Alien*. "So, I'm this high school dropout in a conference room on Sunset Boulevard, listening to pitches for poster taglines. Everybody's talking typical horror sci-fi stuff about screams and space until someone says something about screaming in space. The wife of the producer overhears and interrupts to make fun of us like, 'You idiots! You can't scream in space because there's no air and no sound!'" The surfer-producer across the desk paused smugly before the obvious climax in which, he, a teenager in his first week on the job, wrote, "In space, no one can hear you scream!"

"Hold on," I said. "Why was the producer's wife there? And why was she able to overhear what was going on in the conference room? Was the door open? She was standing outside the meeting room, listening, and then barged in through the open door to correct the room? And, before that, no one there had considered that there was no sound in space? How many people were in the meeting?"

The producer swiveled in his chair, stunned. I shouldn't have been surprised; Hollywood was famous for its liars. But I tried to be positive, imagining that maybe his lying benefited him when navigating the movie business. I changed the subject to something complimentary.

"You know, I looked you up before this meeting," I told him. "And you've produced a couple movies my friends really love."

"Oh yeah?" he said. "That's always cool to hear."

"I didn't personally like them," I added. "But I still feel positive about our being able to work well together."

The producer smoothed it over best he could, thanked me as if I hadn't insulted him.

It wasn't long after this meeting that they attached a director to the project, a brilliant cinematographer who had shot many movies I loved. I couldn't imagine why he'd be attached to some kid's theoretical script that wasn't even written yet.

When the producer, the director, and Sidney were all in New York at the same time, they set up a meeting. The moment before Sidney, the producer, and I entered the conference room to meet the director, I joked, "Wouldn't it be crazy if I walked into the meeting and instantly transformed into a Hollywood caricature, speaking in all the clichés, like 'Paulie, baby! Love your work! Big fan! We should do lunch! I'll have my people call your people!'"

The producer looked unnerved. Sidney grinned uneasily and said, "Michael, that wouldn't be crazy; that would be normal."

I laughed. "And what I'm actually gonna say will be considered crazy." My friend laughed, the producer shrugged, and we went in.

I listened as the surfer-producer and the brilliant director praised a movie that didn't exist, going on about the masterpieces it would resemble, mired in self-congratulation about what a hit it would be. They spoke as if unlikely fantasies were certainties, toasting successes in advance. I tried interrupting, but my reminders that the script hadn't yet been written and that it was best to manage our expectations somehow had no dampening effect whatsoever on their enthusiasm.

Funerals for Fish

EVE LOVED ANIMALS and wanted a pet. I hadn't been raised with pets, was allergic to cats, and we had no space for a dog. So Eve bought a blue fighting fish to keep in a bowl by our front door. She named the fish "Josh," not after my brother; the name match was a coincidence. Eve loved to watch Josh swim around and loved feeding him.

One day, Eve noticed Josh swelling up on one side and wobbling in his swimming. She searched online for possible diagnoses and read that Josh was very ill and likely to die. She ordered medicine off the internet and sprinkled it into the bowl, but Josh continued to swell grotesquely as if he'd soon burst. He continued to swim in a disturbing zigzag. Eve took it hard. I asked her if we should euthanize Josh since he was suffering. She insisted that the medicine would cure him.

Eve was away for the weekend visiting her family in Boston when I noticed Josh dead at the bottom of the bowl. I knew Eve would be devastated. I flushed Josh down the toilet, found a black pillowcase to put over the fishbowl like a shroud, and waited for her to come home. When she opened the door, she immediately saw the fishbowl with the pillowcase. "He died right after you left," I told her. "It was like he waited for you to leave because he knew how much you loved him."

The empty fishbowl sitting there depressed us. We decided to get another fish. I actually said aloud, "That's what Josh would have wanted." I said it seriously, but Eve laughed, jolting me to reality, and then I laughed too.

We got a little red goldfish this time, that Eve named

Banana, but pronounced with a funny accent so it sounded like "Bananer." Bananer liked to sit in a little green fake tree in the fishbowl. He barely swam. I marveled at how even fish could have unique personalities. I'd never truly understood why people loved them so much. I noticed now how animals embraced their actual selves in ways that humans couldn't. Animals didn't fake anything, didn't protect anyone's feelings, didn't pretend to love; you could trust them. I wondered if they embodied a subconscious fantasy of showing all joy or pain or sorrow, of loving openly without hesitation, without shame.

Eve and I, again, stared into a fishbowl crying happily. After a while, Bananer's tree became encrusted with algae and Eve took it out to clean it. It still looked gross, so she planned to go out and buy another tree when she got a chance. The next day, I was in the living room writing when I heard Eve scream from the kitchen. I ran across the two rooms and found Eve on the kitchen floor next to Bananer.

"He jumped out of the bowl!" Eve said, looking up at me, sobbing. "Because I took away his tree!" Bananer was still on the floor. "That tree was his only reason to live!"*

"You were just trying to help him," I said. "You couldn't have known or you would've just gotten a new tree before taking out the old one. It's not your fault. You were just trying to make him happy!"

"All I wanted was for Bananer to be happy," she said, still sobbing.

"Me too," I told her. "Me too."

---

* It would have been advisable to comfort her by insisting that it couldn't have been about the tree, but we'd emotionally committed to a certain world and there was no turning back now.

Welcome to the Real World

EVE'S TWIN SISTER, Lila, was a musician too, so one weekend we had the idea to all play together in my practice space. I rented and shared the space with a dozen other musicians, so I checked the schedule and told the twins Saturday night was the only time that week the space wasn't reserved. We planned to play that night. When the time came, we were sitting on our velvet couch with Lila. Eve said, "I'm not feeling like playing music tonight. Let's just do it tomorrow."

"The space is occupied tomorrow," I reminded her. "Tonight's the only free time this week."

"It's okay," Eve said. "Let's just do it tomorrow."

I looked at Lila to see if she noticed this odd response, but Lila showed no sign of anything unusual.

"What's going on?" I asked. "I just told you tonight is the only time the space is available."

Eve glared at me and repeated herself. "I don't feel like it tonight. We'll just play *tomorrow*."

"I don't get what's happening," I persisted. "Are you pretending to not understand what I'm saying?"

"Let's go get a drink instead," Eve said. "We'll play music tomorrow."

Eventually, I had to let it go, but the conversation haunted me for the rest of the night. When I was finally alone with Eve again, I asked her what it was all about. She seemed annoyed by my bringing it up.

"Lila didn't feel like playing music tonight," she said. "I didn't see why you made it such a big thing."

"You kept saying we'd play tomorrow."

"I wanted Lila to feel like we'd play music with her another time."

"Why didn't you just say that? Or something that made sense? And why did you say *you* didn't want to play instead of Lila just saying it herself?"

"What's the big deal?" Eve said. "Who cares?"

"Well, you must care enough to make it worth a bunch of weird lies! It seems like *you're* the one who thinks it's a big deal."

This escalated into a fight, Eve acting as if she were defending Lila against me, like I'd mysteriously become possessed to attack her family. I couldn't follow the logic, and it eventually just petered out without resolving.

Not long after that, Eve invited me to Christmas with her mom in Boston. Her dad lived in the same area, so I'd be able to meet him too on the same trip. Given how much she loved her family, I felt certain that she'd only stay with me if I could charm them. Never before in my life had I felt that I needed specific people to like me. I'd never pandered before, had no idea how.

"I'm worried your family won't like me," I told Eve. "I don't know how to get people to like me."

"You knew how to get *me* to like you," Eve said.

"No, I didn't!" I said. "I was just myself and you happened to like it. That's not how it usually works out."

Eve laughed, not as concerned as she should have been.

Eve's mom smiled at me warmly, expecting to like me. I'd imagined having to prove myself to her before receiving any positivity. Her house had a whole Christmas setup with a tree and decorations, and I talked a lot about how strange it was for me to celebrate Christmas, how I wasn't sure how I'd feel about giving and receiving presents. I told Eve's mom and sister the story of my moment of truth with Santa and about my dad's mother rejecting gifts. Eve's mother laughed at my stories, but I could also see behind her positivity that she was collecting information, deciding what she thought of my telling these stories of my troubled family so quickly, of my speaking ill of my grandmother.

When it was time to exchange presents, they had a lot of tradition and ceremony; they'd been doing this the same way for decades.* I kept commenting on it and asking questions, unpleasantly reminding everyone over and over that I was an outsider instead of just running with it. "My family had no traditions," I said. "And we didn't want to do anything that mass amounts of other people were doing."

Eve's mother, her sister, and her sister's boyfriend gave one another presents like they really knew one another, like they'd done research and planned surprises. Eve didn't have money for gifts, so she'd made everyone personalized drawings and comics. Almost from the start of the giving and receiving presents, I was crying. I tried to explain to them why it moved me so much, but again I was imposing my experience on everyone, taking over the scene. Given the circumstances, it went pretty well.

In the morning, we visited Eve's dad, who enjoyed the fatherly tradition of cutely intimidating his daughters' suitors. Because I wasn't conventionally masculine, certainly not the type of guy he'd dreamed of his daughter being with, I made an appealing target. He cracked a joke about how every man should know basic carpentry, and I responded as if he'd made an actual argument. "Have you ever noticed that whenever somebody suggests what everyone should know how to do, it always happens to be something *they themselves* know how to do? What a wild *coincidence!*" Eve and her dad weren't laughing, so I tried to

---

* I'm now aware that this is not extreme at all but rather the way most families celebrate holidays.

be clearer. "What if I insisted that a *real* man should be able to play piano? Or write a story? Or cry on cue? Who gets to decide what everyone should be able to do?"

Whatever response Eve's dad expected to his innocuous jab, this wasn't it—I watched him decide how to take it, whether to laugh, be insulted, or to engage in argument. He laughed politely.

Eve changed the subject, complained about the typical troubles of freelance life as a twenty-four-year-old, and her father said, "Welcome to the real world."

I launched into another rant. "When we talk about the 'real world,' why is it always negative? I'm gonna start saying that about good news, like when someone wins the lottery, I'll say, 'Welcome to the real world!' or 'You fell in love? Welcome to the real world!'" Eve's dad liked this bit more than the last, though I could also see him feeling disarmed by the unpredictability of our back-and-forth.

Afterward, as we walked to the car, Eve held my hand and said, "He'll love you. It'll just take him a minute."

It occurred to me that I was taking part in a common experience: setting out to convince a girlfriend's parents to like me. Setting out to be liked by *anyone* had always struck me as such a doomed enterprise that I'd never attached to it any feelings of self-worth. And it seemed hypocritical to feel proud when someone liked me unless I was willing to feel ashamed when they didn't. Giving away the power over my feelings seemed a dismal gamble. I ran this train of thought by Eve in the car while she drove back to her mom's. Gazing out the windshield, she said, "That's just what it means to care."

"I don't think it's good to define yourself according to other people's arbitrary opinions," I told her.

Eve shrugged, now in a much worse mood. "I just know I like it when you care."

When we returned to her mom's house, everyone sat around the kitchen table to make plans to see a movie. Though I was usually pretty particular about what I wanted to see, I thought they would like me more if I was willing to see whatever they wanted. Eve's mom looked at the list of movies in the newspaper and said, "Michael doesn't like dramas, so let's see a comedy."

This claim baffled me. "I like dramas," I said. "I'll see whatever you want to see." Eve gave me a hard look like I was making a big mistake, but I couldn't imagine what that mistake could be.

"It's okay," Eve's mother said. "We'll just pick a comedy. We know you like comedies."

"What makes you think I don't like dramas?" I asked.

"A comedy would be great," Eve said, grabbing my hand under the table and shooting me another look that meant I should shut up. I guessed that I was supposed to agree with her mom that I didn't like dramas, but I couldn't bring myself to say that. I tried to stay quiet and let them choose. Eve's mother suggested a movie. "Michael, do you want to see that one?"

"I'm open to whatever you want to see," I told her. Eve frowned for reasons I couldn't understand.

"Okay," Eve's mom said as if I'd vetoed her suggestion. She then asked about another movie.

"Whatever you guys want," I said again. Eve looked exasperated, and I was so confused that I just cracked. "Sorry," I said. "I'm trying to follow the rules of this conversation but I can't figure them out! Can someone please just explain it to me? Are you saying I don't like dramas because *you* want to see a comedy? And when I told you I'd see whatever you wanted, you acted like I'd rejected your suggestion. I honestly meant that I didn't need to take part in choosing the movie. I'm trying to be nice but Eve's looking at me as if I'm being rude, and I can't figure out what to say!"

I was laughing, but Eve's mom and sister had their eyes down, mortified. Then, within seconds, they burst out comforting me. "We don't have to go to a movie, it's okay! We can just do something here!"

Eve got up to shepherd me from the room, saying something like, "Hey Michael, I just remembered something to show you." She brought me to our bedroom and said, "Don't worry, just stay here a few minutes and I'll take care of it. When you come back, don't mention anything about this."

"Are they gonna want me to apologize?" I asked. People always wanted me to apologize.

"Acting like it didn't happen is the apology," Eve said.

When I returned, the movie had been decided and everyone was in a good mood again.

Later that night, when we were alone in the guest bedroom, I asked Eve what had happened. She paused with a quizzical expression and then whispered as if communicating a sensitive military secret. "My mom tries to make everybody else feel comfortable. My whole family tries to make everyone feel comfortable."

"How was the bit about my not liking dramas supposed to make me feel comfortable?"

I could see that Eve had never tried to explain the way her family communicated, which blew my mind because explaining how my family and I communicated was like my part-time job. "When you want something, you can't just say you want it," Eve said.

I interrupted with a little obnoxious rant. "People say this all the time. 'You *can't* just ask for what you want!' or 'You *can't* just tell them how you feel!' Where's this *can't* coming from? Just open your mouth and move your tongue and vocal cords!"

"They don't mean you *literally* can't!" Eve scoffed. "They just mean it's rude!"

"Okay, so if they want something, how do they go about it?" I asked.

Eve answered quickly now, but was still whispering. "They give you a hint and then you notice and make them comfortable by saying it's what *you* want." Eve paused, impressed at her discovery that she could translate social life for me so clearly. "So, when Mom said you didn't like dramas, that was her way to say *she* didn't want to see a drama. And when she asked if you wanted to see a specific movie, that was the one *she* wanted to see. You were supposed to act excited about whatever movie she asked you about. When you said 'whatever you want,' she took that to mean that you didn't want to see it."

"That's the most complicated thing I've ever heard," I told her.

Eve laughed and softened, got onto the bed to hug me. "For you, it's complicated," she said. "It makes sense to us like how your family makes sense to you."

Though Eve had warmed now, I was still frustrated. "But how does this make anyone comfortable? To not be able to admit what you want? To know everyone's only pretending to want what you want? Doesn't that feel terrible?"

"No! Why would that feel terrible? Everyone's being nice!" Eve said. "I mean, sometimes there are miscommunications, I guess, but it's worth it."

"Why?" I asked.

This was another question she'd not previously considered.* She thought a moment and said, "Because we're always showing

---

* We live so much in our own styles of communication, it's hard to know why we prefer it, if there's even a reason.

that we care and giving chances for other people to show that they care."

"Can't everybody caring about each other just be assumed?" I grumbled. "Can't they just say 'I love you' or something?"

"No!" Eve laughed. "It's nice to show you care over and over."

"A broken record of love," I said, at first with some bitterness, but then moved by it. "I'd like to show you that I care over and over," I said. "I don't get this whole avoidant, indirect way of doing it, but . . ."

"I know," Eve sighed.

"I love how great you are at translating," I told her. As I finished this sentence, I plummeted into a neurotic spiral. I'd previously rolled my eyes at those who always played to the room, donning the most advisable mask. I'd prided myself on only wearing one face. Not everyone was allowed to exist that way. For most, switching personas wasn't a matter of preference but of survival. Beyond that, my speaking one language burdened everyone else with translating. Who knew how many had ushered me away and smoothed things over without my noticing? I watched Eve mull over my comment, taking in that being my girlfriend meant also being my translator.

ONCE I'D MET Eve's family, she started asking when she could meet mine. My family never came to New York and were really only all in the same place at family camp, so I joked, "You could come with us to family therapy camp!"

"I could come to family camp?" she said. "I'd love to!"

I'd told Eve a lot about family camp over our first year and a half together. A lot of movies reminded me of camp, so I'd pause them to tell her stories.

"You'd really want to come?" I asked. "*Why*?"

"You like it," she said. "Why wouldn't I? And I could spend

time with your family. And it sounds fun to go camping with you."

I took this explanation at face value. After all, Eve was really into "family" in general. And lots of people enjoyed camping. Besides, family camp would surely be twice as interesting with Eve's commentary. So I didn't question it. It didn't occur to me that bringing my girlfriend to family therapy camp might be a bad idea.

It's Fun to Be Nice

WE DECIDED TO spend a week in Los Angeles staying at Mom's house before camp. When I discussed it with Mom over the phone, her voice was ecstatic. "I'm so excited to meet her!" With the same enthusiastic tone, she added, "All that matters is that she likes me!"

When Eve walked in the door, Mom gave one of her near-violent hugs. "I'm so excited to meet you! I hope you like me!"

Eve laughed in the hug, surprisingly not thrown off, and said, "I hope you like me too!"

We put down our stuff in Mom's office, which had a bed and doubled as a guest room. As Eve took in the room, she noticed the affirmation Post-it notes Mom stuck on the mirrors and walls, things like, "You will sound professional and confident in all phone calls," "You deserve to be seen," and "You will be appreciated for your authentic self." I stood next to Eve and watched her read each Post-it, her expression shifting from discomfort to amusement to sadness and back. I remember she lingered with a melancholy smile at the one that said, "You are a good person." Though she didn't comment on the Post-it notes, she *did* comment on the lighting, that my mom used blinding energy-saving florescent bulbs without shades or dimmers. "It's the least-flattering lighting possible!"

"Hmmm," I said. "That would explain why I always found myself so ugly."

While Eve was in another room on the phone with her sister, I told Mom Eve's observation about the unflattering lights. "Huh," Mom said. "That's funny. Well, I guess it's good that we see what we really look like."

"But those bulbs make us look worse than we'd look anywhere else," I insisted. She remained unconvinced, didn't change the bulbs.

Mom hosted a breakfast at her house so that her family and Joe could meet Eve. It was a big deal to her that I had a girlfriend.

When Joe walked in the door, he beelined for Eve, said, "Wow! You're Eve! It's so great to meet you!" He hugged her and said, "We knew it wasn't gonna be easy for Michael to find somebody, but we never lost faith that *someone* would understand him!"

Eve's eyes widened. "Wow," she said emptily, filling conversational space. "That's so nice."

I'd warned Eve about my grandparents, but she showed no sign of irritation or recognition of their unpleasantness. It was wild to watch Eve smiling and laughing while Grammy regaled her with repetitive tales of nasty people she'd encountered (waiters, doctors, random people on the street). Under the light of Eve's attention, Grammy got on a roll, recounting endless stories of alleged nastiness.

At one point, Mom couldn't stay quiet anymore and said, "Mommy! You're still mad about that? You told me that story when I was *a teenager*!"

Eve intervened, "But it's such a funny story!" Mom and I exchanged looks, desperately hoping that Eve was only acting.

As Eve sat through Pa's dirty jokes and creepy comments on her appearance, I kept trying to interrupt and save her, but Eve always waved me away to keep Mom's parents comfortable. Eventually, they ran out of things to say and the conversation degenerated into repeating how "sweet" Eve was.

That evening, I was excited to have time alone with Eve to hear her true thoughts about all she'd seen, but her take wasn't what I'd expected.

"Your grandparents aren't so bad!" Eve insisted. "You made them sound like monsters!"

I sputtered, "I assumed you were pretending! How could you possibly have enjoyed talking with them?"

"They're your family!" Eve said. "Sure, they're not great conversationalists, but it's fun to be nice to your family."

"What's fun about being nice!?!" I asked in horror. "Being nice is excruciating!" Eve laughed at the state I was in so I calmed down. "Well," I said. "For what it's worth, I've never seen them love someone so much. You might be the only person outside the family who's ever listened to them."

Eve sighed. "Wouldn't you be unpleasant too if no one ever listened to you?" Eve overestimated how many people listened to me and underestimated my unpleasantness.

WHEN I TOLD Sidney that I was in L.A., he insisted that while in town I work with the director of my theoretical horror movie in person.* I feared that they would fire me if I said no.

Eve didn't sympathize with my predicament. "You're leaving me alone with your mom?"

---

* I shouldn't have mentioned that I was in town. Once I'd mentioned it, I should have made up an excuse why I couldn't work, but hiding information and making up excuses were not in my vocabulary.

"It'll just be for a part of the day each day," I said. "I'll leave you the car in case you want to go somewhere and I'll be back in the afternoon."

But by afternoon, she was in an even worse state. "You told your mom about me criticizing the lightbulbs! Why would you tell her that?"

"I thought it was good advice. And I wasn't gonna take credit for your observation."

"But it was awful. I tried to tell her I didn't say it and she didn't believe me."

"Don't lie to my mom!" I told her.

I'd never seen Eve so exasperated. "While you're out, she keeps trying to talk to me for hours and take me shopping, and she doesn't notice that sometimes it's too much. Even when I try to say no, she doesn't understand."

I could imagine Eve's version of "trying to say no" being a series of imperceptible hints we'd never pick up. "Did you try just telling her explicitly that you want to do something else?" I asked.

"No! I can't just say that!" Eve said. "I want her to like me!"

"With my family, you can make boundaries," I told her. "She won't be offended. And even if she is offended, that's okay."

"No, it isn't!" Eve said.

I continued working on the script in the mornings, and each time I met back up with Eve, she was more in the mood to fight than to go out and have fun. I could tell that she wanted to break up but couldn't figure out how to do so in the situation—we were staying at my mom's house, about to leave for family therapy camp. I figured it'd be best to address this instead of leaving it unspoken. "I can tell that you want to break up," I told her. "And I'm afraid you're gonna spend the whole week of camp pretending everything's okay, refusing to admit that you want to break up. So, I want to talk through it. Maybe you don't want to go to camp. Maybe we should break up and go to camp as friends? I don't know. What do you want to do?"

Eve glared. "Are you *dumping me*?"

"No!" I said. "I'm in love with you. I'm trying to make *you* feel better about dumping *me*. If you need to break up, I don't want you to feel bad about it."

Eve shook her head. "Believe me. If I'm breaking up with you, you'll know."

"Okay," I said, starting to cry. "Just please don't pretend to like me more than you really do or pretend to be happy when you aren't. If I can tell that you're pretending, it'll be so sad. And if I fall for it and believe that you still love me when you don't, that'll be even worse."

Eve was moved by this speech and embraced me. "I wouldn't do that," she said. "I promise to be honest." I still didn't believe her.

The next day, we set off on our romantic getaway to family therapy camp.

Rooting for Trauma

THE SNAKY ROAD to camp especially concerned me this trip because of Eve's self-diagnosed "vomit-phobia" which I'd learned about when we watched movies. So many movies featured vomit scenes—comedies, dramas, horror movies, romances—far more than I'd ever have expected. Whenever a character threw up, Eve cupped her hands over her face and lamented, "Why does there have to be vomiting in every movie? Who likes to watch vomiting? Who wants to write about vomiting?"

After a while inching up the mountain road listening to the family-therapy-camp-themed mix-CD I'd made of songs containing the word "crazy," Eve unbuckled her seatbelt, knelt on her seat, leaned far out her window, and threw up. I stopped the car. "It's even worse when I'm the one vomiting," Eve complained between heaves. "Because it makes me hate *myself*." When she finished, Eve settled back into her seat and said, "Never speak of this again." I never would've guessed I'd be so charmed by someone vomiting.

We just listened to music for a while. When the Boswell Sisters sang "Crazy People," I asked, "Should *this* be our song?"

Eve changed the subject. "So, what are you gonna do therapy about this year?"

"Oh, I don't do work," I said. "I just watch."

"You just *watch*?"

"It's all voluntary," I explained. "If you don't want to participate, you can just observe."

She curled her lips, her most disgusted expression. "You're telling me you go to family therapy camp every year and don't do therapy?"

"What should I do work about?" I was literally requesting her advice, but that's not how she took it.

Eve scoffed, "Right, I forgot—you don't have any problems."

"My problems are about dealing with other people and the culture, not my own feelings." I took my eyes off the road, risking death to check Eve's expression. She scowled out the windshield and I tried to recover. "Besides, therapy doesn't work on me because I've seen too much of it. I've built up an immunity."

"I'm still disturbed that you think you don't have any problems," Eve told me.

"You know that's not what I said."

"It's what you *meant*."

"Therapy doesn't do anything on its own anyway," I told her. "People don't change unless something crazy happens that messes with them enough to reconfigure their brain. Ebenezer Scrooge only changes because he's visited by ghosts. Dorothy is only convinced that there's no place like home because a tornado takes her over the rainbow. You can't just do therapy. You have to be traumatized."

I turned to Eve again, and her face plainly expressed her position. The only woman who had ever loved me hoped I'd be traumatized.

WHEN WE REACHED the campsite, I stopped in the middle of the road and kids mobbed the car, hopping and shrieking, "Family camp! Family camp!"

"This is awfully cute," Eve said.

I peered past the greeters and spotted Dad on the roadside, reading in a lawn chair, still wearing what he'd worn my whole childhood, an old tie-dye band T-shirt and shorts. When he saw us, he closed his book, leapt from his chair, and dashed in our direction.

Dad nudged past the laughing kids to my window and waved to Eve. "Hi!"

"I'm so excited to meet you," Eve said, her voice higher than before, smiling out of nowhere. It unnerved me that she'd hide her awful mood and turn on this fake performance of warmth.

I think Dad might have noticed it and found it uncomfortable too, because he shifted his attention. "Michael, you grew a beard. It looks good. Did you grow it to look like me?"

Before I could say no, Eve leaned over me to answer. "I told him to grow it," she said. "I like him with a beard."

Dad raised an eyebrow and smirked. "I have to be vigilant.

Michael rips me off a lot." Eve looked at me as if I should say something. Dad backpedaled. "I rip him off too. We rip each other off." Eve eyed him expectantly, perhaps waiting for a fun fatherly display, but there would be no shoulder-punch. "Go put up your tent," Dad said.

"We're sleeping in a tent?" Eve asked. "I figured we'd sleep in cabins or something."

"No, we rough it out here," Dad said. "At least some of us do. Michael still wears fucking suits all the time." He chuckled. "Eve, I hope you know how to put up a tent."*

This jab confused me because I'd been putting up my own tent at camp for nine years and it was unlike Dad to make fun of me for something he knew wasn't true.

"Are you implying I can't put up a tent?" I asked.

Dad scoffed. "Are you implying that you *can*?"

Eve broke in. "I'm sure Michael can build a tent."

I drove Eve through the camp, thinking aloud about Dad's remark. "Maybe he's never been present when I built a tent? So he's just assuming? Who would he think builds it for me? Mom? Josh?" I asked. Eve didn't say anything; she was in a bad mood again. We got out of the car and headed into the woods. "So, I'll build the tent with you watching and you can tell Dad you witnessed it."

Eve grabbed my shoulders and shook me. "He knows you can build a tent! He's just joking!"

"No," I said. "Dad only says what he means."

Eve looked off into the woods. I wanted to argue more but she changed the subject again. "This forest is so beautiful," she said.

I shrugged. "I don't get very excited about scenery."

---

* This wasn't a double entendre; he was literally talking about tents.

Eve clenched her teeth comically in an exaggeration of annoyance and said, "The forest is most beautiful when it's *quiet*."

AT CAMP, MOM was usually with Joe, who none of us wanted to be around, so she wasn't present for Eve's first camp dinner. Dad, Miriam, Josh, and me sat around the picnic table, watching her swiftly sketch depressed-looking characters. In our two years together, seeing her draw hadn't lost any novelty. At each character, we all cracked up or gasped.

"You are so cool!" Dad said. Then he stage-whispered, "Why would you be going out with *Michael*?"

Eve's ballpoint halted on the page. I recognized the same exasperation she sometimes aimed at me now directed at Dad.

"I'm kidding," Dad said. The collective discomfort remained, and Dad's eyes widened. "I'm sorry," he said. "I joke around and give Michael a hard time. I guess sometimes I'm just mean." Dad turned to me and said, "Michael, I'm sorry I was a jerk. I hope you'll forgive me."

I couldn't believe anyone would expect me to be upset by this joke, which was really more of a truth. "I've made similar jokes myself," I said. "I'm just as surprised that she's my girlfriend."

I thought everyone would laugh, but they didn't. Eve was the only one at the table with any experience avoiding awkwardness. She turned to Miriam. "How are you doing?"

Miriam shrugged. "I hate camp."

Dad said, "Don't worry about Miriam. She likes complaining. No one *makes* her come to camp. She chooses to come."

Miriam shared a look with Eve and went back to eating, her eyebrows scrunching and unscrunching as she internally grouched.

Eve suggested, "Maybe Miriam doesn't like camp itself, but she comes to spend time with her family."

"If that's how she feels, she should say that," Dad said.

"I *do* say that," Miriam said.

But Dad just continued. "Every year, she *chooses* to come and then complains about the choice she made."

Eve looked to Miriam and me as if Dad had said something cruel, but then saw that this was, to us, everyday conversation.

After dinner, Eve and I headed up to the tent to change into warmer clothes and get flashlights. In the twilight, the forest appeared dull and gray.

"That was upsetting," Eve told me.

"Oh? Because of the joke about you being too cool to be my girlfriend?"

"That was upsetting too," Eve said. "But I meant how your dad talks to Miriam. She comes all the way here every year even though she's still upset about your parents and your dad makes fun of her."

"He only pointed out that she chooses to go to camp and then complains about it," I said. "He didn't say anything inaccurate."

"But she's upset!" Eve said.

"Everyone has a right to feel and say whatever they want," I told her. "But everyone else has a right to feel or say whatever they want in response."

Eve was finding my obliviousness exhausting. "But nobody's trying to make Miriam feel better!"

"If your family were in our place, Miriam would be pretending to love camp to make my parents comfortable. We'd all fake loving Joe to make Mom happy. Everyone would be lying. Would you like that better?"

Eve wouldn't look at me. "It's not about lying! It's about showing that you love your family." She was struck with a way to explain. "If your family is so honest, why don't they say how happy they are to be around each other or how sad they are that Miriam is going through a hard time or how happy they are that their son is in love?" I had no answer. Having struck me dumb, Eve calmed. "Being honest doesn't have to mean that you don't care."

"Yes, it does!" I said, revitalized. "The truth hurts people's feelings. If I cared whether I hurt feelings, I couldn't tell the truth." Eve's mouth fell open, but I went on anyway. "And if I cared what people thought of me, I'd be hurt when *they* told me how they felt. If you want to be honest, you *can't* care."

Eve's pale face had flushed. "Michael," she said slowly. "You should be upset about the way your family talks to each other."

"You think I can just be upset on demand? That I can choose to believe whatever you want?" I started crying and said, "You're making arguments like a normal person! But I can't dismiss you like I'd dismiss a normal person because I'm in love with you."

Eve started crying too and hugged me. "You're defending your family. You love them so much that you defend them even when they hurt each other. Maybe that's how *you* show you care."

"I'm defending them because they're right, not because I care." Eve ignored this correction, kept hugging. We were quiet for a while, hugging and crying in the woods like a classic family therapy camp couple.

That night, Eve and I hung out at the fire pit with Josh and Miriam and a dozen camp teenagers. Dad, the only adult there, sat alone on the opposite side of the circle, out of earshot.

Eve's extremities tended to freeze, so I warmed her fingers in my hand. I told her about Bubbe's response when Dad complained that he was cold: "No, you're not. This isn't cold."

"That's awful," Eve said.

"I think it's one of the reasons it bothers us all so much when someone demands that we feel the same thing they're feeling." Once I said it, I recognized it as an accidental callback to our earlier fight. Eve turned to the fire, pretended not to notice.

"So, Josh," another young adult asked. "How's college?"

"It's okay," Josh said. "Now I gotta go for even longer to get a degree in molecular biology and chemistry."

"Molecular biology and chemistry!?!" I said. Josh had always hated school, and I'd never known him to be interested in science. I couldn't picture Josh in a chemistry lab.

"I had an internship with the coroner," Josh said. "And they told me a criminal justice degree wasn't enough, that I need molecular biology and chemistry." Josh and I rarely talked, and when I spoke to my parents, he never came up, so I hadn't heard until now about his pursuit of a career in forensic crime labs.

Dad came over to our side of the fire and took a folding chair beside us. "Hey Miriam, how are you doing?"

"Why don't you go to sleep?" Miriam asked. "You're always trying to hang out with the young people."

Josh said to Miriam, "Why do you have to be so mean to Dad all the time?"

"Thanks, Josh," Dad said. "But she's just telling me how she feels." Dad turned back to Miriam. "I'm sorry that you don't like my being here."

Miriam noted to Eve, "That's how he always apologizes." Then Miriam brightened as if her mind had moved on to a happier subject. "Want to hear a horrible story?" she asked Eve. "When I was ten, Dad took me to see *Chicago* on Broadway. After, I said I wanted to be on Broadway when I grew up and Dad said, 'Come on, Miriam. How could you be on Broadway?

You've never done any acting and you can't sing or dance!' I started crying and he just rolled his eyes and walked me back to the hotel."

Dad's shoulders slumped; he reminded me of a child dunce on a stool. "Miriam, I'm sorry you were upset by that."

Miriam gave Eve another nod, drawing more attention to how bad Dad was at apologizing.

His fire-lit face looked tired and wilted. "Is there something you want me to say?"

Miriam kept her eyes on the fire. "That's not how it works," she said. "There isn't some secret perfect sentence you're supposed to say that I'm just refusing to tell you. Why would I write *your* apology?"

Dad started weeping quietly next to us, and the fire flickered and cracked chaotically. Then he got up. "Good night, guys," he said before shuffling off into the dark.

"Don't let him walk away like that!" Josh said to Miriam.

Miriam stayed stoic. "It's not my job to comfort him."

"You're so mean," Josh said.

"It's not mean to acknowledge meanness," Miriam said.

"But it's in the past. You should just get over it."

Miriam threw a stick in the fire. "The only reason my relationship with Dad is remotely tolerable is because I can tell him how intolerable it is."

At Eve's first session, the man doing work called her up to play his young mother. His mother had poked holes in her diaphragm to get pregnant, so her lover would have to marry her. But when she got pregnant, the lover left. Out of desperation, she'd married another man to raise the child. The man doing work had hated this stepfather and his mother's unwillingness to stand up to him or protect her son from him. The stepfather was German, apparently a Nazi sympathizer, so the man doing work kept shouting at Eve, "You're the reason my father was a Nazi! You were afraid to be alone, so I had to have a Nazi for a father!"

Eve stood in front of the audience in her plaid jacket and jeans, her hands clasped anxiously in front of her, her eyes wide, staring down the large man yelling at her.

When the session ended and everyone was asked to give up the roles they were playing, the facilitator asked Eve how she felt in the role of the mother. "I felt like I'd spent my life with an awful man to make my son's life better, that I did it for him. And it didn't help. I felt like I'd wasted my life for nothing." Eve was crying, not in a role, but as herself. "It's so easy to do that," she said. "To only think about making someone else happy. And all along you could have made everyone happier by doing what would make *you* happy." All around me, I heard tissues whisked from boxes.

ON OUR THIRD day, Eve went off to women's group while I was at men's group, which continued to be consumed by Dad's conflict with Joe. After the group, Dad and I were walking back to the dining area and I brought up Josh's education. "Josh getting two science degrees is blowing my mind. He always hated school. And getting multiple science degrees sounds so impossible!"

"Yeah," Dad said hazily. "Josh has great hand–eye coordination."

I laughed at this because I assumed he was making fun of his past self, satirizing the dismissive line he'd used for Josh's whole childhood: "Michael's a writer, and Josh has great hand–eye coordination." But I realized he wasn't joking. I said, "Wait a minute. Are you not joking?"

Dad still appeared spaced-out, perhaps distracted. "What did I say that would be a joke?"

"In response to me mentioning how impressed I am that Josh is getting a science degree, you said he has good hand–eye coordination."

Dad shrugged and said, "Come on, you know what I mean."

"No," I said. "What does hand–eye coordination have to do with getting a science degree?"

Dad moved his hands, miming juggling something. "You know, for lab work."

"You think Josh is able to get a chemistry degree because he's good at juggling beakers?"

"I only said Josh has good hand–eye coordination," he told me. "I didn't say that hand–eye coordination is important to a science degree. That was your interpretation."

"I just asked you what hand–eye coordination had to do with chemistry and you answered that it helped with lab work and you mimed juggling beakers! Why aren't you admitting this?"

"Sorry, I don't know what to say," Dad told me. "You're not making any sense. And whatever argument you're trying to make seems petty anyway. Seems like a waste of time."

I looked up into the sparse leaves of the trees above and noticed a single leaf spinning. All the leaves around it were perfectly still. This leaf was being blown by the world's smallest, most focused gust of wind. I had the urge to point and tell Dad to look, but then the leaf spun its way right off the branch.

"So, how is Eve enjoying camp?" Dad asked, oblivious to the internal freak-out I'd just experienced.

"I think she's still getting used to it," I told him.

"You two have gotten pretty serious," he said.

"Serious" was such a joyless word, all wrong for me and Eve. But at the same time, it felt like an extreme understatement; I couldn't imagine a relationship more serious. I stuttered out something like, "Yeah, we're in love."

"Well," Dad said. "Don't you think you're awfully young to settle down?"*

"I'm twenty-five. What do you think is the appropriate age to have a serious girlfriend?" I asked him.

"I just think you're awfully young," he said.

I fell into a subconscious impression of how he spoke to me on the walks to and from synagogue. "To hold the opinion that someone's too young to settle down, you have to be able to define the appropriate age," I said. We continued like this, Dad refusing to name an age.

I immediately set off to find Eve. She was sitting at a picnic table in the dining area, drawing.

At the sight of me, her face fell. "Hey, are you okay?" she asked. "What happened?" I hadn't realized how frazzled I looked.

"Oh, nothing," I said. "I was just talking to Dad."

I explained the part about Josh's hand–eye coordination and Eve laughed. "All parents do that. My mom still always calls Lila the writer even though she hasn't written anything since she was ten."

"Yeah," I said vacantly.

Eve sucked in her lips. "Did something else happen?"

I shrugged. "He also told me he thought I was too young to have a serious girlfriend."

Eve stiffened and put down her ballpoint. "He said *what*?"

Here we spiraled into theorizing what this statement meant.

---

* I could've interpreted this in a number of ways: perhaps he disliked Eve or wanted to upset me. But, still naively taking everything at face value, it seemed to me that he was just arguing that twenty-five was too young to fall in love this hard, which read to me as even more obtuse than his juggling phantom beakers.

I told her that my first interpretation, that he disliked her, seemed both impossible—she was too cool and charming—and out of character for Dad. He'd have just told me explicitly. Eve suggested that he might fear her influence over me becoming more powerful than his. With every interpretation we proposed, Eve asked if I was okay. "You seem to be having thoughts you're not saying."

"No," I told her. "For some reason, I'm just not having any thoughts."

AFTER CAMP, EVE spent the whole car ride down the mountain complaining about Dad. "He doesn't believe in being considerate. He acts like it's superior to do whatever you want without accommodating anyone."

"I don't want anybody accommodating me," I said. "Everyone should be themselves and do what they want."

Eve rolled her eyes. "Are you nuts? Everybody's accommodating you all the time! You just don't notice."

This baffled me. "Who's accommodating me?"

"*Everyone,*" Eve said. "Everyone's walking on eggshells so they don't say something you'll disagree with. You don't see that everyone just goes along with whatever you want to talk about?"

I didn't want to believe this. "You're telling me everyone is lying to me? Why?"

"Because you give them no other choice! If they don't do what you want, you won't like them," Eve said.

"What you're saying is horrifying," I told her.

"Look," Eve said bitterly. "I know you don't compromise to make me happy. I can deal with that. But it *does* bother me that you don't notice all my compromises."

"Like what?" I asked, proving her point.

"For instance," Eve said. "I'm freezing right now because you like air-conditioning."

"That's crazy!" I said, turning off the air-conditioner. "Why would you do that?"

"Because I care about you."

"There's nothing romantic about you being secretly uncomfortable for my sake," I told her. "Do you do other things like that?"

"Of course, like a zillion."

"I don't do *anything* like that. Not one thing."

"I know!" Eve said.

"Tell me all the things you do to accommodate me without my noticing."

Eve proceeded to tell me that she made sure in advance that anywhere we went would be air-conditioned, not too loud or crowded, with music I'd like, that there wouldn't be anyone there I'd clash with, that she'd involved her family in many of these plans, calling in advance to restaurants to be sure they were air-conditioned and asking what music they'd be playing. She told me she cleaned the apartment when I wasn't home, dealing with the dust I thought didn't bother either of us.

"Don't clean secretly! I'll help!" I said.

"But I don't want to bother you!" she said.

"This is the strangest fight ever," I told her. "I'm angry at you for secretly helping me and you're angry at me for not appreciating it."

"Exactly!" Eve said.

Then she started listing times she'd disagreed with me and pretended to agree and times she was upset by a story I told her and pretended to like it.

"Why didn't you say something?" I asked.

"Because that would upset you and then we'd only have to talk about it even more, which would upset *me*."

I was so thrown off that I considered stopping in the middle of the one-lane mountain road. "You promised you'd be honest with me."

"I know," Eve said. "But how can anybody promise that?"

"*I* promise that," I said.

"But if I told you every time I was upset, you'd hate me."

"What feeling could you possibly express that would make me hate you?" I asked.

Eve thought about it, came up with no examples either, and laughed to herself. "I'm sure we'll find something."

Chapter 7

To Know Her Is to Love Her

THE YEAR FOLLOWING Eve's first time at family camp was particularly eventful. My theoretical horror movie fell apart boringly and unsurprisingly, Eve's book of doodles was published to some very deserved acclaim, I released a ukulele album to little acclaim but still more than the zero I expected. Eve and I went on tour together playing music all over the country. Eve was getting more illustration work, and I got some freelance writing work ghostwriting children's picture books for celebrities. I helped Eve record her new album with her mother playing violin and her sister singing, a family band. Her family had gotten used to me, even often found my honesty charming. Eve told me that she could feel me changing them, that they were getting more comfortable admitting when they were sad and wanted to talk, or when something meant a lot to them. For Eve's next graphic novel, she wrote short illustrated stories intended as personal messages to specific people she cared about, telling them what she'd most longed to say. She dedicated the book to me.

Our friends weren't going to the Clubhouse anymore and we missed those old open mics, so we started our own version, throwing monthly parties in our little apartment, inviting our musician friends to play a couple songs each. Eve and I were falling deeper in love all the time. I'd never imagined that I'd have friends I loved or a great romance; at twenty-six, my life had already far surpassed my highest expectations.

Having been to camp and spent time with my family, Eve knew a lot more about the origins of my bad qualities. We'd talk about my family often and she'd give her takes on all my old stories. Eve spoke as if I were under a spell that she hoped to slowly break. It frustrated her when I parroted Dad's arguments or wouldn't acknowledge his wrongness. Eve said that when we quarreled, she felt like it was Dad she was fighting.

No matter how much I asked Eve to stop doing secret nice things for me, I kept catching her. She refused to stop, and I started to recognize that it made her feel connected to me, that maybe my compromise was to try to notice and express appreciation. I was awful at noticing things that weren't talked about.

Each time Eve admitted to me that she was upset, I thanked her because I knew it was hard for her to admit. There was nothing I wanted more than to trust that she was really telling me how she felt.

We continued watching lots of movies, pausing to discuss. Eve talked about her past more and more. I think we learned the most about each other while movies were paused.

We rewatched a lot of children's movies and told each other about how we'd responded when we first saw them as kids. During *Fantasia,* Eve explained that the satyr dance had epitomized her vision of romance: each satyr had a nearly identical counterpart as if born to be together. I told her I'd loved the Muppets, *Edward Scissorhands*, and *Who Framed Roger Rabbit*, in which lovers looked nothing alike and romance was unpredictable and inexplicable. Eve stopped *Oklahoma* to tell me how as a child, she'd loved "I'm Just a Girl Who Can't Say No," how Gloria Grahame's character sang about her boy-craziness without shame.

We joked that we chose movies superficially, purely based on the sexiness of the actors and situations, but this joke was more than half a truth. Eve pushed to rent whatever starred Robert Redford, Winona Ryder, Paul Newman, or Sam Rockwell until we'd watched their whole oeuvres. These movies so full of seduction and flirtation finally got Eve telling stories of men she'd been with before me, telling me sexy things they'd said and done, stuff straight out of the movies and miles from anything I'd ever say or do. I asked if she had any pictures of the men she described. She hesitated at first, but then trusted that I could handle it, and dug through her memory boxes to show me photos of ex-boyfriends much better looking than me. When Eve asked me why I wasn't jealous, I didn't have much of an answer. "I don't understand jealousy," I said. "Why *wouldn't* I be happy that you've had romantic or sexy experiences with really attractive people. If you found out I'd been with really hot, cool people before you, wouldn't you be happy for *me*?"

"Yeah," Eve answered, clearly lying.

One night, Eve paused *Cat on a Hot Tin Roof* to tell me about one man she'd dated who acted like Paul Newman, avoidant and mean in the perfect way to inspire obsession. She eventually learned from someone else who had known him longer that his fiancé had died in a bike accident a year before. When Eve confronted him about this, he denied it, called her crazy, accused her of irrelevant character flaws, until eventually he broke down and admitted it was true. Then he disappeared and stopped answering her calls.

"He was afraid to let you know him," I said.

"I know!" she answered as if I'd stated the obvious, which maybe I had.

"Imagine," I said. "If your girlfriend died and you didn't want anyone to find out, if you preferred your most profound experience to be invisible."

Eve's green eyes looked angry and sad at the same time. "I don't have to imagine it. That's how I am. You don't even notice."

It wasn't long after that conversation that Eve and I were sitting around the apartment listening to a compilation I'd made of my favorite doo-wop and slow-dance music when the Teddy Bears' "To Know Him Is to Love Him" came on. Eve stopped talking to listen. The recording played all the way through while we cried together. We understood what this meant: regardless of what Eve had just told me, she wanted me to really know her. When the recording ended, we took in the unspoken moment, perfect for me to ruin by clumsily announcing the obvious: "We found our song!"

Teaching Hopelessness for No Reason

SOON, OUR JOB situations worsened and freelance work was too intermittent to live on. Eve insisted that I should get a regular job but I assured her I couldn't make it through interviews and that even if I did, I probably couldn't keep a job because I was so bad with people. "I'm sure you can get hired if you try to be nice," she told me. "You can be so charming."

"Employers don't find me charming," I told her.

Eventually, she'd get fed up and say, "Just figure it out!"

I started searching for a regular job for the first time since I moved to New York four years before.

I'd had some experience working with kids, even occasionally going into elementary school classrooms with my ukulele to write spontaneous songs with the children. It also helped that I'd published a bunch of books for young people through the literacy program, ghostwriting, and other freelance work. I managed to convince a few friends to connect me with potential jobs playing music and writing songs with kids at the schools where they taught.

A teacher friend invited me to spend a few days assisting him at a nursery school before I applied to work there. I loved observing the social world of these three- and four-year-old kids. My teacher friend intervened in a fight between two boys with the simple question, "What's going on?" and I watched them struggle to articulate themselves. Adults couldn't answer that question most of the time either. Describing their feelings really calmed the kids down; they loved being listened to, even though they had little to say. "Music time" was much more depressing. A separate teacher handed out drums, xylophones, and toy pianos, and the kids banged unpleasantly, unable to play notes that fit together. The teacher sang out of tune over the cacophony. It wasn't much like music at all.

After my few days there, I interviewed with the head teachers and told them what I'd observed, including the problems with music time. "All you have to do is give the kids instruments designed to complement each other, that play in the same key, don't have any dissonant notes," I told them. "That way, everything the kids play will automatically sound like music. If you plan it well, they could sound really beautiful."

The interviewer said, "Oh, that's very interesting." I recognized that she used the word "interesting" to express a lack of interest.

"Regardless of whether you give me the job," I told her. "You should do that."

"We'll consider it," she said, implying that she would not consider it and that I should move on.

Instead, I tried to figure out why she was against my suggestion. "Is it about the cost of new instruments? I'm sure you could get really cheap ones."

"Oh, we have plenty of funding," she told me.

"Do you have some argument against this?" I asked her.* She looked at me now as if I was being very rude. "This isn't about me," I said. "It's so the kids have a positive first experience making music. As it is, they're only learning that whatever they play will sound awful. You're teaching hopelessness for no reason."

They didn't hire me.

At the second school where I applied, my interviewer was an ever-laughing, rose-cheeked, gray-haired woman in a suit. In each room, well-dressed children sang or improvised plays. Young cool teachers read to cuddling masses of gasping and laughing kids. The walls showed off the children's exquisite drawings and comics. My only issue was that this wonderful place was reserved for rich kids. "I wish all schools were like this," I told the interviewer.

"Thank you," she said, not catching my meaning.

"I mean, I wish public schools were like this," I said. "Not just private schools."

"Thank you," she said, still not catching my meaning.

---

* I imagine she just had a policy of ignoring the unsolicited advice of raving strangers.

Though I'd originally applied because I needed a regular job to ease Eve's stress, the prospect of spending afternoons at this school making music with kids was very dreamy. I really wanted the job.

I followed my interviewer into a conference room lit sublimely by a skylight, and faced three expensive-suited interviewers behind a luxurious wooden desk. Their eyes landed on my ukulele case.

"I brought my ukulele so I could play you some songs I've written with kids," I said.

The interviewers looked at one another, flustered. "Oh," one said. "We don't need to hear you play."

I rested the case on the hardwood floor and took a seat. I labored to hold myself back from asking how they could possibly decide to hire a musician without hearing him play. "Okay," I said. The interviewers sensed my judgment. "It's just that I've written a lot of songs with kids and they're really funny and beautiful. I expected that playing them for you would convince you to hire me." The interviewers hesitated, none of them wanting to be the one to figure out how to respond.

I could tell that the interview was over already. I got up and lifted my ukulele from the floor. "This clearly isn't working out," I said.

The woman who had given me the tour grimaced. "What do you mean?"

"Come on," I said. "It took two sentences for this to go wrong. I don't see any reason to sit here and hide my feelings while you go through with the rest of the interview just as a formality."

"Wow, okay," one of the other interviewers said.

"Are you sure?" another asked. That question struck me as odd and purposeless; did she seriously expect me to sit back down and go ahead with the interview after this outburst?

"In the future," I said. "Let potential music teachers play for you. At the very least, you'd get to experience a little private concert. Maybe you'd hear something you liked, assuming you enjoy music, which maybe you don't? I imagine if you enjoyed music, you'd want to hear applicants play."

The interviewers glared as if I'd told them off, which made no sense to me. I didn't see any "fuck you" in the suggestion that it could be beautiful to listen to some children's songs.

When I told Eve about these interviews, she went back and forth between finding them funny, agreeing with whatever objection I'd made, and being furious at me.

After a while, I refused to bank on the possibility that I might please an employer. I hatched a scheme to teach one-on-one ukulele lessons out of our apartment. Eve designed me posters to put up around town, and I advertised lessons to my mailing list of fans of my ukulele album. A handful of students responded immediately. Then a popular Brooklyn blog wrote about my ukulele lessons and I got a dozen more. Each day, I received more emails inquiring about lessons. It turned out that when someone searched for "ukulele lessons" with "ny" or "Brooklyn", the post about me came up first. Soon enough, I had twenty students a week, an arrangement that paid more than any of my previous jobs. My students needed to know how to improve; for once, my truth-telling helped.

The Best Part of Breaking Up

In 2006, Eve went to camp with us a second time and became even more a part of our family. Everyone loved her so much that her name appeared in most of the sentences they spoke to me. Dad would introduce her as the future mother of his grandchildren. Once, he asked her directly if it made her uncomfortable when he went overboard praising her.

As Eve figured us out more and more, she wore me down with constant insights and interpretations. After that second year, she'd become the only one with both the closeness to understand us and the distance to see us as we were, the true expert on our family.

But when I upset her, Eve now told me what was on her mind, bringing up my family and psychology like a therapist, but angry.

"When you were a child, your dad refused to consider your feelings and never let you be upset. And now you act like everyone else's feelings are stupid and unnecessary. But they're not stupid or unnecessary."

"You can't be my therapist when you're mad!" I told her. "That's the opposite of what's supposed to happen in therapy!"

When I couldn't be convinced,* I'd tell her I was sorry that we disagreed.

"Your apologies are the *worst*," she'd say.

"Disagreeing is okay! We don't need to agree," I'd tell her. "This is like you getting upset because I don't like coconut!" Over time, the chocolate defense had become personalized. "If I have to apologize for believing something you don't like, why don't *you* have to apologize for believing something *I* don't like?"

In the cases when Eve's arguments turned me around, I'd say, "I get it now. You're right. You changed my mind. Thank you for spending so much time and energy explaining it. I'm sorry you had to go through that. I won't make the same mistake again."

---

* Eve's being across-the-board right didn't mean I was ready for these ideas.

But my apologizing never ended anything. "Your apologies are even worse when they're sincere," she told me. "Like you're issuing a correction of a factual error."

As we fought more and more, I described it as a problem of "philosophical incompatibility."

"You think it's okay to demand that I change essential parts of myself to please you," I told her. "Does that mean I can demand that you change too? Can I demand that you be more accepting?"

Eve narrowed her eyes a moment and then softened. "You feel like it's wrong to ask for someone to change because as a kid you knew your dad wouldn't change."

"Well," I said, not softening with her, "at least when Dad criticized me, he'd tell me what he thought and let me make my own decisions. You're just as critical but you act like it's my responsibility to become whatever you happen to want. That's way more brutal than Dad."

"*I'm* not like your dad!" Eve said, suddenly joking. "*You're* like your dad!"

I matched the joke. "No, *you're* like my dad!"

With Eve, I never knew when a fight would become a joke or when a joke would become a fight. She was the one who decided. But many of our fights ended with laughter.

Once, in the middle of an argument, Eve stopped and said, "Oh no, does this mean the salad days are over?" We both cracked up. "Who named it the 'salad days' anyway?" Eve asked. "Can we all agree that person was insane?"*

In the midst of the laughter at the end of one of our fights, Eve pulled off a remarkable feat of emotional translation and told me exactly what she needed. "I know you care," she said.

* It was Shakespeare.

"You show it in your own way. But it'd be nice if you could show it in *my* way too."

Not long after that, I came home to a handwritten letter on the bed that said she didn't want to be with me anymore. Though I'd known this day would come since we started dating three and a half years before, I still had to sit down on the bed sobbing and read the letter ten times. Eve wrote about all we'd had together with so much sentimentality, nostalgic already for the past that had just ended. I was at least glad she didn't hate me like most ex-girlfriends. I hoped we could stay friends, that I could keep her in my life. I accepted her decision but I wanted to say goodbye with a gesture that showed I didn't blame her, that I knew what I'd done wrong, and that I hoped to learn from my mistakes.

I considered what Eve had said about wanting me to show her I loved her in *her* way. In the past, we'd talked about how much she liked flowers. I'd parroted one of Dad's mocking rants about the ridiculousness of flowers and candlelight being defined as romantic, how a culture could arbitrarily assign meaning to things that could be easily bought, that could be given emptily or deceptively, that didn't even express one's personality or anything specific about the relationship. "Oh yeah?" Eve had replied. "Then tell me about all the special personalized gifts he gave your mom instead of flowers?" I admitted I'd never heard of him doing anything romantic for Mom. "I rest my case," Eve had said. So I decided to buy Eve flowers, certain she would know what that meant.

Inside the flower shop, chilled by the damp iciness of the refrigerators and overwhelmed by smells that changed each time I took a step or turned my head, I realized I didn't know what kind of flowers Eve liked. She'd been buying flowers for the apartment for years and I'd never really looked at or asked about them. I thought I knew her because I'd heard her personal stories and opinions and could name her favorite movies and records, but I only knew what I'd wanted to ask. There were other things that she'd wanted me to know. I cried in the flower shop and bought hydrangeas from a lady at the counter who was worried about my emotional state. "Don't feel sorry for me," I told her. "It's my own fault."

Eve had said in the letter that she'd stay a few nights with her sister. I figured I'd leave the flowers on the kitchen counter with a note for her to find whenever she returned, but when I got back from the flower shop, Eve was already there on the couch. When she saw me enter with wrapped flowers, she jumped to her feet.

"You got me hydrangeas?" she asked. She embraced me, told me she'd come back because she loved me and couldn't possibly ever leave. She told me how moved she was by the flowers, that I paid more attention than she thought. It turned out hydrangeas were among her favorites. I admitted ruefully that it had been a lucky guess. But I told her the story of crying in the flower shop and we were together again.

Within a few months, our fights came back, this time more frequent and volatile. I asked her, "Do you think you're criticizing me more now because I'm getting worse? Or because we've been together so long that stuff you didn't mind before now bothers you? Or is it because you've become more comfortable expressing how you really feel?"

"All of those explanations are right at different times," she said. "Sometimes they're all right at the same time."

I came home to another letter almost identical to the last. And, like last time, she came back less than a day later to say she loved me and would never leave again.

By spring of 2007, Eve was dumping me once every two

months, sometimes even more. Once, in a happy period, I joked that maybe we should switch our song to the one that claims that the best part of breaking up is making up.

Eve didn't laugh, just looked at me sadly. "I do like making up."

EVE HAD BEEN a hypochondriac since childhood. She told me that once in kindergarten, she'd overheard an adult talk about AIDS. She didn't know what AIDS was, but she felt certain that she or her parents had it or would get it. She'd lie awake in bed at night, secretly worrying about AIDS. Eventually, she began falling asleep at school. When her mother asked what was wrong, Eve broke down sobbing and said she couldn't sleep because she had AIDS. She didn't change much in the next twenty years because she still lived in an on-and-off panic about having cancer or some other ailment she'd just heard about or found on the internet.

Once, lying together on the couch with her head in the crook of my neck, she asked me if I'd leave her if she had cancer. Hypothetical questions had stressed me out ever since Dad started me on them as a child, but Eve's were more dangerous; when I answered wrong, she'd be devastated by what I'd theoretically do in a situation that wasn't happening. But I believed she had the right to ask any question and that I had to answer.

"How can either of us know what we'd feel or do if you had cancer?" I answered, likely with some desperation in my voice already. Eve jerked up. I told her, "No one knows who they'll become in a time of tragedy! Maybe you'd have a nervous breakdown. Maybe *you'd* dump *me.*"

Eve returned her head to my neck. "I know," she said. "I still wanted you to tell me you'd never leave me." She'd learned by now to explicitly state what I was supposed to say.

"You're asking me to promise something that can't be promised," I told her.

"It's not lying," she insisted. "It's saying what you hope will be true."

"Here's a question," I said. "Forget about the cancer part: are you gonna leave me sometime when I *don't* have cancer?" Eve lowered her eyes guiltily. "After all," I continued, "you've dumped me plenty of times. You never needed cancer."

"Oh, Michael," Eve sighed. Her tears landed on my shirt collar. "Sometimes I get confused. But I'll never really leave you." She sounded so honest that I felt I'd been proven wrong. I leaned my head back and stared up at our tin ceiling. She continued. "I love you. And I'll always love you." Now I was crying too. I held her against me, believing a promise I knew to be false. She smiled up at me. "See? That was the easiest thing I could ever say."

Honesty Among Thieves

I WAS WAITING alone at 3 AM on the squalid and silent J train platform at Bowery when I noticed a blond man in an orange-stained white T-shirt speed-walking toward me with one arm behind his back. He puffed out his lips and flexed his jaw to intimidate me and said, "Let's go for a walk." Despite his efforts to appear tough, he mostly read as stressed out. I was about to tell him that honesty about his nervousness and mixed feelings would command more respect and compassion than a transparent masculine facade, with me at least, but before I could comment, he shoved my shoulder, turning me to face the far end of the platform, and pushed me ahead.

I didn't have any money on me. I'd heard that some muggers would stab or shoot people with empty wallets, but I considered it more likely that my mugger would be the one hurt by this interaction, that he'd go to prison for this failed robbery. I felt a responsibility to prevent potential trouble for both of us if I could.

"Before you go through all this," I told him, "I don't have any money."

"Shut up and walk," the mugger said.

I followed his order about walking but couldn't bear to shut up. "Everyone's so used to being lied to," I told him, my hands gesturing wildly, my voice rising. "My family's really honest so I've only lied twice ever, but still, no one trusts me." The mugger didn't stop pressing me toward the other end of the platform. My ranting gained fervor. "Most people lie about having no money on them, right? So now you automatically hear that line as a lie? Everyone performs this futile script: the mugged person lies, knowing he won't be believed, and then the mugger plays his part and doesn't believe him and so on until you end up in prison over an empty wallet." At this mention of prison, his body tensed against me. "It's a perfect example of how the liars spoil everything for people who trust and tell the truth."

As if to teach me the meaning of being believed, he moved his hidden hand into view and showed me a knife. The knife was triangular; it reminded me of a miniature sword. This mugger was like everybody else, so careful about what information he revealed and when. Then it occurred to me he might have hidden his weapon for a legal benefit, that if I'd never seen the knife, he could claim later he hadn't had one. If he'd shown the knife at the start, the law might have punished him for his honesty.

We reached the far end of the platform. "Empty your pockets," he said.

When he saw my ratty brown wallet, he averted his eyes; he couldn't bear to watch me open it. I opened it anyway and held it out beneath his lowered face. I thought he ought to have the strength to look at it even if it bothered him. He fell back a step, looking down at the filthy station floor. "Damn!" he said, his voice pitched much higher than before. I liked hearing his real voice. "Damn!" This mugger seemed like he'd cry if he weren't so pointlessly hung up on hiding his authentic self.

"I tried to warn you," I told him. "Also, for future reference, a subway platform is one of the worst places to mug someone. There are cameras everywhere." The mugger lifted his eyes, now enraged. I resented his emotional reaction to objective fact. This alleged badass couldn't even handle criticism from a stranger. I shrugged and said, "I'm just being honest."

He lunged at me, his knife-wielding hand rising in an uppercut that stopped just short of my throat. His other hand clutched the back of my head, pressing my neck into the knifepoint.

"I've got some advice for you too," he said. "*Shut up.*"

I immediately went home and told Eve about the mugger almost stabbing me for being honest. I considered it hilarious, but she didn't laugh. Eve just looked concerned. "Michael," she said. "Please don't do things like that. If you get yourself murdered, I'll be sad."

The Fear Game

BY THE FEW months before our third year of camp, in 2007, our relationship felt like family camp year-round. Camp's creeping influence meant we often fell into the roles of therapist and patient.

At one point, our unstable landlord was harassing us, demanding money we didn't owe, refusing to turn on the heat or hot water despite formal complaints to the city. We didn't have money to move and we loved the home we'd built, but our landlord banging on our door and screaming incoherently weighed on us. I was upset about it, but Eve was more upset. I asked her if she'd like to play the "Fear Game."

We'd invented the Fear Game months before. I got out a piece of paper and pen to use as a substitute for family camp's forest chalkboard and Eve listed her fears.

"We wouldn't be in this situation if we had money," she said. "And we'll never have money. We'll always be living like this. We're really just broke losers." I wrote this down. "And if we don't have money, we can't have children or give our children the life they should have." I wrote this down too. "And if you really wanted children, you'd get a job and figure out how to make enough money. And you don't do that because you don't even expect us to be together forever." She was crying a lot now. "And that's because you don't really love me." I continued to take notes. "And you don't love me because I'm a monster and I treat you so horribly. And you shouldn't even be here. I break up with you over and over and you take me back, and you're so patient and I don't deserve it because I'm a horrible person." Then she pulled herself together. "But that doesn't matter because I'm gonna die of this brain tumor soon anyway."

"Okay, that feels like enough," I said. "Let's look at the list." We moved close together on the couch and I handed her the page and a pen. "Why don't you put check marks next to the ones that have something to do with our landlord problem."

Eve cracked up. "This list is bananas. It all sounded so true when I said it."

When Eve and I argued, it was never clear at the start which of us would end up acting as therapist. Sometimes we'd even swap roles mid-conversation.

Though I was teaching lessons and making more regular money, Eve continued telling me to get a job. "Writing and teaching lessons *is* a job," I insisted. "And it pays more hourly than other jobs I could get. And I like it."

Eve then became the facilitator. "How does it make you feel when I suggest that you get an office job?"

"Well," I said. "It's the same message that the rest of society gives me, that living outside of normal culture is stubborn and stupid and that I'll inevitably fail and I'll deserve it. I feel like you're siding with society against me."

Eve said, "You talk like society is one big bully out to get you."

"I know!" I said. "The culture en masse acts in a creepy unison!" I flailed my arms like a family camper doing work. "If you don't do what society wants, society gets revenge. If you make money out of your apartment instead of joining the corporate empire, they'll do their best to arrange it so you can't see a doctor, so potential friends or romantic partners don't respect you, so that your obituary makes you sound like you accomplished nothing. If you don't consent to your culture's social rules, they'll do their best to starve you into submission." Eve abandoned her warm therapy face and traded it for an extended eye-roll. I finished anyway. "When you get upset at me about my job, it feels like the culture maliciously whispering in your ear that I'm a loser, hoping you'll believe it and leave me."

Eve scoffed. "So if I want you to get a better job, it's because I'm a sucker brainwashed into a minion of evil capitalism?"

"When you put it like that, it sounds ridiculous," I said. "But yes."

Eve snapped, "If I leave you, you're gonna blame me and society. But you should know, just for the record: if I leave, it's your fault."

This "if" felt more like "when."

ON THE LIST of our troubles, under hypochondria and general neurotic spiraling, was jealousy, Eve's tendency to arbitrarily decide that I must be secretly in love with random women we knew. The more I denied having feelings for whatever woman she found threatening that day, the more guilty she claimed I sounded. Strangely, she only focused her jealous attacks on women I wasn't attracted to. Eve never commented on the women whom I lusted after, perhaps because she knew if she asked I'd admit the truth; maybe she specifically liked hearing me assure her over and over.

This whole scenario was complicated by the fact that Eve was open about her own feelings for other men we knew. She'd get depressed or manic and tormentedly ask me whether she should try being with someone else. I'd say things like, "I'm not the one to give unbiased advice because I'm in love with you and I want you to stay."

In these discussions, Eve often found a way to get angry at me, but with a confusion regarding what exactly to be angry *about*. Once, she became angry that I wasn't more upset about her having feelings for someone else; she insisted my not being jealous meant I must not love her. I told her I *was* upset, but that I was focusing on trying to comfort her. Then she became angry that I'd suppress my own feelings to deal with hers. So I focused on myself, telling her more about how upset I was.

Then she accused me of guilting her, trying to control her. When I told her I wanted her to do whatever would make her feel better, she again became upset that I wasn't jealous and the spiral started over.*

Once, Eve and I were lying on the couch together after resolving one of our breakups when she asked directly if I ever fantasized about women we knew. This question felt particularly pointed because we'd just made up after a jealousy-related dumping. I was dismayed that she wanted to start on this again already. But she asked the question softly, as if she she'd find it romantic to know some of my more dangerous thoughts and feelings. "It's okay, I fantasize about other people too," she said. "It's something everybody does."

I wanted to tell her that my whole life before her had been all about fantasizing, that I'd always found fantasy to be joyful and comforting, something I had when no one liked me. I was about to launch into this speech but I stopped myself. Eve had explicitly given me permission to tell her the truth, but if she really believed everybody fantasized about other people, why was she asking?

I had to think fast because she was looking right at me. I imagined my transparent face betrayed that I was deciding whether to be honest. I'd seen that weaselly look on many faces. They usually chose to lie.

If I lied, she'd surely know. But I had an unpleasant suspicion that she *wanted* me to lie. I felt nauseated again, and it was hard to push the words out of my mouth. I probably sounded like I was stuttering or slurring or both. "I

---

* As bizarre as this whole conversation might sound, I think the wildest part was that her being honest with me about all this only further convinced me that our relationship was special. I figured she'd never be so honest with someone she didn't love.

don't fantasize about other people," I said. It was my third proper lie.*

Eve smiled gloriously and embraced me, a reaction that seemed unwarrantedly positive. My first response was to feel awful that she'd believed me, to feel possessed by a compulsion to confess. But then it occurred to me: maybe she didn't believe me. Maybe it moved her that I'd lied to protect her feelings. I desperately wanted to ask if she'd been fooled by the lie or if she recognized it and appreciated it. But I knew that question would ruin everything so I stayed quiet, wondering if this is what people meant when they said lying could be an act of love.

My Infant Self

EVE SPENT OUR third drive up the mountain to camp insisting that I confront Dad about how my view of him had changed and tell him I wanted to be less like him.

"I can't just say that," I told her, noticing myself sounding suspiciously like most people, explaining what one "can't" say. "He'll just call me crazy. He might never speak to me again."

Eve rubbed her hand on my shoulder. "That would never happen."

"Who knows?" I told her. "My family is full of estrangements. People sometimes stop talking to each other. Dad's sister hasn't talked to him in fifteen years. She refuses to say why. When they're at the same family event, they stay on opposite sides of the room."

---

* To recap, my first was at five when I let the kindergartners believe in Santa. My second was at eighteen when I told Amanda during her work that she'd be appreciated for her authentic self. For this third lie, I was twenty-six.

Eve said, "Just the fact that you think telling your dad how you feel might make him never speak to you again shows that you need to tell him."

I asked Dad to talk and we left the camping area for the thin road that passed by family camp, an ideal place for a private conversation; you could talk for hours without a car passing. The surrounding forest provided shade and the sounds of the running creek and the wind through leaves and birdsong.

We strolled up the mountain, alongside the uninhabited woods. I felt ill at the thought of what I would say; I couldn't remember a time when saying something true made me so nervous. There were too many potential angles or places to start. I never felt more like I needed to express myself perfectly. I was prepared for this to potentially be our last conversation.

In the past, when I had something to say that I knew would get a bad reaction, I'd treat speaking as a simple physical act, like putting a letter into a mailbox. I'd push the words out of my mouth as if they had no meaning.

"I don't think you were always honest," I told Dad.

"I can't think of a time when I wasn't," he said. His eyes didn't look up and to the right like someone trying to remember.

"I don't know if you lied consciously," I told him. "I think you repeated to me the lies you told yourself."

"What would be an example?" he asked.

I felt tremendous pressure to choose the right first example to convince him. Combing through the past, Eve and I had found dozens. I picked one, uncertain if it was the best.

"When we walked to and from synagogue when I was a kid," I said. "You'd give me hypothetical questions and mock any answer I gave you. You acted like I could get your approval if I could just make a good argument, but you never acted proud or told me I was right."

"What was I supposed to do? *Pretend* I thought you were right?" His pace quickened and I hurried to keep up, re-creating the very walks we were discussing. "In a debate, you don't tell your opponent that he's right or that you're proud of him," he said.

"I wasn't your opponent," I said, my voice cracking already. "I was your son."

Dad's hard-walking didn't flag. "It would have been hypocritical for me to give you special treatment just because you're my son." I felt this line settle in my stomach. Dad stopped walking. "I don't know what to tell you." In the silence, he shrugged over and over as if shrugging at each individual thought that came to him. "If this is all you've got, I don't know how to go on with this conversation," he said. "I'm sorry, if this is the level of your thoughts, it's probably best if you just don't say anything at all."

BACK AT THE dining area, I told Eve I'd talked to Dad and she started crying and hugged me. "I'm so proud of you," she said. "You're so brave." I hugged her for a whole minute. I suddenly understood why other people had always been so into long, silent hugging.

I recounted to Eve what had happened with Dad and she sucked in her lips, her most disappointed expression. "I thought he'd respond better," she said.

"You overestimate us," I told her.

Later that night, after dinner, while much of camp was milling about or playing cards or engaged in quiet intimate conversations in duos and trios in the forest dusk, I returned from the bathroom to find Eve looking shaken.

"Your dad just came up to me sobbing," she told me.

"He didn't say anything?" I asked.

"He said, 'Thank you so much for appreciating Michael and understanding him. I don't know how to show him that I love him. At least he has someone in his life that can show him.' And then he hugged me and cried."

"I don't know what to make of that," I said.

"It means talking to him helped! You're solving your family's problems!" Eve said. "Are you gonna do work?"

"Oh no," I said. "You want me to do work now?"

"Yeah!" Eve said. "How many years have you come to camp without doing work?"

I had to do the math. "This is my eleventh year."

"In all this time, you never did work?" Eve said. "It's ridiculous. You have to!"

"But they're gonna make me get on the rug and play myself as a baby!"

Eve laughed. "Come on!"

"But I don't want to play my infant self!"

Eve kept on me about it and I figured I might as well since I was already trying whatever Eve thought I should and, as far as I could tell, she'd been right about everything so far. And, at the very least, this could show her I was trying to change and compromise, which I hoped would convince her to stop dumping me.

AT THE NEXT session, Max asked for a volunteer to do work, and I raised my hand. As I stepped up to the front the audience audibly responded, some laughing or whispering to each other. Maybe, like Eve, they'd been waiting years for me to do work. Or maybe they suspected my session would involve the Leviton family camp scandal and everyone was ready for a sensationalistic thrill. Or maybe they were rooting for me to learn to be less obnoxious.

"So, Michael," Max asked. "What's bubbling?"

"I have lots of problems," I said. "And I think that they're connected to my dad."

I felt an excited tension in the audience and I wondered if they hoped to see me fall apart. I could understand how camp would find that satisfying. Even for me, falling apart had some allure.

"I want to list my problems," I said. "But I feel like it's gonna take an hour." The crowd laughed.

Max said, "Once you start, you might realize it's all just different facets of the same thing and you'll get your point across quicker than you think."

"Yeah, please cut me off if I get redundant," I said. "I've always thought you don't cut people off enough." Everyone laughed, including Max. Then they waited for me to tell my story. "So, Dad always had a lot of rules and demands. He had opinions about what was right and what made sense and I had to be in line with those things." The audience was with me. They could relate. It was unusual to have people relating to me. "I thought it was all worth it because, you know, most people's minds are disordered, they don't know how to express themselves or they're afraid to, they're cowards and liars who don't even care whether they're right." I'd lost the audience now. I spotted Eve in a lawn chair near the front, also uncertain about where I was going.

Max interrupted. "You just wanted him to love you." It only took one line for me to be relatable again. Max continued, "But I don't think that was the end of it. I think what you really wanted was for him to love you without your having to earn it."

A groan pushed its way through my throat. Now tears poured from my eyes. "It's difficult to talk while I'm crying this hard," I whimpered, barely able to dribble out the words.

"You don't have to talk," Max said. "We don't need words to understand."

At this, I broke down in classic family therapy camp fashion. It felt dizzyingly physical, more like retching than crying. In that moment, I wished someone would photograph me, like on a rollercoaster when they catch you mid-scream.

"Let's go back to a time before you could speak," Max said, and I knew what was coming. "Why don't you call up someone to play you as a baby?" I snapped out of my emotional state and laughed.

"What happened?" Max asked. "Stay with me—"

"Do I really have to call someone up to play my infant self? That's my least favorite camp cliché."

The audience laughed. Max said, "I've never heard someone stop his work on the grounds that something was 'cliché.'" The crowd loved that. They were more receptive to jokes about therapy from people taking part in it. That felt like a lesson to apply elsewhere.

Max continued. "Some things are cliché because they're true." I resisted my impulse to say that sentiment was also cliché. I looked into the crowd to pick someone to play my infant self. Without any conscious reason, I chose one of the teenagers I knew from the campfire. The teenager got down on the blanket on the forest floor, with leaves scattered around him.

Max called into the audience for Dad. "Would you come up? I'd like to talk to you for a moment now, if that's okay."

I found Dad crying in the audience. He slunk up to the stage, hanging his head.

"How do you feel about what Michael's been saying?" Max asked.

"I'm so sorry!" Dad keened.

"Look down at baby Michael there," Max said. "And talk a bit about how you felt when he was a baby."

Dad straightened, his body expressing his instant distraction from what he'd just been feeling. "I don't remember much about how I felt when Michael was a baby," he said.

"Try to remember."

"I loved him so much," Dad said, his voice now clear.

"Why did you love him?" Max asked.

Dad's face screwed into a pained scrunch. "I tried to find reasons," he said.

Max's eyes narrowed and his voice shed its therapist warmth. "You tried to find *reasons* to love your baby? What would be an example of a reason to love a baby?"

"He rolled over early," Dad said. "He could move along with music; he had a good sense of rhythm. He said his first word when he was only six months old. He said 'ice cream.'"

Max warmed again and asked softly, "Why did you have to justify loving your baby?"

"I don't know how to love without a reason," Dad said.

"Why don't you lie down with baby Michael and let yourself love him without a reason."

Dad crouched and rolled onto the blanket to hug the teenager pretending to be my infant self. Dad wept and groaned, "I love you so much. I love you so much."

As the session grew more redundant and comic, I spaced out. After a while, I interrupted Max and Dad and said, "I feel like there's a lot of other stuff to talk about."

Dad looked up at me from the rug, disappointed that his spooning this teenager hadn't solved anything.

Max rose from his kneeling position. "I don't know what you want to say, but I have a suspicion that you intend to build a case against your father. You want to list all the ways he's hurt you. Is that right?"

"I guess," I said.

"Your whole life, you've built cases," Max said, "You have a talent for describing in detail what's right or wrong and why. As a child, you needed that skill to survive. But did it ever get you anything you wanted from other people? Even from your father?"

"No," I said, again choking on the weird physically manifesting feelings.

"You can't convince someone to love you with a good argument. People don't love each other for being right."

It seemed suddenly that a vast percentage of life had been a sham, a prank on me. I'd worked so hard for something that should have required no work at all.

Max asked Dad to get up so we could face each other. Up close, I could see his big nose pores and hairy nostrils and his penetrating dark brown eyes, which looked beautiful crying. Max asked me if there was anything I wanted to tell him. A breeze blew and I heard birds. I assumed the squawking was in response to the breeze but then decided the two weren't connected.

"You taught me that being honest meant not caring," I said. "But now I want to care. And I guess I needed you to care."

Dad embraced me and sobbed into my ear. "I don't know how!" He wept in my arms for a moment. "I love you so much," he murmured. "I just don't know how to show you."

"I don't know how to show that I care either," I told him. "I think I don't know because you don't know."

Max said, "Has there been anybody in your life who's been able to show you that they care, where you felt like they loved you even when you couldn't earn it?"

I looked through the audience of family campers sobbing, with crumpled tissues all over the dirt floor. I found Mom among them, her face wet and blotchy. "I always knew Mom loved me," I said. "She loved me before I could speak."

Mom came up front and gave me possibly her most crushing hug of all time; the crowd applauded. Then Max invited Eve up to the front. I told her, "I feel that you love me too, even though I often make it difficult."

"Loving you isn't difficult," Eve said. I could tell she meant this despite the statement's technical inaccuracy. We pulled together for a teary group-hug, and it appeared that all present found it cathartic and satisfying.

Afterward, Eve was a broken record telling me how proud of me she was and how brave I'd been. "Well, don't get too excited yet," I told her. "Let's see if it makes any difference."

Chapter 8

Uncomfortable Questions

ON THE PLANE home from camp, I started writing down what had happened, just so I could get some distance and wrap my mind around it. I continued writing when I got home, and soon I was spending most of my free time writing about family camp.

As much as we'd returned feeling hopeful, I hadn't changed much. Eve regularly expressed her disappointment. I told her, "I guess I still haven't been traumatized enough."

As I wrote more and more, I noticed her focusing on a new hope, that writing about myself would change me more than therapy. Though I talked about trying to publish what I was writing as a fictionalized novel, Eve told me she recognized its real purpose, that it was a message to Dad.

Eve and I moved together into a much nicer apartment with a proper office for Eve and space for a dining room table. We once again searched the junk shops. We spotted the base of a wrought iron Singer sewing machine probably from the 1930s.

It didn't have the sewing machine attached, but its foot pedal sent gears spinning. Eve had the idea to make it into a table. We bought a walnut tabletop and attached the two ourselves. The table was the centerpiece of the apartment, the first thing you saw when you walked in. When we sat there, we could pump the wrought iron foot pedal and look out at the whole neighborhood through our fourth-floor window. A man on the roof of the building next door trained pigeons; at twilight, Eve and I would lie on the fire escape and watch his cloud of birds circle.

Within a year, I had a four-hundred-page manuscript.* I hadn't told my family about it because it seemed cruel and unusual to say, "Hey, I'm writing a book about you. I'll send it to you in a year or two if I actually finish it. Try not to stress till then!" I'd never kept a secret so talking to my parents felt like lying; for a year, I dodged or cut short phone calls. Luckily, the next family camp fell at the same time as Eve's sister's wedding, so we had an excuse not to go. If I'd had to tell them I didn't want to go anymore and they'd asked why, I surely would've blurted, "Because I've been secretly writing about you!"

Miriam had just graduated college and moved to New York. We'd put a bed in Eve's office so it could function as a guest room. Miriam planned to stay there while she looked for her own apartment. On the night she arrived, I told her about what I'd written. She read the manuscript first. Josh, who was still working on his master's degree in criminology, read it second. They were both moved by it but expressed concern that Mom and Dad would be upset. Mom read it next. She said she was just glad the book didn't make her look as bad as Dad.

I decided to mail Dad a physical manuscript because it

---

* It focused mostly on family camp but involved some of the childhood stories that also appear in this book.

seemed wrong to make him print out what would only upset him, like assembling the rifles for his own firing squad. The thick manuscript barely fit into the postal envelope. Cramming it in was rendered more difficult by my sweating, shaking hands.

I quaked my way through writing a short note, asking him to call me before reading it. It looked as if it had been scribbled in a moving car. I imagined that the bumpy scrawl probably made me appear unhinged. I considered rewriting the note but decided it was more expressive if the handwriting looked as unsteady as I felt.

When I gave the postal worker the envelope, my pulse hammered as if I'd mailed an envelope full of anthrax. I watched the postal worker shuffle over to a pile of envelopes and drop mine on top. It sat there looking just like the others.*

The postal worker had told me the date the package would arrive and Eve and I waited that whole day in the apartment for Dad's phone call, crying together on and off, Eve saying over and over, "I'm so proud of you. You're the bravest person I've ever known."

Eventually, Dad called. "I got your package. Definitely unexpected and interesting." He didn't sound surprised or interested.

I cried into the phone. "This book might make you hate me, but I needed to write it."

"I can't imagine it'll bother me," Dad said.

Through the phone receiver, Dad's disembodied voice possessed a special power. It was a radio voice. It sounded correct no matter what it said.

When I got off the phone, Eve embraced me.

"What did he say?" she asked.

"He doesn't expect the book to bother him," I told her.

---

* I'd never again look at a pile of mail without curiosity.

Eve backed out of the hug. "He *said* that? You told him you wrote a book about him and he straight-out told you he doesn't care?"

"I was telling him I was afraid he'd be upset."

"And he told you that you couldn't upset him."

"Not exactly."

"It's what he *meant*," Eve replied.

"It would be awful if the book didn't bother him," I said. "But I can't even picture what a positive response would look like."

Eve wrapped her arm around me and pressed her face into my chest. "What if he read it and understood what you've been through?"

I started crying again. "That won't happen," I said.

Eve smiled warmly and laugh lines crinkled beside her teary eyes. "You're showing that you care."

But this gesture of care seemed indistinguishable from a declaration of war.

When Dad called back, I took the phone into the bedroom but left the door open to allow Eve to listen to my half of the conversation.

"So, I read the book," Dad said, his voice casual, as if referring to a stranger's book I'd recommended.

"Okay," I said.

"I'm sorry," he said. "I didn't think it was any good."

"Okay," I said.

"For instance, on page two, it says there's a family on the side of the mountain throwing up from carsickness?" I could sense his rolling eyes through the phone. "A whole family throwing up? Maybe one person would be throwing up or maybe just the kids, but *a whole family*? No one would believe that. It undermines the author's credibility. Then on page three . . ."

I interrupted him, "Hey, Dad. I can get comments from other people. I thought we'd talk about our relationship."

"Oh," Dad said. "You don't want comments?"

"I want to know how you feel," I told him.

"Oh, okay," he said. "Let me call you back."

I emerged from the bedroom and told Eve about this response. "I shouldn't blame you for anything," she said. "Everything bad about you is clearly his fault."

I appreciated this sentiment but knew she didn't mean it; she'd definitely still blame me.

Dad called me back in about a half an hour and I retreated again to the bedroom with the door open. "Okay," he said, sounding less certain than he'd sounded on the last call, pausing and hesitating instead of his usual rapid-fire. "So, I guess I have to ask a kind of uncomfortable question." My brain reeled, trying to imagine what question could possibly be uncomfortable enough for Dad to feel he needed this preface. "Is this fiction?" he asked. "Or do you think these things really happened?"

That was indeed an uncomfortable question, but it required me asking one even worse. "Do you not *remember* these things happening?"

Dad paused again. "Well, I guess they technically *happened*, but the way you wrote them is . . . odd."

"In what way?" I asked.

"You wrote what I said and did, but you didn't explain why I was right."

Uneasy laughter rattled out of me. "I left them up to interpretation."

"Yeah, but that's misleading," he said, now speaking at his usual speed. "Like, you only have one side of the story here. If you'd wanted to portray me accurately, you could have asked me why I said these things and then included that explanation so the reader doesn't have to read my mind."

My cell phone was wet with sweat from my hand, maybe even from my ear. I wished I could be having the conversation on a phone with a real receiver. A cell phone didn't feel heavy enough.

"Let me ask you something," I said. "What did you think of the father in this book?" Dad let out a labored, groany laugh. "Actually, let's imagine that I told you the story of a friend who wrote a book about his father. Imagine I told you he sent the book to his dad and that dad called and started giving him notes on the book, like an editor."

Dad now let out an authentic laugh. "That's a great example!" he said. "If you told me that, I'd say this father was avoiding his feelings and criticizing his son out of cowardice, because he was too weak to face what was in the book!"

"Yeah—" I began, suddenly hopeful.

"But that's not why *I* gave you notes! That's just what it would mean for *most people*."

I paced the bedroom and caught sight of Eve through the doorway. She stood in the living room holding a coffee mug near her face as if weighing whether it was too hot to drink. Our eyes met and she smiled just in time for me to say to Dad, "You're not the expert on your own feelings. Or on whether you're right."

"Of course I am," he replied. "You think you know my feelings better than I do?"

Eve's smile fell and I wondered if she somehow could hear what Dad was saying. Then I realized she was reacting to my expression, which must have looked awful. She put down her coffee on the sewing machine table and headed toward me to comfort me. After a few steps she stopped herself, deciding that I needed to do this alone.

I only realized how hard I was crying when I next spoke; my voice barely came out, half rasping, half cracking. "Look," I said, "I understand that the choice you have to make here is difficult. If you decide I'm just crazy and you're right about everything, then you don't have to accept anything hard about yourself. But, for the record, if I'm crazy, you probably have something to do with why anyway. Your other choice is to think that maybe I'm worth listening to."

"This is emotional blackmail," Dad said, his voice intact, not breaking at all. "Just because you're my son, I'm obligated to believe your perspective has value? Sorry, but I can't just choose to believe whatever you want me to."

I got off the phone and told Eve, "He's just saying to me the exact things I've said to you. It's my ironic punishment that I have to hear them now from the other side. I guess I was following a pretty limited script too."

Eve smiled lovingly. "Well, you're not following any script now."

The Girl Who Cried Wolf

ONCE I'D SENT my family the manuscript and it still hadn't transformed me, our breakups escalated until Eve was dumping me and coming back every few weeks. Sometimes she'd give me a clear reason, but sometimes she'd just disappear and stop returning calls, only to show up in bed that morning, telling me how much she loved me. By this time, she'd broken up with me because:

— She decided I was secretly in love with the violinist
in our band
— Teaching ukulele wasn't a job and I kept insisting
it was
— I didn't take it seriously enough when she felt
certain she had a brain tumor
— She didn't want to put me through watching her
die of cancer
— I criticized the band arrangement of one of
her songs
— She wanted to go back to family camp and
I didn't
— She was too sad to go to a wedding we'd RSVP'd
for and I insisted on going without her instead of
staying home to comfort her
— She had crushes, which meant we shouldn't
be together
— I wasn't jealous enough about her crushes
— I was too controlling about her crushes
— We watched *Indecent Proposal* and I supported
Demi Moore sleeping with Robert Redford for a
million dollars
— I wasn't upset enough about death
— She mistreated me and she wouldn't let me be with
such a monster

I kept all of Eve's goodbye letters. Once, I brought them out
to show her the stack of about a dozen. I tried to hand them to
her but she wouldn't take them. "There are so many," she said,
horrified. "I didn't realize there were so many."

"Also, they're all almost the same letter," I said. "They're
pretty much identical."

Eve looked down, despondent, and wrung her small hands. "Every time I break up with you, it feels like the first time."

One weekend when Eve was in Boston to visit her family, I invited some of our friends over to watch *A Nightmare on Elm Street 3*. When our friends arrived, the mood was mysteriously tense so I asked if everything was okay.

"Are *you* okay?" one friend asked.

"Yeah," I said. "Why wouldn't I be?"

"We ran into Eve yesterday," he said. "She told me you'd broken up so we figured that's why you'd invited us over."

I sighed. "Okay, hold on a second."

I called Eve while our friends were in the room;* I wasn't sure Eve would pick up because she so often disappeared, but she answered. "Oh, sorry," Eve said. "On the way to the bus yesterday, I was mad at you so when I ran into those guys, I told them we'd broken up. But then I felt better so I didn't break up with you and I forgot I told them that." Eve sighed. "I probably look like such an idiot. Can you tell them I'm sorry for the false alarm?"

When I got off the phone, I told them, "We're fine. Apparently Eve was just in a bad mood. She says sorry for the false alarm." I could sense that my friends didn't believe me.

A few months later, Eve returned from a visit to her family and told me she'd rented an apartment in Boston and wasn't coming back, that we were done. She didn't give me the usual letter saying she loved me; this time she sat coldly at the table we'd built and demanded that I call my parents to tell them we'd broken up.

"But you're just gonna change your mind again," I said.

"I'm moving to Boston," she said. "You have to accept it."

---

* It didn't occur to me that I should have this phone call in private, that I was forcing them to listen to something insane.

"They're gonna be so upset," I told her. "You're gonna put them through this and then I'm gonna have to call them to say we're back together."

It felt disrespectful to continue insisting that she was lying. So, with her still sitting across the table, I called Dad and told him, crying, that Eve and I had broken up. "Oh my god," he said, starting to cry himself. "You must be devastated." I told him yes, I was devastated.

I covered the phone and told Eve, "He's crying."

"I wanted her to be the mother of my grandchildren," Dad said.

I reported this to Eve as well. "He says he wanted you to be the mother of his grandchildren."

"I hope we can still have her in our lives," Dad said. "I'll call her directly to talk about it."

I told her, "Dad is gonna call you directly to ask if you'll still be in our lives."

I didn't talk to him long. Then I called Mom and had a similar conversation.

"Why?" Mom asked. "Why would you break up? You're so in love!"

I said, "You'd have to ask Eve. I don't really understand." I told Eve that Mom asked why we were breaking up when we were so in love. I kept that call short too.

I hung up and Eve wiped away a tear, smiled warmly, and said, "How am I supposed to break up with you after seeing that?"

IT WASN'T LONG before Eve dumped me again, left her stuff in our apartment in New York, and went back to Boston. She found a friend to sublet her office to cover her half of the rent and was gone. I suspected she'd call me back again soon and tell me she didn't want to break up after all, but even if I received that call, I didn't know what to do. Eve no longer cared what I went through. Now she just acted according to whatever she felt. In other words, she was doing exactly what I'd asked of her; she was just being honest.

Predictably, Eve called me a few days later from Boston to tell me she wanted to move back to New York to be with me after all. I couldn't go on like this. But I also couldn't ask her to go back to hiding when she was upset, to feeling ashamed about her shifting feelings and indecision. I couldn't take her back. I didn't want to tell her over the phone so I asked her to meet me that weekend. I intended to break up with her then.

When it was time to meet, she called to tell me she was in a bad mood and didn't want to see me. I was more insistent than usual, told her I really wanted to sit down together and have a conversation. She asked, "Why? Are you gonna break up with me?"

"Yes," I said. "I wanted to do it in person but you're not letting me."

Eve screamed and wailed into the phone, mournfully, like something from family camp. I couldn't bear to hear it; I told her that I loved her too much to continue listening, that I had to hang up.

The next morning I awoke to Eve in bed with me, sobbing, trying to convince me to take her back. I told her that I couldn't, but she could feel how much I still loved her. Over the next months, I never knew when I'd hear a knock and open the door to find Eve standing there in tears. Once she showed up unannounced to give me a comic book she'd drawn, portraying her favorite moments from our relationship. "I thought I could remind you what it was like," she said. "I hoped I could make you remember."

She started sending me daily emails describing her shifting feelings. Some days they were accusatory, about how she felt betrayed by my giving up on her. Other days, she wrote that she understood why I couldn't be with her anymore and that she wanted to be friends. Other days, she'd send me recordings of heartbreaking songs she'd written about us, about how sorry she was for what she'd put me through. I told her that we should take a break from contacting each other, but she kept writing and sending me songs anyway.

One day, I heard a knock at the door and found Eve outside smiling at the sight of me. "Hi," she said.

I didn't invite her in. "Eve," I told her, choking up already myself. "I asked you to please stop coming by like this."

"But this is my home," she said.

"It's not anymore," I said, really crying now. "I'm gonna move out as soon as I can. It's not our home anymore."

"How can you do this?" she asked me for the hundredth time. "You lied to me."

I rubbed my palm over my face. "How did I lie?"

"You let me think you'd never leave me, no matter what I did," she said. "If I'd known you'd leave me, I would never have treated you so badly." She wiped her eyes. "This is like that horrible story about the boy who cried wolf. You're punishing me just for being myself."

I had to hold back from laughing. "*That's* your interpretation of the boy who cried wolf?"

"Sometimes he sends out a false alarm. That's not his fault. It's just who he is." Eve started crying harder but kept talking anyway. "Everyone convinced him they loved him. Then they let him get eaten by wolves. Really, everybody *else* lied."

Chapter 9

The Polite Way To Say No
Is to Say Yes

My EMOTIONAL STATE made teaching difficult. I warned my ukulele students that Eve and I had broken up. "So if we're playing a love song, don't be caught off guard if I start crying."

I'd recently found a part-time job teaching adults how to write children's books. For a group workshop, a student had turned in a picture book about an octopus. The octopus sewed himself various disguises to trick others into being his friend. At the end, he met someone who loved him for the octopus he really was. As I gave my critique in front of the class, my voice kept cracking and I eventually just stopped talking to cry. "Sorry," I told them. "I just broke up with my girlfriend so, at the moment, this book has personal meaning for me." Some of the students seemed moved or concerned, others looked down at their desks in discomfort, others held back awkward laughter. I found it funny myself and said something like, "Doesn't this feel like a scene from a cute romantic comedy? A children's book author goes through a breakup and falls apart in class while discussing a picture book about a lonely octopus?" The class didn't find this as funny as I did.

I wasn't talking to Dad much. When we did talk on the phone, the conversations weren't about the manuscript or our relationship or even about my breakup. We talked about movies we'd seen recently or about politics. We resorted to small talk and avoidance, all that we'd once hated.

Mom mostly wanted to talk about Eve. She was trying to be supportive, but she was pretty unhappy about it. "She still wants to be with you," Mom would say. "You could go back to her." Mom was open with me about how much she missed Eve. I told her I missed Eve too.

Miriam, who was now twenty-three, had expected Eve to be part of her life in New York. She was the least sympathetic. "Eve's definitely the best person you'll ever go out with. Dumping her is just dumb. Like, who do you think you are to dump Eve?"

Josh was the most detached and accepting. "It's sad," he said. "But these things happen."

Though this response was verbatim something I'd often said, I found it suddenly false. I wanted to tell him that great romances barely ever happened, that this was not normal.

Because I'd never really been with anyone but Eve, I assumed I'd just go back to isolation, getting by on fantasy the way I had before I moved to New York. But I didn't see anything to lose in asking out friends and acquaintances I found attractive. Family camp had taught me long ago that I should always ask for what I wanted, even if I'd likely receive a no. I saw dignity in asking and no shame in rejection; I'd been raised to expect it.

I was pleasantly surprised that everyone I asked out said yes. I was then unpleasantly surprised when they each canceled, stood me up, or stopped replying. I assumed that I must have done something wrong to change their minds between the yes and the stand-up, a mistake in where I'd suggested they meet me or the way I'd phrased the invitation. I mentioned this to a friend and she was the one to break it to me that these women had said yes without meaning it. I considered myself well-trained in recognizing lies, but I clearly had blind spots.

"Why would someone say yes when they mean no?" I asked. Before she could reply, I spewed out various incorrect theories: "Maybe they're scared to say no because men in their pasts freaked out at rejection? Or maybe they find sadistic enjoyment in getting my hopes up just to dash them?"

My friend suggested that most who gave me a false yes either generally shied away from confrontation or believed saying yes and canceling was more polite than saying no.

This reminded me of when, as a child, my teachers would ask, "How would you feel if someone said that to you?" This was the wrong question. My feelings worked differently. I couldn't understand others by asking myself how *I'd* feel. Because I had no trouble saying or receiving no, I'd overlooked that others would do anything to avoid it.

Every once in a while, a woman who agreed to go out with me would show up, and usually it only took a few lines of conversation for her to regret it. Despite her obvious urgency to leave, she'd stay the minimum time politeness demanded. I tried to acknowledge what was happening and tell her she could leave if she wanted, but that only tortured my date further and never resulted in her leaving any earlier. I wasn't sure why I was so immediately off-putting, and it occurred to me that the ones who knew, the experts on this subject, were sitting right across from me. I began asking the unfortunate women who I'd just put through bad dates what I'd done wrong. Yet again, I felt I had nothing to lose by asking; the date had already gone sour.*

The first several times I stopped a date to ask for advice, the woman lied, claiming that she was having a great time. "Come on!" I'd laugh. "Isn't it more awkward to deny it?" No matter how much I pushed for answers, they'd stick to the story we both knew to be false. Then, soon as they could, they'd make an excuse and get the hell out of there.

Two months after my breakup, a friend directed a music video for my newest song called "You're Somebody Even If Nobody Loves You." On set, I noticed one of the crew members freely giving artistic suggestions to the stylist, choreographer, and director. Her notes were brilliant, and people listened to her because she was kind and charming. She managed to be both outspoken and liked. The director introduced us—her name was Connie. We only interacted for a few minutes, barely spoke to each other, but I sensed a mutual interest. From afar, I didn't seem so bad. After the shoot, I looked her up and found that she kept a journal on her website that went on for pages, with personal stories and observations. I read far too much of it and then asked her out for coffee.

Connie chose a coffee shop in SoHo, quiet and empty and lodge-like, with wood and taxidermy and ironic paintings of old white men in hunting outfits. She wore a black turtleneck and black suit pants. Connie's bangs ended in a straight line, framing her expressive arching eyebrows and long eyelashes. I told her I'd read a lot of what she'd written. She clearly didn't like my saying that, but I couldn't be certain which part bothered her: my reading it or my telling her about it. I moved on to

---

* My brain was having a hard time with the concept that I was supposed to spare these women the awkwardness.

other subjects but could sense that she just wanted to get away, so I said, "Hey, Connie. Can I ask you some advice?"

"Okay," she said, curious about this change in tone. "About what?"

"I was raised by unusual people," I said.

"Everybody thinks that," she interrupted. "Everyone thinks they're weird and their family is crazy."

"Some people are *actually* unusual." Connie looked over my shoulder as if searching for any escape. "I only brought it up to say that I'm trying to be *less* unusual," I told her. "I want to learn normal social life."

Connie laughed, attentive again. "Okay?"

"This date obviously failed and I'm sure it was my fault," I told her. Connie's face plasticized into a grotesque smile intended to mask her embarrassment for me. Still, I persisted. "You're exactly the kind of person I want to like me," I told her. "So maybe you can tell me what I'm doing wrong." Connie's face was expressive enough that I could clearly read each step in her thinking. I watched her abandon her fake smile. She didn't soften to comfort me like others had. She raised a judgmental eyebrow and scrutinized my face coldly, guessing whether I really wanted to hear what she had to say. "I've asked other women for advice like this," I told her. "And they all lied or avoided the conversation."

Connie laughed. "Of course they did! What do you expect?"

"But you seem honest. In your writing, at least."

Connie loosened and leaned forward again. Her fingertips perched on the table as if cradling stacks of poker chips. "Yeah," she nodded. "I *am* honest."

"Great," I said. "Then tell me your side of the story."

Unlike the other dates I'd badgered, Connie smiled, enjoying this. "You said so many things you shouldn't say on a date that

I thought you were trying to manipulate me, playing games I hadn't heard of. But then I realized you were just awkward."

"What did I say?" I asked.

Connie went off listing inappropriate first-date subjects I'd broached, glowing like she'd never felt so free to trash someone.

"You said you couldn't imagine having another girlfriend because the one you just broke up with three months ago was the great romance of your life? That was the part I thought might be some kind of game to make me want you."

It had never occurred to me that my honesty could be misinterpreted as game-playing; that really bothered me. Her hands chopped at the air and fluttered around her head as the honesty spilled from her.

"You told me you disliked most people and most people disliked you and you'd only learned to have friends when you moved to New York?"

She paused, suddenly hesitant, but then shook it off.

"And don't tell someone about your fetish before you've even made out. It could be hot if you reveal it at the right time but otherwise, it's creepy."

At my lack of freak-out, she became comfortable again.

"You told me about your weird family camp cult? And you said you had money problems and you were afraid that the video shoot had made me think you were rich?"

I tried to explain myself. "I just felt like you should know what you were getting into. Wouldn't you rather know in advance . . ."

Connie interrupted. "Do everyone a favor and just don't."

"I was doing the right thing," I insisted. "If I had herpes, wouldn't you want me to warn you before we had sex?"

Connie rolled her eyes so hard that she reminded me of Dad. "Obviously," she said.

"How early would you suggest I warn you?" I asked. "The first date? The second?"

"I don't know!" she said, exasperated. "If you have herpes, it's complicated. Do you have herpes?"

"No, I'm using herpes as a metaphor for my personality."

She laughed and waved her fingers in my face. "Don't go on a date with me and list reasons why I shouldn't like you. It's *idiotic*. It's self-centered. Like, you brought me somewhere and gave me this shitty experience."

"You think it's okay to hide the bad things about myself so that someone will like me?" I asked. "To trick and mislead people? That isn't right."

Connie wrapped herself in her own arms and blurted out, "If doing the right thing makes everyone hate you, what's the point?"

This struck me as a very good question.

I LEANED BOTH elbows on the sewing machine table with Eve's vase still on it, emptied months ago of its last dead hydrangeas, and played the Fear Game. It wasn't as fun to play alone. Without Eve there to cut me off, my list of fears was too long. These troubled me most:

- Now that I'd experienced being in love, I couldn't be as happy alone
- Ukulele lessons will dry up and I'll have no other way to make a living
- Eve is the only woman who would appreciate an honest boyfriend
- I won't be able to get along with a landlord enough to get another apartment
- I'm oblivious and misguided and everything that feels right is, in fact, wrong

Then I listed reasons to be less honest:

> — Eve, the wisest person I knew, and others I
>   admired lived dishonestly
> — I wanted to be different from Dad
> — I'd make other people happy
> — If so many loved dishonesty, there had to be
>   something to it I couldn't see

There was also a reason I didn't have the insight to write down but that hid somewhere in my mind: if no one really knew me and no one let me know them, I'd never have to fall in love or feel loved, and I wouldn't have to go through any more pain. So perhaps my truest reason for becoming dishonest wasn't so uncommon.

Part 3

The Dishonest Days

Chapter 10

Forbidden Subjects

To kick my honesty habit, I'd need steps, probably more than twelve. I started by listing subjects I'd no longer let myself discuss. The first ones that came to mind were:

— Unpleasant truths
— My parents
— Eve
— Most people
— My opinions
— Family therapy camp
— My personality

It didn't occur to me that I could adjust my tone for my audience. All I knew was that certain topics irked or unnerved. I figured it was safest to outlaw them completely. I told myself that every time a conversation went wrong, I'd add whatever topic ruined it to my list of forbidden subjects.

I came up with dozens of other rules as well, all in the service of the same overarching scheme: to learn to read people and give them what they wanted. Instead of asking questions, I'd pick up hints. Instead of expressing myself, I'd pander. I'd reverse the golden rule and do unto others what *they* wanted me to do unto *them*.

When I decided to censor myself, I told everybody. It didn't occur to me to keep my dishonesty-aspiration private. I hoped to get advice from friends savvier at social interaction. At a Christmas party in a friend's crowded little apartment, I announced my plan to be less honest.

Everyone around the coffee table laughed. "I'm not joking," I said, gesturing madly. "My honesty has rendered life impossible." I continued in all seriousness as everyone laughed, and my fingers tightened around my whiskey. They told me over and over that it was crazy to aspire to be a liar. Eventually, I cracked. "I'm only trying to be as dishonest as all of you." At that line, no one laughed. I added "honesty" to my list of forbidden subjects.

Within a week, I'd banned everything I usually talked about.

For years, I'd been told that I misused words, swapping connotations, that what I called "honesty" was really "rudeness" and what I called "lying" was generally known as "politeness." Because "rude" and "polite" had come up so often, I thought it might benefit me to read a bit about etiquette.

At the time, I viewed etiquette as a web of arbitrary rules written by the powerful to maintain psychological control. Some rules shamed or exposed outsiders, such as complex table manners. Others discouraged dissent by defining boundary-drawing as "confrontational." Exposing wrongdoing was "making a scene." Calling out racism was worse manners than saying something racist. For me, etiquette was most insidious when presented as morality. Perhaps using the wrong fork wasn't immoral, but eating before the whole table was seated would be compared to an act of violence, a "slap in the face." I saw nothing moral about these rules that benefited some at the expense of many, that encouraged class-worship and conformity. To put it mildly, I went into my study of etiquette with some skepticism.

As I studied some etiquette guides, I observed that that they mostly served to collect and categorize lies. What if you don't want to attend a party? There's a lie for that. What if you feel hurt about something? This lie is most appropriate. What if you've betrayed someone and he confronts you? We've got the perfect lie for you! Of course, these books and articles never used the word "lie," instead described acts of untruth and evasion with a litany of more positive words. But referring to lying as "grace" or "kindness" didn't convince me. I skimmed the books, as well as advice columns, for any circumstances in which the authors advised the reader to behave in a manner that I could loosely interpret as honest. As far as I could tell, the etiquette experts regarded dishonesty as the salve to all ills, humanity's finest invention.

As much as I thought I knew about lying, I was unprepared for how complex it really was. I marveled at the countless purposes of different lies: lies intended to be understood as empty pleasantries; lies to stop or redirect a conversation; lies to prompt a specific response. The books explained so many of my last few decades' worth of interactions. Among many other examples, I now knew why many on the phone had behaved strangely after they told me, "I know you have to go." It turned out all along that I was supposed to repeat the line they'd given me and agree I had to go. Instead, I'd replied with confusion, saying I didn't have to go, asking where they'd gotten that impression. I couldn't imagine the uncountable hints I'd missed; my obliviousness overwhelmed me. I found most of it hilarious but also remained aware that there had been no humor in it for the people who had gone through the mortification and awkwardness of dealing with me.

Though I'd learned a lot from the etiquette experts, I resented how they delineated any behavior on the sacred spectrum from polite to rude. I saw no reference to etiquette being subjective, a matter of personal taste. And yet, I noticed dozens of disagreements between the "experts." How could one be expected to follow these rules if no one could even agree upon what they were? Was it a violation of space to say hello to a stranger in line beside you or was it unfriendly to *not* say hello. When was it uncomfortable to compliment and when was it insulting to *refrain* from complimenting? Was the whole world a series of no-win situations? When one encounters a rude person, should one draw his attention to his gaffes or respond with kind deflection to avoid embarrassing him? I couldn't quiet my brain's satirical rants. How had these fools come to be considered etiquette experts anyway? It seemed to me that claiming to be an etiquette expert, in itself, ought to be considered rude.

I reminded myself that I was supposed to be learning, not quibbling. When I tried to take the worldview of the etiquette experts seriously, I recognized that their vision of humanity matched my family's, but with one crucial difference: they regarded the offended and hurt with compassion. The etiquette experts didn't see caring about what other people thought as a flaw or tragedy, but as an easy-to-accept reality. Perhaps this was a truth that the Levitons were unwilling to face. What the experts wanted to accommodate, my family had tried to satirize, fix, or escape.

During this period, I'd often run into friends or acquaintances at my usual bar and ask questions about normal social life. They'd have a drunken laugh poking holes in my theories. It was more fun for them than it was for me. I couldn't decide how reliable they were, but they still influenced my thinking. Because they involved a rotating cast of characters, and in many cases I can't remember who was there and who said what, and because they mostly judged me, I'll refer to them in our dialogues as "the jury."

I told them, "If the etiquette experts are to be believed, everyone's constantly embarrassed and trying to avoid embarrassment. I don't understand why."

The jury glowered, sensing where this was going. "Yeah, that's because you have no shame."

I told them it would be helpful if I could hear the kinds of daily interactions that embarrassed them. The jury told me about being forced to admit to rich friends they couldn't afford something and being snubbed by cool girls, about showing up overdressed or underdressed to parties, about public rejections and disastrously timed toilets that wouldn't flush. The jury responded most to one story about a man who got money out of an ATM while his date stood close to sneak a look at his bank balance. "At the time, I only had forty dollars," he said. The jury's hysterics embarrassed him all over again. He insisted, "I was gonna get paid soon!"

"Here's the part I don't get," I told them. "These things happen all the time. Toilets clog. People have forty dollars in their accounts. That's probably happened to all of us. What's the big deal? There's no reason to be embarrassed about not having money. Statistically, almost no one has money. The embarrassing thing is to be someone who would care so much if someone isn't rich! If this woman on the date judges you, she buys into foolish cultural dogma. *That's* embarrassing."

This comment offended the jury because it turned out most of them would judge their date for only having forty dollars.

One of my new rules was to backpedal if I offended people, so I used the classic strategy of adding "all I'm saying" to the beginning of every statement. "All I'm saying," I told the jury, "is that the jerks who've embarrassed you are the real embarrassments."

The jury drew my attention to the absurdity of me considering myself the arbiter of embarrassment, so I moved on to another question. "The etiquette books assume there's a lot that we all know but still can't stand to hear someone speak aloud. Can you think of things you feel that way about?"

The jury started listing:

— Not everyone will like you
— Some are more moral than you

"Is this why so many people hate vegans?" I asked. "Because we agree they're morally superior?" The jury proved its point by avoiding this question to continue listing.

— When you achieve something, it isn't necessarily because you deserved it
— The one you're with now was with others before you
— Your relationship likely won't last, and you'll likely hate each other after it's over
— There are other values one could have, other ways to live

"Oh, maybe that's why some people with kids feel offended by people who don't want kids? And why some people who devote their lives to making money get upset about people who don't?"

— You'll never be rich
— Someone is better looking than you

"How can they possibly be upset at the idea that someone is better looking!?!" I asked. "*Of course* someone is always better looking."

I got the sense that this list could go on forever, but I stopped them because it depressed me to imagine needing to avoid these common truths visible everywhere, referenced a thousand times a day. They needed sheets to throw over the mirrors. I'd always been the mirror when I should have been the sheet.

Nobody Calls Them Lies but You

MY EARLY LIES were simple attempts to misrepresent myself as normal. I answered each "how are you?" with "great" or "fine" no matter how I felt. I gave disingenuous compliments to be nice. When I received an invitation, I said I planned to be there even if I had no intention of going. When greeted by someone I didn't remember, I feigned recognition. If I'd forgotten someone's name, I pretended I knew it. When someone didn't pay enough on a split dinner bill, I didn't call it out, I just covered it. When something went wrong, I acted as if I hadn't noticed. I pretended to like people I didn't. I littered my speech with standard questions, clichés, and pleasantries: "How are you?" and "What do you do?" and "Where are you from?" and "So nice to see you!"

All of these felt like small-time cons. I'd get nauseated and stuff my hands into my pockets to hide their involuntary clasping and unclasping. An omission would leave me hungover for hours. I was a goldfish in a plastic bag. I kept reminding myself, "Nobody calls them lies but you. Nobody calls them lies but you."

A few months into my experimentation with dishonesty, I attended a party at a newly opened restaurant where the tables encircled a white grand piano. After dinner, they removed the tables for a dance party around this piano. When most of the crowd had cleared out, the restaurant's manager, a friend of a friend, turned off the music. We stayed after hours in the silence and I asked her if I could play the piano. She gave me permission so I played a jazz standard I'd taught myself. This manager told me they needed a piano player to play background music for brunch on Sundays and asked if I'd like the job.

I needed any jobs I could get and I liked the idea of being a brunch pianist, but I knew this gig would require playing for hours and I didn't know enough piano music to last more than thirty minutes. And when it came down to it, I just wasn't good enough at piano to deserve a paid gig like that over other pianists. In the past, I would have told her to find someone else, and I would've recommended better pianists I knew, but I thought instead I'd experiment with pure bullshit. I said yes and acted as if I was an appropriate candidate for the job. She bought it and asked me to start this coming Sunday, in two days. I needed at least a week to learn music and practice, but instead of telling her that, I lied, saying I already had plans that weekend, but that I could start the following Sunday.

I spent the whole week preparing. When Sunday came around, I still sounded pretty bad and I felt certain I'd start playing and the manager who had hired me would be humiliated and they'd have to find some polite way to fire me. But, to my surprise, they were satisfied. I could have taken this as validating, told myself it proved I was better at piano than I thought. Though I was learning to lie to others, I couldn't stop being honest with myself. The owners and manager possessed no knowledge of music and paid little attention. No job could convince me I was a good pianist. But I resisted my impulse to let them know.

I WASN'T SURE how I'd get a new apartment without Eve. She'd found our first apartment herself. And in our second apartment search, she was the one who could politely deal with the landlords and brokers. Aside from my troubles interacting with most people, I was a freelancer without guaranteed income or a boss to give me proof of employment. A ukulele teacher was no landlord's dream.

I'd heard that lying was so common in these situations that it was expected, part of the ritual.* I spoke to a friend who occasionally hired me to collaborate on music for commercials and asked him to write me a letter on his company stationery that claimed I worked for him full-time, earning six figures. I braced myself to be called a degenerate swindler, but he had no problem writing me this fraudulent letter.

A landlord showed me a crumbling old one-bedroom in a great location that cost half as much as it should have. I wanted to tell him that he could charge more, but I censored myself, ignoring the stabbing stress pains in my stomach. I noticed the place had no fire escape and thought to ask if they'd priced the apartment this cheap to make up for it being a fire-hazard death

---

* Because all lying felt equally insane, I couldn't easily differentiate between what was normal or abnormal, reasonable or selfish, or truly immoral.

trap. But I stayed uncharacteristically silent again. The landlord inquired about my job information and income and I told him about my fictional job and invented salary, my most extreme lies yet. He immediately offered me the apartment. I tried to show him my friend's letter but he said didn't need to see it, that he trusted me.

Each time I lied, my mind swirled with guilt, stress, and dread. I eventually recognized my stomach sickness as what others called shame. I wasn't used to doing things *I* considered wrong. When I neurotically spiraled, I found comfort in the fact that these crimes had no victims. If anything, even my most self-interested lies were mutually beneficial—the restaurant got a piano player, the landlord a tenant. Still, I couldn't help feeling that I'd be caught and called out any time. I ran through my mind how these confrontations would play out. In every imagined version, I found myself indignant and resentful. "You're the ones who wanted me to lie!" I'd say. "You rewarded me for it, pressured me into it!" It soon became clear that most people weren't constantly on the lookout for lies like I was. Even if someone had caught me and despised me for it, they'd likely have been too polite to say anything. Besides, even my most reprehensible falsehoods weren't considered noteworthy. It didn't take long for my anxiety to dull. I was getting used to being a liar.

IN SUMMER OF 2010, eight months after my breakup with Eve, a year after giving Dad the manuscript, I still wasn't talking often with my parents. My experiments in deception saved our conversations. My parents found the subject as bizarre and funny as I did.

"It's crazy," I'd say. "When you're behaving normally, you live in this alternate world. No one recoils in disgust! Everyone's happier. And even if they're not happier, they'd never let me know it!"

"I guess that's positive?" Dad laughed. When I told him about adding dozens of clichéd pleasantries to my speech, he said, "At work, people always thought I was mad at them. I couldn't understand it. My therapist told me it was probably because I got to the point immediately without saying 'How are you?' or 'Nice to see you.'"

"Did you try saying that stuff?" I asked.

"Yeah, actually. And it solved the problem immediately!" He laughed, I assumed, at his past obliviousness. It took me a second to recognize that he was laughing at the absurdity of this small change making a difference. "I went through with it," Dad said, "but I felt a low-level resentment about them wanting that stuff." He sighed. "I used to get so many reactions that I didn't understand. I needed a therapist to explain. Back then, I didn't know how other people saw me." I held myself back from telling him he still didn't understand how people saw him.

When I told Mom about my newfound dishonesty, she tried to be positive. "I've always said that a smile is free. It doesn't cost anything to smile!"

"It costs feeling known," I said. "And it costs the person I'm smiling at an accurate sense of my feelings. But I guess they don't care if I mean it; they just want a smile." Mom was quiet. I tried a slight change in subject. "I heard once that fake-smiling releases dopamine into the brain, so faking a smile makes you smile for real."

"Fake-smiling doesn't make *me* happier," Mom said, switching sides.

"Yeah," I told her. "I didn't believe it either."

Go for the Bold Statement

I SUSPECTED THAT packing up the apartment I'd shared with Eve would be a sob spree, and I was right. Moving can be very moving. I couldn't take a book from a shelf without a photo of us falling out, a heartbreak booby trap. When I moved the couch, I discovered several of Eve's drawings under it covered in dust.

I didn't want Eve to go through what I'd just gone through, so I packed her stuff for her and left it in boxes around the sewing machine table. I didn't have room for the table in my new apartment. I feared that, wherever Eve moved, she wouldn't have room for it either. I didn't want Eve to sell it or throw it away, but bringing it up would give away how much I still loved her; that was the sort of thing I was supposed to keep hidden. I had to decide if it was more painful for Eve to believe I didn't love her anymore or to know that I did. I'd heard that a breakup was easier if it cut off cleanly, even if the truth wasn't clean. As I packed up Eve's stuff, I remembered how just being honest required no weighing of different types of pain, no gambling on which strategy would be kindest or get the most desirable result. It was so much simpler to say whatever I felt and take no responsibility for the response or consequence. Family camp had assured me that "you can't control events but you can control your reactions." I took that to mean it was everyone else's job to manage their own feelings. It was becoming clearer and clearer that these therapy lines were intended for those who felt bogged down by the longing to please others, not to validate the reckless and inconsiderate like me.

IN MY NEW apartment, the walls were unevenly painted and cracking, the floors a patchy linoleum from the 1970s with sinking spots. The "living room" had space enough for my fake-Victorian couches and my broken-down half-size speakeasy piano but not a coffee table. My bedroom only had room for a bed and dresser. The shower was in the cramped kitchen. Since only the living room had any space, I knew I'd be spending all my time there. I invited over an interior decorator friend to advise me. He noticed a couple of vintage mirrors I'd collected and suggested I buy more and cover the wall with mirrors all the way to the ceiling. "Salon-style," he said. "Like Versailles." He said mirrors would make the room feel bigger. Even my apartment would now be about illusion. I asked him if people would be put off by a room full of mirrors. After all, I was supposed to be trying to appear normal. He flicked his hand and said, "Always go for the bold statement!"

So, I set about collecting mirrors. My neighborhood in Brooklyn now had its own junk shops, so each time I found a new mirror, I'd walk it home, carrying it like a shield. Passersby would check themselves out, instinctively adjusting their face to the angle that made them look how they wanted. Even when looking in a mirror, they'd trick themselves.

Within a few months, my walls were covered with mirror constellations. When visitors came over, I would notice them trying to sit in spots where they could avoid their reflections. I had unwittingly created yet another situation where spending time with me required looking at yourself whether you wanted to or not.

Lunch with Chekhov

OVER MY EIGHT years in New York, I'd had some jobs playing vinyl records at bars or parties. I mostly played old rock and roll, soul, and jazz, which meant it was common for strangers to criticize the music and make irrelevant requests.

One New Year's Eve, I was playing records for a dance party of about four hundred people when a young man approached and asked me why I wasn't playing hip-hop. I told him I loved hip-hop but that I had a different specialization. He persisted. "You know, most deejays play hip-hop." I told him I understood that he personally wanted me to play hip-hop, but that the audience appeared to be satisfied with old rock and roll; I gestured to the crowd of hundreds of people dancing. He just repeated himself. "But most deejays play hip-hop."

On another occasion, a young drunk woman simply asked me, "Could you play *better* music?"

In the honest days, I found it hard to get these people to leave me alone. They considered it disrespectful to refuse to engage in conversation or express plainly that I wouldn't take their requests. On a couple occasions, they demanded apologies, threatened me, or invited me outside to fight.

In the winter of 2010, I got a gig playing vinyl records one night a week at a small fake-vintage cocktail bar with distressed mirrors and furniture. My first night at this new job, a young woman requested a modern pop song unrelated to the style of music I'd been hired to play. Instead of my old method of telling her I didn't play requests, I tried dishonesty; I made a big show of telling her how much I loved that song, though unfortunately I didn't own a copy. This was my first time attempting to hint. Encouraged by what she misread as a positive reply, she told me that she could play the song from her own device if I plugged it into the bar's stereo system. A missed hint was just as tiresome as others had claimed. I almost broke character and got candid but I kept my cool and told her I was only allowed to play vinyl. She laughed and told me I was too uptight about the rules; she thought she was being fun. I now imitated an evasion I'd witnessed hundreds of times: inventing someone to blame. I replied that I really wanted to play her request but the owner was a big drag, that he only liked old music, and I didn't want to get fired. She replied that I should tell the owner this music wasn't what people wanted to hear. Though I could recognize the positive sides of these new strategies, the conversation wasn't ending. She was encouraged by all I'd said. I was losing my mind, so I buckled and made a mocking joke: "It sounds like you should be the deejay!"

She broke into a huge grin. "I *should* be a deejay!" she said. "I'd be an amazing deejay!" Then she hopped away, much happier than when she'd arrived. I watched her return to her friends, excitedly gesturing to me, probably telling them the story of how I'd ordained her a deejay.

After that, when a stranger approached me at the turntables, I'd smile, invest my voice with warmth and enthusiasm, and suggest that *they* should be the deejay. Each time, the person left happy. I'd been mistakenly assuming these people cared about music. They only wanted connection and validation. I had to keep reminding myself that few meant the words they said. Even fewer knew consciously what they wanted, why they did what they did. I made another rule:

> — *Don't take seriously what people say. Their minds are chaos.*

When I told a friend about my strategy of telling strangers to be deejays, she told me how she'd conquered one of her own problems. Whenever a man asked what she did and she answered that she was a painter, the man would lecture her unpleasantly about painting. If she interjected or tried to leave, the man would become aggressive and insulting. After a long time experimenting with how to get out of listening to these men, she found that it only took one sentence: "How do you know so much about painting?" The man would puff with pride, say something vague, and strut away satisfied. I asked her if it bothered her to let these obnoxious guys feel like experts. She said, "It does, but it's better than a confrontation or suffering through the conversation."

Alerted to the possibilities of giving people whatever interaction they wanted, I started to try it—not just to cut off aggravating interactions, but to make everyone happy.

One of my children's book writing students wrote a picture book about a mother who felt unappreciated. In the book, the mother's kids didn't say thank you when she drove them to school or made them lunch and didn't notice how much work she put into planning their birthday parties. It wasn't a big leap to intuit that she herself was a mother who felt unappreciated. Even the description of the mother in her book seemed intended as a depiction of herself. She'd turned in this manuscript for workshop, which meant the other twelve students had read it and we were all going to take turns giving comments in front of the class.

As a teacher, I felt it was my responsibility to mention all she could potentially do with her concept. As written, her picture book for children was focused solely on the mother—the children barely appeared. And the book was more likely to shame kids than to entertain. I could imagine her making the concept more fun by cartoonishly exaggerating the mother's self-sacrifice and her kids' obliviousness. Or maybe she could focus it more on the kids by reversing the concept, writing about a self-sacrificing child whose *mother* never noticed or said thank you.

Usually, giving notes on children's books was fun for everyone, but I could feel how, in this case, she was likely to take criticism of the book as criticism of herself. Not only would I be telling her that the mother in the book wasn't self-sacrificing enough, but also that she as author had made herself the hero instead of empowering children. It felt to me like the exact opposite of what she wanted to hear.

With the class watching, I began my comments by saying that it was nice to read a book about such a great mother, that it was a tragedy so many mothers did so much for so little appreciation. My student beamed. I continued talking but she didn't seem to listen. I'd already said the only thing she wanted to hear.

AROUND THIS TIME, I heard a story about a young Russian in the 1800s who ended up with an opportunity to meet the writer Anton Chekhov for tea. This young man felt certain he'd make a fool of himself; he couldn't imagine saying anything interesting enough to impress this famous genius. But once he was seated at a table with Chekhov, the young man found that everything coming out of his own mouth was brilliant. Chekhov laughed and gasped, barely speaking except to ask him more intrigued questions. The young man left that day amazed at how he'd underestimated himself. He took in Chekhov's interest and spoke with a new freeness, a trust in the value of his voice.

Decades later, long after Chekhov's death, the formerly young man encountered someone else who had once drunk tea with Chekhov. He was excited to trade stories. The formerly young man retold the story he'd now told hundreds of times about the day he enthralled Chekhov. The other man smiled affectionately and explained that he'd heard this story before, that every time someone spoke of meeting Chekhov, the description was identical. In fact, the man said, his own vision of himself had been changed by those very same laughs and gasps. The formerly young man was shattered at the thought that Chekhov had only been polite, showing equal interest to everyone as if they were his children. The other man recognized his disappointment and reassured him that Chekhov had been an honest man. This was the magical effect of his curiosity and his admiration of humanity. He showed people how to fall in love with themselves.

This story haunted me, plagued me with questions. Did Chekhov inspire them to become more moving and interesting than usual by inviting them to be their truest selves, like I'd always tried to do? Had Chekhov really been honest? Or did he just make people feel good about whoever they happened to be, interesting or not? Did Chekhov just reflect back to them their fantasy of who they longed to be? Chekhov couldn't have loved everybody! If he helped people he disliked to love themselves, wasn't that still a great service?

Honest or not, I wanted to be more like Chekhov.

The Profundity of Small Talk

My list of forbidden subjects required me to seek new genres of conversation. I was willing to bore myself if it would spare others' awkwardness. I was getting used to the once-foreign concept that if someone in an exchange was going to be uncomfortable, that person should be me. So I decided to attempt "small talk."

Years before, in a dentist's office waiting room, I'd read a magazine interview with a movie star in which she said she liked introductory conversations to be "stupid." She suggested starting out by discussing favorite colors. As bizarre as this sounded to me, I tried to keep an open mind. Other people found meaning in places I didn't. I was curious what would happen if I went out for a night to my usual bar and, when introduced to someone new, tried discussing our favorite colors.

Almost immediately upon arrival, a friend introduced me to a musician who seemed the worst possible subject for this experiment. I recognized her from photographs of her performances at fashion events and art galleries; she wore dark red lipstick and a black beret. My friend went to the bar for a drink, and she looked dismayed to be left alone with me. I felt certain that if I asked her favorite color she'd laugh at me or flee, but I still proceeded with the plan. I found it unexpectedly calming to go into this conversation without the intent to be interesting.

She asked the standard question about what I did and I answered, "Lately, I've mostly been trying to find the right color to paint the bedroom in my new apartment." This was true.

"Oh yeah?" she said.

"What's your favorite color?" I asked her.

To my surprise, she embraced the question, listing her favorites and how they'd changed over time. She showed no sign of condescension or boredom. "Your favorite color isn't necessarily right for your walls," she said, while I privately laughed at how well this deliberately stupid conversation was going. "What colors are you considering?"

I had a story ready. "My favorite color is eggplant," I said. "I kept going to paint stores but none had the right shade of purple. Eventually, I found an independent paint company that had a perfect match, but when I looked at the sample jar, I saw the label, and the color was named 'Bachelor Pad Jazz.'"

She laughed. "Oh no."

"I imagined this business meeting in a boardroom where they name colors, that someone in a suit gave his pitch." I did an impression of a cigar-smoking executive. "'I know the guy who wants this eggplant. He's probably thirty years old, just broke up with his girlfriend, moved into a new apartment by himself, probably plays jazz piano at restaurants. He's a total cliché. There are a million of this guy. Bachelor Pad Jazz! It's gonna be a hit.'"

The musician laughed and grinned, not even slightly put-off. I longed to tell her why I was talking about colors and what it meant to me, but I knew the truth would ruin it. The whole thing made me want to cry, but I kept it together.

I tried this conversation about colors several more times that night. If anyone was just being nice while waiting for an excuse to escape, I couldn't tell. As hard as it was for me to believe, they were charmed.

I'd always thought conversation was for expressing myself or learning about someone else, an exchange of information. There was clearly a whole type of communication I'd overlooked. I remembered the children in school who didn't need to talk in order to play. I thought of when Max at family camp told me a person could be loved without saying anything to earn it. Some close friends just played video games in silence. Even some lovers didn't speak to each other. I'd thought these people were just bores with nothing to say or, worse, afraid to speak. But I now saw they just communicated differently, showing affection in ways that had nothing to do with words.

I spent the next few weeks small-talking with strangers. After a few dozen of these conversations, I finally encountered someone who hated it. "You're seriously asking me my favorite color?" she asked. "What is this? Kindergarten?"

I cracked up, so excited that I'd found someone like-minded. "I know!" I said. "I just started experimenting with small talk and it's been blowing my mind. People really do want to talk about things like favorite colors. You're the first person who's resisted or even noticed that I was doing anything out of the ordinary!" The stranger looked me up and down in disgust. I assured her, "*I* don't want to talk about colors. Other people like it. I'm trying it to make other people happy."

The stranger glared at me. "You asked me my favorite color because you assumed I was stupid."

"No," I replied. "Small talk isn't stupid! I used to think that too, but I've realized that it's an alternate system of communication just as legitimate as ours!" I was waving my hands in the air, so excited to have someone to talk to about this.

Unmoved by my speech, she said, "If someone talks to you about their favorite color, they're either just being polite or they're a vapid idiot."

Her condescending expression and her voice's judgmental certainty gave me a small sense, for just a moment, of what it might have felt like for other people to meet *me*.

Chapter 11

This Is Normal

THOUGH I'D MOSTLY acclimated to lying in many casual situations, I'd procrastinated applying my rules to dating. I couldn't stomach the blatant immorality of wooing someone under false pretenses. The jury advised me to present myself in the best possible light at first, to wait a few months into a relationship before revealing any potentially off-putting information. I called that a bait-and-switch; they called it normal.

I read some books and articles about dating; the alleged experts wrote as if it were assumed that no one would be loved for who they really were, that romance was no more than well-executed sleight of hand. I found "hard to get" hard to accept. One book recommended that I face my body away when talking to someone attractive to subtly express an alluring lack of interest. Another article claimed that I should look at the bridge of a woman's nose instead of directly into eyes; that way, my eye contact would be steadier and sexier. Even if I managed to woo someone with tricks, I'd know she didn't love *me*, that she loved my psychological manipulations.

The idealized characters in movies and literature acted as if they'd read the same dating books. Jane Austen's characters attracted each other with unavailability and insults, treated each other just as terribly as Wesley and Buttercup from *The Princess Bride*. Even the most charming characters from old movies—Astaire and Rogers, Hepburn and Grant, Belafonte and Dandridge, Stanwyck and Fonda—spoke indirectly and showed little of themselves. As much as it bothered me to admit it, even in my favorite stories, romance had rarely been about honesty.

My first dishonest date was in August of 2011, about a year and a half into my research and experiments. I'd met Malaika at the restaurant where I now played piano. She wore loose, colorful clothes that felt "summery" and white gardenias pinned in her hair like Billie Holiday. I didn't usually appeal to people who smiled constantly, but she sat down at the table closest to the piano and spent brunch having staring contests with me while I played. Her light brown eyes remained unblinking; she had more talent for staring contests than I had for anything. When I asked her out, my hands shook with nervousness. She grabbed my phone and typed the number herself.

For our first date, I'd invited her to a musician friend's concert. I arrived early to pick up the tickets and waited on the sidewalk outside, biting my nails and compulsively checking my watch. Soon, I spotted her waving to me from down the block. She glided directly into a hello hug. As we embraced, it took all my fortitude to hold back from announcing that this date was an experiment in deception. I noticed a pain in my gums and realized I'd been subconsciously clenching my teeth to keep my mouth shut.

As my friend performed, Malaika and I danced, not saying anything. Things went so much better when I wasn't talking.

After the show, we got a drink at a wine bar next door so dark that our eyes had to adjust. Candles behind patterned glass cast calculated shadows. Malaika and I perched on stools at a high table. Her flirtatious smile felt to me as if it were saying, "I'll enjoy this, but only if you don't reveal who you really are."

I said as little as I could and stuck to asking questions. I didn't mind this part because I wanted to know all about her and I loved her voice, half-whispered and half-laughing. She'd linger on certain words and syllables, pausing and letting her expressive face carry her meaning. Whenever I interjected, my graceless high-speed chatter reminded me of a stuttering machine gun. I'd once liked the way I spoke. My new attention to how I'd be perceived had already corroded the way I saw myself.

Malaika told me about her job inventing paper craft projects for children. "I can talk about paper all day," she said. She described the paper baubles and origami she'd folded herself, her desk drawers filled with paper samples. "My apartment is a world of paper," she said. I was barely talking, but she didn't look bored.

As whiskey and her presence intoxicated me, I found it more and more challenging to follow my rules. An attractive woman was like truth serum.

Malaika opened her mouth to speak and then hesitated. I wasn't the only one deciding what to censor. She readied herself to say something risky. "This is my first time on a proper date," she told me. She crossed her arms and a line of shadow fell over her eye. "I broke up with my boyfriend a few months ago. I haven't had much experience being single."

Malaika's mention of her recent breakup felt like permission to tell her about Eve, but I had a rule about this already:

— *Don't take someone else's openness as an invitation.*

She could bring up her ex but still judge me if I brought up mine. Malaika told me that in the past she'd only dated friends; she'd never gone out with a stranger.

I'd put "dating" on my list of forbidden subjects for a reason. I flipped through potential strategies in my head for how to dodge this line of conversation. Malaika's eyebrows constricted. "Are you okay?" she asked. "What are you thinking about?"

I panicked. "Let's not talk about this."

Malaika laughed. "Why not?"

Still flustered, I answered, "I have a list of subjects I'm not supposed to talk about."

Malaika laughed, but then recognized I wasn't joking and stopped laughing. I liked that she could tell I was serious. She rested her drink on the table and asked, "Who decides what subjects you're supposed to talk about?"

"It's self-imposed," I told her. "I wrote the list."

"Oh," Malaika laughed, relieved. "It sounded like something from therapy." My whole brain was something from therapy. "Okay," she said, leaning in and smiling. "So you have a list of subjects you won't let *yourself* talk about."

"And I add to it whenever a conversation goes wrong."

She laughed again. "What's on this list?"

"I shouldn't tell you," I said.

She reprised our staring contest. "Yes, you should." I kept in mind that when people believed they wanted to know my thoughts, they were usually mistaken. "You *want* to tell me," Malaika said.

"I want to tell you all kinds of things I shouldn't," I replied, intentionally misleading her. I wanted to tell *everyone* things I shouldn't, not just her. And the things I wanted to tell weren't sexy or fun or romantic; they were off-putting. The flirtatious line only sounded flirtatious because of what it omitted.

Malaika's eyes lowered and lingered upon my lips. I wanted to ask her if this look meant I should touch or kiss her, but I'd come up with a rule about this too:

> — *Don't ask permission. People prefer to be read.*

I felt frustrated that I couldn't just ask what she wanted, but I forced myself to trust my reading of the situation; I placed my unsteady hand on her bare leg.

Malaika smirked. "Maybe the list of subjects you shouldn't talk about is, itself, a subject you shouldn't talk about."

I reminded myself that flirting often involved insincere criticisms. I noted her attentive eyes and open posture and mentally referenced another rule:

> — *Trust facial expressions and body language more than words.*

Soon, we were making out across the table. I was distracted by thoughts of pulling away and telling her she'd been duped, that this date had been a sham, that I'd kept quiet so she would like me, and that this experiment had proven all my most dreaded hypotheses. But I didn't pull away. The kissing stopped and I still didn't say anything. Things went so much better when I wasn't talking.

AT THIS POINT the jury had been listening to my observations and experiments for a year. Two of the jurors had been recently dumped by their boyfriends. Carmen coped by going out drinking every night, crying in public, lamenting her loneliness to strangers who she'd then have to reject when they tried to kiss her. Angie had overnight become a geyser that gushed brilliant break-up songs. They weren't in a great place to be giving advice but that didn't stop them.

The three of us sat in a row at the bar as I recounted my dishonest date with Malaika. Angie half-smiled with crooked teeth. She'd engage with me for a few minutes and then her eyes would float to the corners of her sockets, distracted by memories.

Carmen, who had a way of being glamorous and joyful until the moment she fell apart, laughed at me as usual. "You told her about your list? She must think you're crazy."

"It's possible," I said. "But she made out with me."

"See!" Carmen said, grinning. "I told you. You can be yourself. You just have to find the right person."

"One sincere moment in a whole conversation isn't my idea of 'being myself.'"

"That's just semantics." Someone always said it was just semantics. "Being yourself doesn't mean saying everything you think."

I sipped my drink and retreated into vagueness. "These terms aren't so easily defined."

Angie chimed in softly, "It's great that you're honest. It's everyone's favorite thing about you."

I clutched the edges of my barstool. "That's like telling a recovering alcoholic he's more fun when he's drunk."

Carmen laughed again. "Honesty's a good thing. Everybody knows that."

"When I was teenager, I wished everyone could read each other's minds, that all our thoughts and feelings and histories were automatically public."

"Okay, that's creepy," Carmen interrupted.

"I thought if we were all forced to see the full contents of each other's brains spilled out in front of us, all the stories, the worst things we've done, the insecurity and shame and fear and pain, we'd be moved and we'd all love each other."

"Wow," Angie said hazily, considering.

"But I was wrong," I said. "When we see feelings or behaviors different from our own, we're threatened, and we resent them. And when we see our own insecurities reflected in someone else, we feel disgust instead of sympathy. We catch another person doing exactly what we'd do and call him a jerk."

Carmen laughed. "You're *really* overthinking this." This was another thing someone always said.

I continued, "Honesty rarely helps us love each other. Being loved is more about lying and hiding."

Carmen stopped laughing. "That's so negative."

"But you agree," I insisted. "If you didn't believe that, why would you live the way you live?"

EVE AND I hadn't been in touch since I'd moved out of the apartment nearly a year before. I hoped enough time had passed that we could meet as friends, so Eve and I got a drink.

She arrived wearing a summer dress and normal-size glasses. She looked distinctly younger to me, and I had the strangest impression that she looked *less* experienced, less world-weary. It occurred to me that the whole time I'd known her, she'd always been recently crying.

When she saw me, she gazed at me the way she used to, and smiled nervously. We sat at the bar and she asked me about my new apartment. I told her about the mirrors and about "Bachelor Pad Jazz." She laughed, and I asked her about where she'd moved.

"I didn't move, actually," she said. "I'm still in the apartment."

"You didn't move?"

She smiled, tearing up. "I didn't move," she said. Only a few minutes into this and we were already both crying.

We laughed a moment about our crying together again and I said, "Maybe with us, being friends means always crying. A crying friendship."

She asked about my family and I told her that they missed her. "They weren't so sympathetic toward me about the breakup. They really wanted us to stay together."

"My family misses you too," Eve said. "They still talk about you all the time." She paused to gather herself. "Because now we can tell each other what we mean. And every time someone talks about how they feel, they think of you. You taught us how."

I was having a hard time keeping it together. Eve could move me more than anybody.

Then she looked down nervously, became shaky. "So," she asked. "Are you seeing anyone?"

I had become so used to my forbidden subjects that, without a beat, I said, "I don't think we should talk about that."

Eve stiffened, perhaps at the implication that I'd found another girlfriend already, but I suspect it was more at the shock of hearing me avoid a question.

"But we're best friends," she said, not looking at me. "We can talk about what's going on. Just tell me, do I know her?" She lifted her wineglass, her hands so unsteady that she spilled. She went red, dashed off, and returned with napkins to wipe the table. "I'm sorry, I'm going crazy."

"It's not just that *we* can't talk about it, I'm trying not to talk about this stuff with *anyone*. I'm trying to be more . . ." I hated the words "private," "secretive," "mysterious" so much that I couldn't spit them out. "I'm trying not to tell people what's going on with me. To keep it to myself."

Eve squinted skeptically. "Why?"

"I've made rules for myself. One of them says don't answer any questions." I sighed. "Another one is to not tell anyone about the rules. I'm breaking that one but I felt like I had to tell you."

Her teary vibe dried up quickly. "I get it," she said.

Her lack of response surprised me. "What I just said doesn't require further explanation?"

Eve had spaced out, wasn't really listening. "I'm with someone too," she told me. "I'm with John now."

I'd heard about John, a comedian and writer she knew when we were still together. She'd shown me a few of his sketch comedy videos. Before we broke up, she'd told me about their mutual attraction. So, now he was her boyfriend. I hoped that he'd make her feel better, but she wasn't acting like she felt better.

"He doesn't talk about anything real," Eve said. "If I bring up feelings, he makes an excuse and leaves the room. Sometimes he doesn't even make an excuse. He just walks away." She looked down into her wineglass. "It's kind of good. Maybe that's what I need." Now she looked up at me. "If John was honest, I'd be telling him stories about you and about missing you and I'd be freaking out all the time. But he can't listen, so I don't say those things. I just sort it out myself. Since I've been with him, I haven't freaked out *once*. It's sort of nice," she said. "To not freak out."

"Well," I said. "I'm glad that you figured out a way to not freak out?"

After this admission, she got more comfortable and we were able to talk like before. I told her more about my experiments in dishonesty and she found them as funny as I did.

"How does it feel being dishonest?" she asked.

"Sometimes it feels like being in an iron maiden where you can't move because there are spikes everywhere. Other times, it feels like bowling with bumpers on the gutters."

Eve laughed. "When Lila and I were kids, we loved the

bumpers. We'd get so upset if anyone suggested we bowl without bumpers."

"Everyone else is so much happier," I said. "Which makes me happy too, I guess, in some ways. But it doesn't feel beautiful. It isn't romantic."

"Yeah," Eve said. "I know what you mean."

We sat there quietly a moment, just a couple of liars.

Playing Easygoing

FOR YEARS, I'D left behind me a trail of estrangements. Almost everyone I'd liked had pronounced me an enemy eventually, always for the same reasons:

- I'd criticized them or set a boundary
- The more someone agreed that what they'd done was wrong, the more they resented my pointing it out

It struck me as backward that the one who'd been a jerk would get mad at *me*; if they weren't proud of their own behavior, why not get mad at *themselves*? Either way, I made a rule:

- *When a friend mistreats you, pretend not to notice or care.*

An old friend had asked to collaborate with me on a project I needed done by a specific deadline a few months away. We met several times to plan. As the deadline approached, she hadn't shown me any work but repeatedly told me to trust her to meet the deadline. The day before, I wrote her again and she replied with a snippy message about my bugging her. Then, late that night, she sent me something that had likely taken her ten or fifteen minutes and had nothing to do with what we'd planned. It struck me as odd to send this instead of just admitting she'd flaked, as if she thought I might not notice.* I'd have to stay up late working to meet this morning deadline on my own; she'd known this to be the case and had flaked anyway. Calling her out wouldn't get her to do the work she'd promised, so I took this as an opportunity to see if I could get through this situation without my old friend hating me.

I thought of the nicest things I could possibly say in response to what she'd sent me. The best I came up with was to tell her I trusted she had a good reason for flaking, perhaps a personal tragedy going on unseen, that I understood and forgave her. But then I analyzed the way she'd gone about this in the hope that it hinted to her desired response. She didn't confess, make excuses, or tell her side of the story; she was indirectly asking me not to acknowledge her flaking. She didn't just disappear either; that meant she probably wanted to stay friends. I decided she'd sent me something to leave room for plausible deniability so that we could both pretend she'd turned in what she'd promised. I was supposed to say I liked what she'd turned in. Then she could convince herself that she hadn't done anything wrong, or at least that her actions hadn't had any consequences. I was impressed by this foreign method of smoothing over a betrayal and couldn't wait to see what happened when I followed her lead.

I wrote her to thank her for meeting the deadline and for doing such a great job. She responded to my thank-you note

---

* Of all the rhetorical-sounding questions I used to use literally, oblivious to how offensive they were, the worst of all was probably, "Did you think I wouldn't notice?"

with no sign of offense. Soon enough, we were hanging out like before, as if it had never happened. I had no way to know for sure what she thought or felt,* but someone who usually would have walked away hating me had remained my friend; that was a success.

I'd never depend on this friend again, but I'd learned from experience that notifying someone of a new boundary meant being declared an enemy for life. So, I had a novel idea: I'd set this boundary in my own head, without notifying her. I made another rule:

— Continue setting boundaries, but keep them secret.

These rules ended my monthly falling-outs. Now, if I bought a friend an expensive concert ticket and they canceled last minute, I'd write and say I was feeling ill anyway, that I was just about to call and cancel myself. The friend would never know I'd set a boundary. If they noticed my not inviting them to things anymore, they'd have plausible deniability, could tell themselves it had nothing to do with them.

I'd always heard that some people resented being alerted about food in their teeth, but I'd never understood it. It now occurred to me that this was about preserving plausible deniability. If they came home and found food in their teeth, they could tell themselves no one had noticed. If someone pointed it out, it implied that everyone could see it. Removing plausible deniability, for many, was a crime.

After I'd tricked most I knew into thinking I was easygoing, they spoke to me much more freely about why they flaked so often.

---

* I suspect even if I asked her now, years later, she'd still lie or refuse to tell me.

"The more I care about seeing the person, the more stressful it is," one friend told me. "If I have a date with someone I really like, I spend the whole day trying to keep myself calm. If I'm still feeling anxious when I'm supposed to be leaving, I just cancel." I told her I found it unexpected that she only canceled when she really cared about the person. "Oh yeah," she replied. "If I don't care, it's no big deal to show up. It's like a work event or obligation. I only flake on people I really want to see."

Another friend told me, "Most people are relieved when their plans cancel. *I'm* always relieved."

Another friend said, "I usually imagine they'd have more fun without me."

If someone had accused them of flakiness, they'd be too embarrassed to admit they'd felt anxious or depressed.

I made a new rule:

> — *When someone is lying, there's a chance it's because they're going through something personal that they're ashamed to admit. Instead of getting angry, assume their motivations are sympathetic.*

The less judgmental I appeared, the more people would confess. To hear the truth, I had to deserve it.

Bad Seeds

AROUND THIS TIME, Miriam, Josh, and I spent an afternoon with Dad and his girlfriend, a Scottish psychologist and *Jeopardy!* champion who worked with depressed teenagers. After lunch, she brought out the *Times* crossword puzzle. She worked her way through it, casually inviting the rest of us to help with answers she didn't know, calling us out by areas of expertise, like "Michael, you know about old movies. Try this one." When she called on Miriam to answer a music question instead of Dad or me, I realized what she was doing. She didn't need any help; she knew all the answers. She'd only involved us in the crossword to make us feel valued. She knew giving Miriam a chance on a music question would be unusual and special. Dad glowed as he watched her lead us through the crossword, no sign of his skeptical stare, no need to correct anyone or insert himself. He was well-aware that she had all the answers. He admired her playing easy.

Miriam was now in her mid-twenties, living in New York, running educational programs for young children, complaining to me often about her romantic situations. She'd never had a boyfriend, tended to chase after fickle men who went back and forth about being with her. Her dates often went wrong.

She told me about meeting up for a second date with a guy near his office after work. When he asked what she'd like to do, she said, "We're right by the 9/11 museum." She said she'd been meaning to go. Apparently, the guy politely ran with this and accompanied her to the 9/11 museum. "If he didn't want to, he could have just said so," Miriam told me.

"People are uncomfortable saying no!" I told her, though I'd only recently learned this myself. "And it's just generally wise not to take a second date to the 9/11 museum!"

"If he's weird about going to the 9/11 museum, maybe he's not for me," Miriam said.

Josh was now twenty-eight, finishing grad school and applying for government work at crime labs. He was hired for the exact job he wanted. But at one point in the hiring process, he went through a background interview, a formality for certain types of government work. A panel of three law enforcement officers asked him a series of questions and eventually asked him about his history with drugs.

Josh knew the policies about drug use, that one couldn't be hired as a government employee if he'd ever done psychedelic drugs. When the panel asked him about it, he replied, "I did mushrooms when I was fourteen. In 1998."

I wasn't present for this moment, but I can picture the shocked and pitying expressions on the cops' faces that meant: "Why are you doing this to yourself? Why are you putting us through having to participate in your destruction?"

They informed Josh that they were legally required to document his answer in the system, that his admission barred him from working in this profession. He told them that he'd expected them to appreciate his honesty.

"It's okay," Josh told me. "I don't want to work for anyone who would want me to lie."

At the time, Mom had similar job troubles. Parents would come to her for help with a child they described as a terror. She'd meet the child alone and find that she loved the kid, that he was wonderful and brilliant and communicative about why his parents' behavior bothered him. When Mom met with the parents, praised their child, and told them what she imagined they could do differently, they would become angry. "They'd rather believe their children are just bad seeds, that it has nothing to do with them. And they'd prefer a therapist who will tell them what they want to hear."

Josh, Miriam, and I had all been rooting for Mom and Joe to break up since their relationship began in 2000, twelve years before. But when they finally did break up, we saw it was going to be challenging for Mom to be single for the first time at age sixty. She wanted to tell her kids about her dating experiences. Josh and Miriam listened for a while, but eventually started setting boundaries. So Mom would tell her dating stories to me, recounting speeches she'd given on first dates outlining the pros and cons of being with her.

"I used to do that and it's not okay!" I told her. "You can't be honest. Let go of this now. Other people don't communicate the way we do."

"What's the point of being with someone if I can't be myself?" Mom asked.

After a few years of trying to lie, I'd forgotten this question. It sent my brain unspooling. Then I felt the mental string catch. I longed to believe there was a point. I just had no idea what it could be.

Opposite Day

NORMAL SOCIAL LIFE demanded so many complex on-the-spot decisions. No longer behaving naturally, each date felt like a series of tests. I couldn't tell if a whole life of this would have made it easier or if I'd have ended up an anxious wreck like most people.

Still, I was now often able to get second dates, a huge triumph. But I noticed a frustrating second-date trend: if my date excitedly made future plans with me, suggesting something like going to a particular museum exhibit or playing music together or watching a movie we'd discussed, then after the date, she'd never reply to me again. It happened consistently; if they brought up the future, there wouldn't be one.

As I asked around about this, I learned that many had experienced being dumped mere days after extreme proclamations like "I want to grow old with you" and "I can't imagine ever not being with you." I couldn't comprehend talking like that right before dumping someone. But I began to notice other similar instances of people saying the reverse of what they felt. Someone who said she disliked an attractive acquaintance would soon go out with him. Someone who talked a lot about being over her ex was still hung up. One man I knew tended to go on and on about people he claimed not to care about. "I don't care," he'd say over and over, and everyone else would hear it as, "I care. I care. I care." I named this phenomenon "the rule of opposites."

Because the rule of opposites wasn't reliable or consistent—we don't *always* speak in opposites—I was left to the paranoid task of recognizing what to take at face value and when to search for subtext. I soon also found that the rule of opposites didn't only help me read people; it allowed me to guess how I'd be read. Stating plainly how I felt could ensure that I wouldn't be believed.

To communicate that I was upset, it was better to snap that I *didn't* care; this was how upset people usually behaved. To hide my money problems, I could casually mention being broke; this was how many people with money spoke. If I wanted to appear confident, I couldn't just say I felt confident. The cocky pool shark says, "I play a little here and there." The successful person says, "I do all right." When I admitted I wasn't a real piano player, that I'd taught myself and didn't deserve the gigs I had, some would misinterpret me as a virtuoso.

While I was still in the thick of thinking about all this and applying it to every area of social life, a friend confronted me, wanting an apology. I'd not yet figured out how to say I was sorry in a way that people appreciated and I wondered if the rule of opposites could help.

I'd often annoyed people by apologizing unprompted.* It was my instinct to confess and say I was sorry whenever I felt I'd done something wrong. Still, when someone actually wanted an apology, my most genuine attempts only enflamed their resentment. I hadn't yet determined why.

"You're always talking about someone else!" my friend told me. "There's always someone whose music you love or who's the funniest person you've ever met or someone who told you the most interesting story. It makes me feel so boring and bland and awful."

It was a valid complaint; I did often gush about other people. It was a holdover from the honest days. My usual strategy here would have been to immediately say sorry for making her feel that way, to promise to stop talking about other people, and to try to reassure her that I found her funny, talented, and interesting too. Because this type of apology always failed, I considered the rule of opposites: a normal person might deal with guilt or shame by *refusing* to apologize. My sorries likely rang false because they came too quickly, too easily, too articulately. I hypothesized that she might respond better to avoidance.

I feigned indignation, launching into a series of transparent, clichéd evasions. "I don't know what you're talking about!" I barked. "I don't say anything like that! *You're* the one who's always talking about someone else! What about all the ways you make *me* feel awful!?!" I sensed that I'd done a good impression, that she read my manic denials as expressions of insecurity and shame. After a while of this, I started averting my eyes and pausing for long periods as if I couldn't get the words out.

* After a date, if I felt I'd talked too much or forgotten to ask questions or been otherwise self-centered, I'd text an apology. No one responded. Even women who had seemed to really like me would vanish. So I'd stopped texting apologies, no matter how obnoxious I'd been or how regretful I felt.

When I finally said, "Sorry," she smiled warmly and hugged me, satisfied. This was the first time someone accepted one of my apologies.

Sometimes to be believed, I had to lie.

I felt like I had fallen into a language-immersion program where I couldn't speak without first translating my thought into a new dialect. I'd write an email with what I wanted to say and then reverse each line before sending. Every day was opposite day.

My highest-paying piano-playing job was at a restaurant owned by a woman I disliked named Gwen. The job didn't require dealing with her much, but when forced to interact, I used it as practice for keeping my mouth shut. I listened to her paranoid ranting about conspiracies between her employees and friends, who she believed were out to get her. She'd make impulsive, brutal decisions like firing everyone in the kitchen for not respecting her enough or telling the piano players they no longer got free drinks because they were taking advantage of her generosity. I'd act as if I'd seen nothing out of the ordinary.

One day, I received an email from Gwen with a new employee contract. I'd played background music at several restaurants before this, never with contracts. Perfectly in line with her unreasonable character, the contract was long, full of nondisclosure agreements and gag clauses, and threats of expensive lawsuits. The contract even said she could respond preemptively to any "perceived threat" to her business's reputation. If Gwen could have included "under penalty of death," she would have.

I suspected that Gwen had updated the contract because her employees kept quitting on bad terms and telling horror stories about her abuse. The contract would give her the option of potentially hounding these ungrateful former employees with lawsuits. Though her contract wasn't likely to hold up in any court, I feared it would embolden her to threaten and harass us. She had money and we didn't. I felt certain I'd soon leave the job on bad terms myself, so I couldn't risk signing it. Unfortunately, I wanted to keep the job.

My first instinct was to tell Gwen straight-out that contracts wouldn't solve her personal issues, that she should instead put her effort into getting along with her employees. By now, I'd gathered that this kind of response didn't help anyone. I hoped I could use dishonesty to keep the job without signing anything.

I'd observed that when I made Gwen happy, she'd avoid spoiling the positive moment. I thought if I could compliment her enough on what she felt most insecure about and portray her life in a way that matched her desired vision of herself, she would be more receptive. I came up with a wild scheme to attempt to blame the bad contract on her enemies, to convince her that my refusing to sign meant I was on her side.

I wrote to her; I didn't want my face to give me away. I started by telling her how anxious I was about writing. I'd learned that referring to myself as anxious or embarrassed made people automatically relate and sympathize, or at least feel comforted to know I wasn't taking an offensive or combative position. Then I got to the big lie: I said I'd shown the contract to a lawyer. That way, any criticism of her or the contract would come from him, not me.

I told her the lawyer had said "upsetting things" and that I defended her, insisting that she wasn't the type of person who would sue anyone. I claimed to have told the lawyer that this contract surely arose from other employees taking advantage of Gwen, leeching off the beautiful business she'd built. I told her I understood that this contract wasn't really her, that she'd been driven to it as the only way to protect her hard work. I then asked her if she'd mind if I didn't sign it. "It would really mean a lot to me," I told her. It was, by far, the craziest progression of lies I'd yet attempted.

Gwen replied that she was amazed at how much I truly understood her. She repeated back to me most of what I'd said, echoing that she didn't like the contract either, that she'd felt forced to draft it to protect her family and livelihood, that she'd never sue anyone. She told me she liked working with me because I was someone she could trust and thanked me for being so candid.

Around that time, I picked up my guitar amplifier from the repair shop and I found that it was still broken despite being allegedly repaired. I told the store worker, "It's still buzzing."

"Oh, *that*?" he replied. "It's supposed to buzz like that."

I knew he wouldn't help if I pointed out this attempt to gaslight me. But I still needed to somehow demand that he fix the buzz. A unique lie came to me. "Oh yeah, I know," I said. "It's just that I asked the guitar tech to customize the amp to remove the usual buzz."

The store worker nodded and pretended to look at the repair slip, "Oh, right. Okay, that'll be another week."

The jury had been impressed with how I'd talked my way out of signing the restaurant contract, but they didn't like my lie in the guitar shop. "He was being a jerk," someone said. "You should have stood up for yourself."

I laughed. "I've stood up for myself enough. I know what it feels like. It's time for me to try to make things pleasant."

* * *

SOMETIMES I'D GO out with someone once or twice and not want to see her again. Rejecting people struck me as the greatest etiquette challenge.

Women usually rejected me with a method I called "the infinite flake," in which they made and canceled dates with me until I got the hint. The one time a woman told me explicitly that she didn't want to see me again I thanked her for her directness. She appreciated being appreciated. When I asked why she didn't want to see me again, it became clear that her directness had limits.

The jury couldn't think of a rejection method they liked. They complained about lovers ending it too soon or too late, about being too brutal or condescendingly comforting. They complained if the rejection wasn't face-to-face but also found fault in all rejection locations. One juror said the dumper's main responsibility was to convince the person being dumped that the problem had nothing to do with her. "Say you're suddenly moving to a foreign country," she told me. "Or that your family was just killed in a car wreck. Or that you realized you need to experiment with your sexuality by sleeping with men."

"But what if she finds out I lied?" I asked.

"She'll have moved on already and won't care," the juror replied.

I didn't like this advice, but it got my mind working. A merciful rejection had three requirements: clarity, closure, and an unrelated excuse.

Thinking about my past apology issues gave me a solution: if I didn't want to see someone after a first or second date, I could text an unprompted apology. Then, she'd reject *me*. I named this technique "sorrying."

I tried sorrying a few people and it worked perfectly. No one replied, which meant no one felt rejected. I believed I'd found my most brilliant mutually beneficial lie until I told the jury.

"Your lies aren't normal anymore," they insisted. "You're manipulating everybody. It's creepy."

"But they're mutually beneficial and victimless! I'm considering other people's feelings and giving them what they want!"* I told the jury, "If you didn't know my thought process and dealt with me, you'd feel great about it. It only bothers you because I've explained it. Even in this conversation, the only thing bothering you is my being honest."

Eventually, I stopped discussing my adventures in deception. Others would appreciate my lies only if I never revealed them.[†]

AT THE RESTAURANT where I played piano, I was introduced to a friend of a friend. After ten minutes of one-on-one conversation, she said, "You're the most dangerous type of person." I asked her what she meant. "You make everyone feel special," she said, eyeing me with bitterness. "But they aren't special to you."

Because I felt she'd been straight with me, I felt invited to be straight back. "I used to only make someone feel special if I meant it," I told her. "The ones I didn't make feel special were offended. I was told that it was polite to make everyone feel as if I liked them, even if I didn't. Now you're bothered when I'm disingenuously nice?" I told her the story about Chekhov. She just shook her head.

I realized that she was right, in a way. My comfort with personal questions and stories could create a sense of intimacy

---

* I couldn't distinguish kindness or social grace from manipulation because it all felt to me equally crazy and unnecessary.
[†] This is the main reason I suspect writing this book is a bad idea.

in the other person without my feeling intimate at all. I'd talk like that to anyone who would let me, inviting people to feel vulnerable without risking anything myself. Intimacy without vulnerability was a weapon.

I was still trying to get people to be honest with me. It now seemed I should approach vulnerability the way I'd approached apology: I could fake being guarded and unspool slowly, unveiling one personal detail at a time, hesitating in order to show that my honesty was special, only for *them*.

Once I had this thought—that even real intimacy would, in the long-term, require a tremendous amount of lying—I felt like I'd gone way too far.

At first, it had felt good to be more compassionate, to try to make people happy. But past a certain point, it felt crazy. Jerks thought I was easygoing. Liars thought I believed them. Flakes thought I trusted them. Because others lied like this too, so many walked around with misguided visions of themselves. People thought their friends liked their boyfriends. Heartbreakers and abusers didn't know how much pain they'd caused. Even with people I cared about, I'd support their projects no matter how ill-conceived. When they told me their troubles, I'd have solutions, but I wouldn't share them.

It had taken me four years to get this far, but I was looking for any excuse to forget the whole thing and be honest again.

EVE AND I HAD STAYED FRIENDS, not seeing each other very often but meeting occasionally to catch up. She'd started making electronic music and found some success writing songs and making beats for hip-hop and pop artists while she continued publishing graphic novels. She'd long since dumped the dishonest boyfriend and fallen in love with someone else, a beautiful and soft-spoken musician and illustrator I liked a lot. This boyfriend was also a carpenter and had built himself an apartment behind his friend's house in Los Angeles. When he invited Eve to move in with him, she decided to leave New York.

Eve told me she was moving and selling of a lot of her stuff, including a bookshelf I wanted, so I returned to our old apartment for what would be the last time.

I hadn't been there in a few years, but not much had changed. We sat down at the sewing machine table and I immediately started sobbing. "I don't know if it's weird for me to ask this," I told her. "Especially when I've just walked in. But what are you gonna do with this table?" Eve knew what I meant. "I imagine it might be troublesome to keep sentimental objects from past relationships when you have a new boyfriend, and I know it takes up a lot of space. But if you can't keep it, I don't want you to sell it or throw it away. If I have to, I can figure out some way to hold onto it. I just need one of us to have it."

Eve smiled, tears running down her face. "I'm keeping it," she said. "I found a temporary place for it. I want to have this table in my house when I'm old and gray."

I was moved by this response, that we both felt sentimental about what we'd had even though it was over. But I was also aware that she was speaking from a nostalgic moment. Eve was leaving New York, the city where we'd spent our twenties together, for a new love in another city. It struck me as impossible that we'd value our relationship like this forever. We still felt this way after four years, but there was no way Eve would want this table in her house in forty.

I used to tell her I couldn't just choose to believe something. But now I could. Nothing defined love as much as trusting in uncertain promises, believing the unlikely. So, Eve would be sitting at this table in her house in forty years. This was the truth.

Chapter 12

The Mercy of Censorship

IN 2014, I went to a concert in my neighborhood and ran into some friends who recommended an Italian movie they'd just seen.

"I don't take recommendations for foreign movies from Americans because it's a cultural trend to claim to like every foreign movie," I told them, laughing. "I've never heard an American say something bad about a movie from another country."

My friends groaned at this comment they recognized as typical of me. But a friend of theirs I'd never met looked on, laughing in amused confusion. Her huge smile expanded and contracted as she laughed, stretching and snapping back like a rubber band. With her unkempt blonde hair and unrestrained smiling, she read immediately as funny, one who could probably find humor anywhere.

"Sorry," I told her. "When I get too comfortable, I revert to the kinds of things I used to say."

She cracked up. "*What*?"

"My parents raised me to be too honest," I told her. I elaborated and she asked more questions, and I eventually asked her about herself. She explained that she made radio stories out of interviews and that she wanted to discuss this subject more another time.

We became friends and about six months later, she called me to ask if I'd like to be interviewed by Ira Glass to potentially appear on *This American Life*. She'd gotten a job working for the show. I said yes, but I didn't expect anything to come of it. As far as I could tell, the show mostly featured stories of the likable and relatable; I was neither.

I arrived at *This American Life* and the receptionist sent me to a waiting room. The office made no attempt to be fancy or romantic. The carpets and couches were gray, the chairs reminded me of public school. I noticed, squeezed between an intern and an air conditioner, a plain white shelf cluttered with awards.

Ira Glass eventually appeared, thin, with a big face and huge features—what I called a "show-business head." Conscious that I was interacting with one of the world's most beloved interviewers, I was vigilant, watching for any sneaky techniques he used to get people to open up. As Ira and I got situated in the sound booth, I felt like I was scrutinizing a sleight-of-hand artist, watching for the misdirection, missing the fun of the trick. All the while, his movement was loose and comfortable, like he just wanted to talk.

The sound booth was just as spare and gray as the rest of the office. Ira and I sat across a table with microphones between us. "Can you explain a bit about your upbringing?" Ira asked.

"Yeah," I said. "My parents taught us to be honest."

"But that's normal in a lot of situations, isn't it?" Ira said. "Not usually bad advice."

"I suspect we have very different definitions of honesty," I said. "Most parents teach their kids to be polite, to hide their thoughts and feelings. Barely anyone *really* wants their kids to be honest. As soon as their kids are actually honest for a moment, they freak out and punish them." Ira didn't seem convinced. I became paranoid that he was pretending not to understand to rile me. If that was his goal, it was working. "Look," I told him. "Barely anyone is honest like us. My parents worked out their divorce in front of us in therapy sessions."

Ira recoiled in what appeared to me to be genuine horror. "Hold on," Ira said. "What do you mean?"

Because we were discussing honesty, I felt invited to be 100 percent authentic. I told Ira honesty stories as he gawked, disturbed. I tried to explain why it felt good to express myself, why it felt awful to stay quiet, why I wanted to feel known and to know those around me. Ira responded, "I feel like when you tell some of these stories, you're like somebody from another planet or something who got dropped into our world."

After being interviewed in the little gray booth for what felt like much longer than the half hour I'd been told we'd talk, Ira stopped the conversation and we left the booth. The clock outside said we'd been in the booth over two hours.

"Do you think your family would talk to me?" Ira asked.

I laughed. "My family will tell anything to anyone." Ira smiled, probably assuming I was exaggerating.

"Okay," Ira said. "Let's plan interviews with them this week and have you come back for another three hours or so too."

I called my family, one at a time, to ask if they wanted to be interviewed by Ira Glass about honesty. My mom and brother had no concern about being interviewed, but Dad sounded nervous.

When I called Miriam, she asked, "Are they gonna make us look like assholes?"

"It's hard to stop us from looking like assholes," I told her.

"So many of the stories about Dad make him look horrible," she said.

"Well, we don't have to tell the worst ones. But even if we don't, you know who will?"

Miriam sighed. "Dad."

She went into the office that week to be interviewed and called me when she got out. "It was weird," Miriam said. "He asked me if you were exaggerating and I told him I didn't have your experience, that I wasn't too honest. He said, 'So if someone asked if they looked fat in this dress, you'd just tell them they looked great?' And I told him I'd be honest if they *asked*. He acted like that was crazy. Then he kept asking me what I'd do in different scenarios and acted like every answer was nuts. Maybe I *am* too honest?"

Mom said her interview was fun, but that she found it confusing that Ira didn't value honesty. "He thought everything we did was rude or mean."

Ira planned his interview with Dad back-to-back with my second interview, so when I returned to the offices of *This American Life*, I waited anxiously outside the booth while Ira finished talking with Dad remotely from California. I couldn't hear what was being said, but I could see Ira through the sound-booth window in his headphones, wincing.

Ira shuffled out of the booth, pinching the frames of his glasses. "Wow," Ira said. "Your dad . . . wow."

"Oh no," I said. "What happened?"

Ira led me into a cramped space by a window between interns on computers. He ducked his gaze as if the conversation with my dad had made it hard for him to look at me. The section of the room where we stood was not ideal for conversation, but Ira showed no indication that he wanted to move. "Usually you have to get things out of people, you know?" Ira kneaded the back of his neck. "I just asked him if he had any regrets about how he raised his kids and he launched into telling me such awful stuff."

I laughed, which maybe wasn't the appropriate response. "That sounds like him. What did he tell you?"

Ira shook his head. "Ummm, I don't think it's appropriate to . . ." He was too thrown off to go into detail. Ira pulled himself together. "He just admitted it so quickly, it was like he was proud. But how could you be proud of these things?"

"No," I corrected. "In my family, we talk about things we aren't proud of. It's cathartic."

"But he said this stuff on the *radio*. On *record*. Obviously, we wouldn't use almost any of it. It could ruin his life. Why would he risk that?"

"We like the truth," I told him.

He gazed off blankly, like that response didn't clear up anything. Ira repeated the question, oddly fixated. "Why would he admit those things on the radio? Why would he admit them to *anyone*?" I eyed the booth, aware that we could be having this discussion as part of the episode. "Michael, I have to admit," Ira said, gazing vacantly out the office window. "I don't understand you."

"Should we have this conversation in the booth?" I asked.

Ira awoke from his haze. "Oh," he said. "Yeah. Yeah, good thinking."

A while later, with the microphone between us, Ira paused, deciding whether to censor himself. "When I was a teenager, I figured out I could get people to like me by asking questions," he said. "I had social anxiety. I consciously decided to avoid talking about myself and just ask questions. And it worked. I had friends and I barely spoke. I just asked about their feelings. I interviewed them. Make whatever connection you want to my life now." Ira wagged his head ruefully. "People would feel close to me but I'd feel nothing."

I had a vision of the finished episode climaxing with this monologue, Ira's confession that *This American Life* was his way to avoid showing his feelings. In the face of my family's honesty, even Ira Glass's facade had dissolved, and the emotional break-through had been recorded.

I called Dad after I left the booth and asked him what he thought of his interview. "Ira's such a brilliant interviewer," he said. "I couldn't believe the stuff he got out of me."

When the episode's release approached, Ira wouldn't play it for us in advance or tell us what exactly was in it. He kept assuring me the episode wouldn't include anything contro-versial, that I'd be "likable" and "relatable." His repetition of this claim made me suspicious; I'd internalized the rule of opposites.

When it aired, the episode included a moment when Dad said he had regrets about telling us too much. This was the first I'd heard about it. But Ira didn't include any specifics about *what* Dad regretted. As the episode continued, it occurred to me that was the only way to keep us likable. Regret was relat-able, but what he regretted might not be. Ira had managed to frame us as charmingly naive and idealistic by including only the safest, cutest parts of the story. Ira had sculpted our lives into something positive, mercifully protecting us from our-selves. It wasn't exactly true, but it was kind.

My friends who heard the episode were surprised at its tameness. I'd tell them, "The episode about whether to omit unpleasant truths to be likable omitted unpleasant truths to keep us likable."*

I told an acquaintance in radio who had worked with Ira the story of the confessional monologue that hadn't been included. She laughed. "Oh, Ira gives speeches like that in every interview. It gets people to trust him. I'm pretty sure what he said to you is in his one-man show. He might have recited it from memory." I couldn't believe that my favorite part of the experience had been a manipulation. This acquaintance assured me that Ira's sentiment was genuine; the only misleading part was the implication that I'd inspired it.

I found this information surprisingly devastating. Ira had recognized what I wanted to hear: that my honesty could transform him. He saw who I wanted to be and reflected the vision back to me. Perhaps this is what it felt like to have tea with Chekhov.

The Leviton Honesty Scale

AFTER THE EPISODE, Miriam became more open to indirectness. Only a year after the episode aired, she had a new serious boyfriend. Two years later, they got engaged. Now, they're married.

---

* Years later, the host of the *Tape* podcast interviewed Ira and brought up my episode. The host explained to Ira that he'd met me in real life somewhere and disliked me; because he'd liked me so much more in the episode than in real life, he felt Ira must have intentionally portrayed me as more likable than I really was. Ira replied, "I liked him. My heart went out to him and I enjoyed talking to him." But Ira did admit, "We consciously made him likable." Pressed further to discuss whether he misrepresented his interview subjects as better than they were, Ira said he didn't. "I'm trying to get across my accurate sense of who the person is."

After being locked out of jobs in government, Josh switched careers and found lucrative work doing freelance mold-inspections. "This is much better," he tells me. "I can choose my own hours, work as much as I want. I don't have to lie to anyone or do anything I think is wrong. I'm free."

Mom also wasn't inspired to be any less honest. "As I get older, I just have less and less patience for people who won't accept me as I am." She told me recently that she wanted to start announcing on first dates that she's a unicorn. "If they can't handle that I'm a unique, special person, I'd rather know immediately." Though Mom's attitude makes me worry about her making the same mistakes I used to make, I hope it's empowering for her. Maybe she's still figuring out how to stop drinking sour milk.

ONCE MY FRIENDS were more aware of my honest past, I found that they were quicker to open up to me. Friends who had trouble with confrontation asked my advice about it. Many told me I'd inspired them to be honest with someone they cared about. Nobody seemed to regret it.

A performance venue in Brooklyn invited me to put on events, so I tried my own take on a storytelling series. I called it *The Tell*, named after the poker term for little mannerisms that "tell" the other players what cards they're holding. The series was a perfect excuse to get interesting people to tell me personal stories, even more effective than carrying around a tape recorder.

A year into *The Tell*, a friend of mine got onstage to tell a devastating story about her first love's schizophrenia and hospitalization. She told the whole thing on the verge of tears. Her raw voice and the sniffling audience felt familiar. During the intermission, I found Miriam in the audience and said, "During that last story, I realized—"

Miriam interrupted, "—that *The Tell* is your recreation of family camp?"

"Yeah!" I said. "I can't believe I didn't notice before."

Over time, I slowly let myself slip back more and more into honesty. But, having experienced dishonesty for a while had softened me. Honesty itself hadn't really been the problem. I'd just needed to empathize with whoever I was being honest with, to be honest not automatically, but because I cared.

I still followed one rule:

— Read whether a person wants honesty or not.

If they preferred indirectness or small talk or positivity, I'd try to give it to them. I'd only be honest with those who wanted it.

IN A CROWDED bar, drunkenly shouting over the music and general noise, I talked to my friend Laura about how I might write about my relationship to honesty. Her blonde hair fell messily over her face and her elbows perched on the table, her chin in her hands.

I told her, "On the Leviton honesty scale of one to ten, the *This American Life* episode was a two or three. If I wrote a five or six, I'd still be perceived as really honest but with a chance of some people still liking me."

Laura closed one of her hazy blue eyes and looked at me hard with the other. She slurred, "People who do great things don't think about what will make everybody like them."

"I'm pretty sure they do," I said. "Whether consciously or not." Laura laughed uncomfortably. I asked, "Do you really think I should write a book at honesty-level ten?"

"Why not?" Laura said. "You're seriously gonna write a book about honesty and not be honest?"

"The thing is," I told her, "everyone prefers the more likable version as long as I don't mention that it's the more likable version."

"I'd rather read something true that I hate than something fake that I love."

"No way," I said. "If you read two books, one that made you hate the author and the other that made you like the author, you'd prefer the likable one. You'd probably even mistakenly see it as more authentic. And second of all, let's say you're right and the book would be better if it made everybody hate me. How does that benefit anyone?"

Laura snapped, "Because there'd be more truth in the world! Everybody's people-pleasing enough as it is."

"Let me ask," I said. "How honest are you?"

Laura gazed into her empty glass as if the ice would show her reflection. Her straw almost went up her nose. "I should be more honest," she said. "It's hard for me." Laura cradled her cheeks in her hands again. "It's different for you. You're capable of it."

"Anybody can be honest," I said. "Just move your mouth and your tongue and the words come out."

"No," Laura said. She cocked her head and ran her fingers over the table's wood. "Trust me. You don't know. We can't." She looked up at me, her eyes watery. "That's why you have to tell the truth. You have to be honest for the rest of us."

WHEN DAD NEXT visited New York, we got dinner at a small Italian restaurant that felt like it hadn't changed since the 1970s. He told me, "I've been thinking about a lot of stuff I used to do. Like writing negative music reviews? I used to go to a concert full of screaming fans and write a review about how the band sucked and all these happy people were wrong.

What was the point of *that*?" Dad laughed at himself, which I was seeing him do more and more. "When Josh wanted to throw the chess pieces around, why didn't I just make *that* the game? We could've just thrown chess pieces and had a great time."

He told me about an office reunion some former co-workers had organized, a gathering of people he hadn't seen in ten years. He told his old associates, "I'm getting the sense working with me was a nightmare. How bad was I?" Everyone took turns telling stories about awful things he'd said, about how scared of him they were. "You're very different now," one told him. Dad seemed proud of that.

Soon we were reminiscing about the ridiculous things he used to say. I told him, "Remember how when you expressed an opinion and someone got upset, you'd say, 'What's the big deal? Who cares what I think anyway?' I used to say it too. We'd insult someone and then insult them again for caring."

"Oh yeah," Dad said, shaking his head. "Like, 'I think you're an idiot, but who cares what *I* think?'" Dad scratched his beard and I noticed now he looked into my eyes when he spoke to me. "Lately, I've just been feeling like if there's no reason someone should care what I think, maybe that means I should just shut up and listen to somebody else for once." Dad asked me, "So, can you explain some other things that I never understood?"

He asked me questions in the emptying restaurant and I answered, telling him stories from his past. He'd been present for all of them, but it was like he'd never heard them. I was telling him his own history. And this time, he believed me.

EVE AND I still spoke every once in a while, though I saw her rarely. She married her boyfriend and they built a house together. Last year, nearly nine years after our breakup, she visited New York while pregnant with her first child. She asked me to walk around the city with her—not my idea of what an enormously pregnant woman would want to do, but she insisted. So we walked from the Flatiron through the West Village, catching up. We talked over the street noise about the *This American Life* episode and my plan to write about my "tragic love affair with honesty," which would involve writing about my tragic love affair with her.

"Oh, you can write whatever you want about me," she said. "I'm writing stuff about you too."

"What are you writing about me?" I asked. She laughed and avoided the question and I let her.

We talked about how honest I should be when writing about honesty. "If I'm too honest," I said, "the book itself will be evidence that I've learned nothing. I should probably use Ira's method, focus on being likable and omit the parts that could be off-putting."

"Come on!" Eve said, laughing. "That's no fun! Tell the truth!" Eve smiled at me the way she used to. "It's like our song, 'To Know Him Is to Love Him,'" she said. "Let them know you."

So I did.

A Postscript on Truth

IN THIS BOOK, I've changed or omitted all names and, in some cases, altered details or descriptions to obscure identities. Some featured in this book asked me specifically to do so. Others portrayed don't know the book exists, and I'm guessing they'd rather not relive their uncomfortable date or conversation as a bit part in the story of some random idiot they'd forgotten. I suspect they'd rather not find out how their offhand remarks might have ruddered my life's direction. Surely those depicted were already tortured enough in our original interactions.

I will now stop explaining because, for all I know, most of you think obscuring identities was the obvious right thing to do and I'm the only one having a neurotic episode. If you feel that I should've used real names and outed everyone, you can be comforted by the fact that deep down in my brutally honest heart, I agree with you.

ACKNOWLEDGMENTS

I don't know how I would've survived the honest days without Linda Silverman, Matthew Gleeson, Noa Piper, Clancy Cox, Geoff Rickley, everybody from CTY, Lyron Millstein, Emmett Kelly, Lewis Pesacov, Ariel Rechtshaid, Alan Loayza, Chris Cooley, the Hausz family, Tim Wright, Edna Togba, Meital Hadad, Tom Drury, Kevin Cornish, Noah Weiss, Matt Bauder, Greg Rogove, Devery Doleman, Chris Calhoun, Elizabeth Ward, Lach, Regina Spektor, John Sopkia, Jonathan Benedict, Dashan Coram, Lippe, the Babyskins, the Trachtenburg family, Nellie McKay, Margaret Miller, the Hayes family, Kaia Fischer, They Might Be Giants, Jack McFadden, Sharon Van Etten, Myisha Battle, Rob Bryn, Cristina Black, Shruti Ganguly, Vicky Stanton, Victor Magro, Kate Urcioli, Alex Steele, my ukulele students and writing students, everybody from family camp, and my family.

Between 2010 and 2015, I received a lot of influential advice about how honest to be, most notably from Aerial East, Kristy Muniz, Nazy Karimi, Nicole Alexander, Ryland Blackinton,

Juliana Romano, Charlotte Royer, Assol Abdullinah, Maria Liu, Jonas Sundstrom, Luke Temple, Lauren Heller, Shilpa Ray, Nina Ellis, Dan Estabrook, Justin Cox, Raina Hamner, Adam Green, Jack Dishel, Jeffrey Lewis, Dione Davis, Nicole Atkins, Jimmy Giannopoulos, James Levy, Cottia Thorowgood, Mical Klip, Stephanie Peterson, Jon Wiley, Dima Dubson, Lena Singer, Alan Del Rio Ortiz, and Kaya Wilkins.

As far as those who most directly contributed to this book's existence: Bianca Giaever appreciated my honesty problems enough to tell Ira Glass. Ira interviewed me, sitting through hours of my ranting. Then Liz Pitofsky sent Elyse Cheney the radio piece Ira had made. She introduced me to my agent, Adam Eaglin, who endured a few years of my ranting. Luckily, the brilliant and moving Caitlin Hodson talked some sense into me about how to be at least a little bit less obnoxious. I also received particularly helpful advice from Annie Correal, Jenna Sauers, Dev Hynes, and John McElwee and inspiring support from Hailey Wierengo and Stephanie Fischer. Then my editor, Jamison Stoltz, who I still can't believe I was lucky enough to work with, sifted through hundreds of pages of my ranting. Those portrayed in this book (especially Dad and Mom and Eve) were impressively understanding about this whole crazy thing, kinder than I could have ever hoped or imagined. In summary, this book is only here because a lot of wonderful people suffered through a lot of obnoxiousness. Thanks, everybody!